W9-CCD-185

W̲H̲I̲T̲E̲
M̲ISCHIEF̲

WHITE MISCHIEF

THE MURDER OF LORD ERROLL

by James Fox

VINTAGE BOOKS
A Division of Random House
NEW YORK

Vintage Books Edition, April 1988

Library of Congress Cataloging-in-Publication Data
Fox, James, 1945–
   White mischief.
   Reprint. Originally published: New York: Random
House. c1982.
   1. Murder—Kenya—Nairobi.   2. Erroll, Josslyn
Hay, Earl of, 1901–1941.   3. Broughton, Henry Delves,
Sir, 1883–1942.   4. British—Kenya—Biography.
5. Upper classes—Great Britain—Biography.   I. Title.
HV6535.K43N343   1988   364.1'523'0967625   87-40272
ISBN 0-394-75687-8 (pbk.)

Grateful acknowledgment is made to New Directions
Publishing Corporation for permission to reprint two lines
from ''Fu I'' by Ezra Pound from *Personae*. Copyright 1926 by
Ezra Pound; and to The Rungstedlund Foundation for
permission to reprint excerpts from *Letters from Africa* by Isak
Dinesen. Copyright © 1981 by the University of Chicago Press.

Design by Robert Bull Design

Manufactured in the United States of America

10 9 8 7 6 5 4 3 2 1

For Thomas

CONTENTS

ACKNOWLEDGMENTS

I owe a special debt of gratitude to Francis Wyndham, Tom Maschler, Cloe Fox, Joanna Bridge, Faith Evans, Jonathan Galassi and Fred Seidel. And, of course, to Cyril Connolly.

I would also like to express my sincere thanks to the following for providing me with their reminiscences, their advice, their help and, in many cases, with their generous hospitality, both in England and during my visit to Kenya in 1979: David Allen, Jim Allen, Petal Allen, Lady Altrincham, Hermione Baddeley, Sandy Birkbeck, Anstis Bewes, Jack and Doria Block, Sir Michael Blundell, Patricia Bowles, Sir Evelyn and Lady Delves Broughton, Lady Elizabeth Byng, Julian Byng, Juanita Carberry, the Earl of Carnarvon, Bruce Chatwin, Lady Clark, Quentin Crewe, Lady d'Avigdor-Goldsmid, Hugh Dickinson, Nina Drury, Dicky Edmondson, Lady Erskine, Charles Erskine, Francis Erskine, Mary Ann Fitzgerald, Alastair Forbes, Udi Gecaga, George Githii, Alfred Harwich, Cockie Hoogterp, Alan Horne, Sir Charles Johnston, Tim Jones, Deirdre Levi, Paula Long, Beryl Markham, Sir Iain Moncreiffe of that Ilk, Lady Mosley, Mark Peploe, Lady Antonia Pinter, Peggy Pitt, Benjamin Pogrund, Arthur Poppy, Peter Quennell, Tessa Reay, Dushka Repton, Mirella Ricciardi, Sylvia Richardson, Pamela Scott, Sir Sacheverell

Sitwell, Louise Stjernsward, Xan Smiley, Dan Trench, Errol Trzebinski, Sbish Trzebinski, Humphrey Tyler, Lady Jane Wellesley, Martin Wilkinson, Stella Wilkinson, Marie Woodhouse.

I would also like to thank Xan Smiley for his permission to use extracts from the diaries of his grandmother, Lady Francis Scott.

The epitaph *Fu I* on p. 30 is reprinted by permission of Faber & Faber Ltd from *Collected Shorter Poems* by Ezra Pound.

Above all, my special thanks to Diana, Lady Delamere, for talking to me about the events of 1941.

1982   J.F.

NOTE

In earlier editions of this book I mistakenly wrote that Sir Iain Moncreiffe of that Ilk had inserted in *Debrett's* the information that Lord Erroll had been mentioned in despatches for his part in the Eritrean operations when Italy entered the war. In fact, there is no such insertion in *Debrett's*. *Burke's*, however, does link Erroll's despatches with the Eritrean campaign, which took place in June and July 1940, at which time Erroll was a staff captain. But I believe that the mention in despatches (posthumously gazetted) was for Erroll's work at East Africa Command in Nairobi and for his organising the troops for the subsequent Abyssinian campaign, which was launched on the day he was murdered.

February 1983   J.F.

WHITE
MISCHIEF

INTRODUCTION

IN THE EARLY hours of January 24th, 1941, when Britain was preoccupied with surviving the Blitz, the body of Josslyn Hay, Earl of Erroll, was discovered on the floor of his Buick at a road junction some miles outside Nairobi, with a bullet through the head. The two Africans who came upon the car, lying almost on its side in the grass beside the road, found its headlights blazing but no trace of an assailant.

Lord Erroll was the hereditary High Constable of Scotland and, by precedence, the first subject in Scotland after the Royal Family. At thirty-nine, he was a leading figure in Kenya's colonial community and had recently been appointed Military Secretary. He was notorious, locally, for his exploits with married women, and had been much praised, ever since he was at Eton, for his charm and his great good looks. It was only in the last five years that Erroll had devoted himself to anything more serious than the pursuit of pleasure. But already he was projected as the future leader of the white settlers.

There were many people in Kenya who had a motive for killing Erroll, and many who had the opportunity that night. Yet nobody was convicted of his murder, and the question of who killed him, who fired the gun at the junction, became a classic mystery. It was at the same time a scandal and a *cause célèbre* which seemed to epitomise the extravagant way of life of an aristocratic section of the white community in Kenya at the moment of greatest danger for Britain and the West.

Erroll was killed on the very day that the campaign was launched in Nairobi to remove Mussolini's army from Abyssinia. It was Erroll, ironically, as Military Secretary, who had been responsible for gathering the European and African troops for that campaign. The Dunkirk evacuation in May and June 1940, and the bombing of Britain's cities, weighed heavily on the conscience of the white community in Kenya, who were keenly aware of their isolation from the main war effort. The last thing they wanted was for Nairobi's social élite to be paraded in court, making world headlines which competed on page one with news of the war itself. It was a source of acute embarrassment. One headline read: "Passionate Peer Gets His."

The story confirmed the licentious image of the Colony in the popular imagination in Britain and America, and revived the legend of "Happy Valley," an area in the White Highlands which had been notorious since the 1920s as a playground for aristocratic fugitives of all kinds.

Happy Valley originated with Erroll himself and with Lady Idina Gordon, who later became his wife, and who set up house there in 1924. Friends from England brought home tales of glorious entertainment in an exhilarating landscape, surrounded by titled guests and many, many servants.

In New York and London the legend grew up of a set of socialites in the Aberdares whose existence was a permanent feast of dissipation and sensuous pleasure. Happy Valley was the byword for this way of life. Rumours circulated about endless orgies, of wife swapping, drinking and stripping, often embellished in the heat of gossip. The Wanjohi River was said to run with cocktails and there was that joke, quickly worn to death by its own success: are you married or do you live in Kenya? To have gone

anywhere near Happy Valley was to have lost all innocence, to have submitted to the most vicious passions.

With Erroll's murder and the scandal that followed,
the spirit of Happy Valley was broken for ever. For the
whites in Kenya it signalled the end of a way of life which
stretched back three decades. The spell was broken, the
ruling confidence that underpinned their unique occupation
was gone, and it was never to be the same again.

Yet the mystery of who killed Lord Erroll survived
and flourished, and continues to exert a strange power over
all who come into contact with it. In Kenya's remaining
white community, it is still talked about as if it had happened yesterday. The virus of speculation has become
endemic, and even today the place is alive with experts.
One is told of many different people who alone hold the
key to it all, but who will never be persuaded to tell.
Others, including a former Governor of Kenya, achieved
local fame by promising to leave the solution in written
testimony in their wills—but the executors have always
been left empty-handed. Much of this oral history is en-
crusted with distortion and incestuous folklore, each version fiercely held to be the truth—a warning to anyone
broaching the subject in the Muthaiga Country Club.

So compelling was the mystery that throughout the
1960s it dominated the thoughts of a man of letters as
distinguished as Cyril Connolly. In the spring of 1969,
twenty-eight years after the event, Connolly and I decided
to investigate the story for the *Sunday Times* Magazine,
where I worked as a staff writer.

We discovered that everything written on the
subject—including the only book—depended on the public record of the trial, adding nothing new, and came no
closer to a solution than the Nairobi High Court in 1941.
To our surprise, no one had returned to the original sources,
or had gathered and sifted the popular wisdom, or had
filled in the glaring empty spaces in the evidence collected
by the Nairobi C.I.D. in the weeks after the murder.

Our article, which we called "Christmas at Karen," turned out to be the prelude to a much longer quest. It generated an unexpected response, awakening memories and producing a mass of new evidence in its wake. The trail led us on. And Connolly, the literary critic par excellence, did not take his obsessions lightly. The volumes of notes that he left me in his will testify to that. My own fascination with the story, shared with Connolly as I played Watson to his Holmes in that year when we worked closely together, was revived when I opened the notebooks again, soon after his death in 1974. I decided to pursue the trail that we had embarked upon together.

Our joint obsession was primarily with the enigma, which Connolly approached like a novelist, believing in a solution through the study of character. But the story also touched off his social phobias and his curiosity about the *beau monde* of the 1930s, about the titled aristocracy and their dense network of kinship. He swotted up *Debrett's* with scholarly reverence, as if it were the Old Testament itself.

One aspect that particularly appealed to Connolly was that several of the male characters in the story, including Lord Erroll, had been contemporaries of his at Eton—the Eton he described in *Enemies of Promise*. They had been transplanted, moreover, to the great Kenya landscape which he had so often eloquently described. The coincidence had a potent effect on his imagination, his envy, his fevered curiosity.

Beneath the surface lay another rich seam: the extraordinary story of the British aristocracy in Kenya, subjected to a tropical climate and high altitude, suspended between English traditions and African customs, answerable, more or less, only to themselves. These British colonials remained aloof, always on guard, determined that Africa conform to their needs, and accept without question an imported, heightened ideal of class privilege, with all its rules and etiquette and yearning for service and luxury.

They struggled to teach their servants the crucial lessons —the setting out of the silver, the heating of the water, the Majesty of King George. The Africans responded to this invasion with infinite patience, often to the fury of the memsahibs, who mistook their attitude for sullenness and even stupidity.

In the colonial imagination, Africa was a dangerous country which inspired extremes, liberated repressed desires, insinuated violence. At the furthest end of the scale was the subconscious fear that someone might even break ranks, betray his country and his class by "going native," though just what form this might take could never be put into words.

The colonials often shared that strange sensation common to exiled Englishmen living in groups of being "out of bounds." Many of them had money. Many were remittance men who had been paid off by their families and sent away in disgrace. Once their spirits and sense of status had been restored by this feudal paradise, the temptation to behave badly was irresistible, and both men and women often succumbed to "the three 'A's" —altitude, alcohol and adultery. No wonder there was suspicion of the colonies at home, and that the Erroll case touched off a tinderbox of resentment.

THE HISTORY of the quest is often inseparable from the evidence itself and lies at the heart of the main narrative. In the first part the story, which comes from many different fragments collected over a long period, is put together like a jigsaw. In Part II, which deals with the search for a solution, many gaps, quandaries, blind alleys and breakthroughs are included in the narrative where they might usefully add to the store of information and evidence and where they give momentum to the quest. There are also some detours along the route which seemed too good to be left out.

In homage to Cyril Connolly, a diligent investigator, I quote his own advice (to be taken, he would have said, before embarkation). It comes from "The Missing Diplomats," another, though more transient, of his obsessions: the case of Burgess and Maclean.

Those who become obsessed with a puzzle are not the most likely to solve it. Here is one about which I have brooded for a year and now wish to unburden myself. Something of what I have set down may cause pain: but that I must risk because where people are concerned, the truth can never be ascertained without painful things being said, and because I feel that this account may lead to somebody remembering a fact or phrase which will suddenly bring it all into focus.

PART
ONE
THE
MURDER

1

THE
WHITE
HIGHLANDS

It is generally a benefit we confer when we take over
a state. We give peace where war prevailed, justice
where injustice ruled, Christianity where paganism
ruled. (Whether the native looks on it in that light is
another matter. I'm afraid that possibly he does not
as yet appreciate his benefits.)
LORD CRANWORTH, 1912

I would add house management [to a list of hints for
prospective settlers' wives] were it not that the
supervision of native servants is an art in itself. One
could not, for instance, learn by experience in England
when is the right time to have a servant beaten for
rubbing silver plate on the gravel path to clean it, and
this after several previous warnings.
LADY CRANWORTH, 1912

Lady Cranworth had been given a chapter to herself
in her husband's textbook for the new arrivals, which
described the first decade of white settlement and portrayed
Kenya as the white man's heaven on earth. He called the
book *Profit and Sport in East Africa*, and a later edition,
with more restraint, *A Colony in the Making*. He described
the sheer pleasure of the experience, the undiluted nobility

of the landscape with which Englishmen and Scotsmen from landed families would instantly feel familiar; the unlimited scope for game shooting, the richness of the soil and the millions of acres of virgin grazing land waiting to be settled. Although public schoolboys, he suggested, had acquired a bad reputation as colonists elsewhere in the Empire, Kenya was different. Here they were particularly suited to local conditions. Their high opinion of themselves was shared by the natives, particularly the Masai, their ignorance, "often colossal," of farming would give them the benefit of a fresh eye on the unusual obstructions that the tropics would put in their way, and as for their devotion to sport, there was nothing the native liked better than eating large quantities of meat. Clearly Lady Cranworth, like the strident memsahibs that Karen Blixen described later, had already succumbed to fierce measures on the domestic front.

The British Government had officially taken over the country, as East Africa Protectorate, in 1895, to compete with German imperial expansion in East Africa. The Germans were building a railway into the interior from the port of Tanga. The British raced ahead and built their own line, 580 miles long, from Mombasa on the coast to Lake Victoria. It took five and a half years and was completed in 1901, to great acclaim.

Before that, any journey inland was an Arab slaving expedition to Uganda or a gruelling Rider Haggard romance undertaken by a lonely white man, a Thompson or a Livingstone, with an army of deserting porters and under continual threat of attack by the nomadic Masai.

The Indian railway workers imported by the British died in great numbers, not on the spears of the Masai "Moran" (young warriors), who seemed to accept the railway and the superiority of British weapons, but from dysentery, malaria, Blackwater fever, tsetse fly and from the heat itself. Many others fell prey to the man-eating lions of Tsavo, who held up the work for several weeks and seemed for a time to be invincible.

The railway was a splendid and ambitious piece of engineering, undertaken in appalling conditions and with truly Victorian confidence. The track crossed deserts, wound up mountains, descended escarpments and cut through forests and across swamps. It rose from sea level to almost 8,000 feet, running across the grazing land of the Masai and the homeland of the Kikuyu tribe, who were less well disposed to this invasion. It looked absurdly unequal to the task, this clockwork toy, with its four carriages and its dumpy tank engine, on a track that looked as pliable as soldering wire. But it was a stupendous journey, for the first part in the intense heat of the Taru desert, with no relief from the clinging and caking red dust which lay in ripples on the floor of the compartment. At Voi, in the coolness of the plains, there was the unforgettable sight of the great massed herds of zebra, giraffe, kongoni, wildebeest, Grant's and Thompson's gazelle, grazing across the savannah or running eight or ten abreast.

Nairobi was established in 1899, on the frontier between the Masai and Kikuyu, as the last possible rail depot before the track climbed 2,000 feet up the Kikuyu escarpment, the eastern wall of the Great Rift Valley. For anyone looking down into the vast floor of the valley for the first time, the sheer scale of the landscape was overpowering—something quite new to the senses.

Tea was taken at Naivasha station, the beginning of the highlands, and from there on, up to Gilgil and then to Nakuru, the promised land was slowly revealed, in all its immense variety and beauty. After some miles of thorn and red rock, you emerged into thousands of acres of rolling English parkland, a haze of blue lawn rising and falling to the horizon, untouched by the plough and apparently uninhabited. Some of it resembled the landscape of the west of Scotland, with the same dramatic rock formations, grazing pastures, dew-laden mists. Streams rippled through the valleys, wild fig (sacred to the Kikuyu) and olive grew in the forests; the air was deliciously bracing, producing an ecstasy of well-being, and the quality of the light was staggering. There were scents too, the indefinable flavour of peppery red dust and acrid wood smoke that never fail to excite the deepest nostalgia.

And yet unless the land was productive and profitable, there was no point to this "lunatic express," as its opponents had described it in England. It had been built for prestige and super-power competition, and its only effect was to drain the Colony's budget.

The Commissioner for East Africa, Sir Charles Eliot, a distinguished Oxford scholar and diplomat, produced a scheme in 1901, soon after his arrival, of recruiting settlers from the Empire to farm the land. The idea was simply to make the railway pay for itself, by hauling freight from the uplands to the coast. The development of the Colony was a secondary consideration, indeed almost an accident. A recruitment drive was launched in London, and the first wave of settlers arrived in 1903 from Britain, Canada, Australia and South Africa. The photographs depict them as "Forty-niners" from the Yukon—a much rougher crowd than the later arrivals, who were drawn mainly from the Edwardian aristocracy and the British officer class. Nevertheless, there were many peers among these first arrivals —Lord Hindlip, Lord Cardross, Lord Cranworth, for example—and victims of the English system of primogeniture, such as Berkeley and Galbraith Cole, younger sons of the Earl of Enniskillen.

There were millionaires, too, like the amply proportioned American, Northrop MacMillan, a close friend of Theodore Roosevelt. There was the fabulous Ewart Grogan, a fiercely chauvinist Englishman who had walked from the Cape to Cairo. There were fugitives, wasters, speculators.

Above all there was the man who became the settlers' unchallenged leader from the turn of the century until his death in 1931, Hugh Cholmondeley, 3rd Baron Delamere, who had first set eyes on the Kenya Highlands in 1897, at the merciful end of a 2,000 mile camel ride from Somalia. He had returned to England for six unhappy years, to look after his estates, but the Kenya bug had infected him too, and he returned in 1901 to buy land.

Lord Delamere was a natural leader of the settlers. He had inherited an enormous estate in Cheshire and vast wealth besides, soon after leaving Eton—where he had distinguished himself as a reckless and unruly boy, untouched by the civilising classics. He was arrogant and wasteful, with a sudden, violent temper; his political instincts were austerely feudal, and physically he was small and muscular, and in no way handsome. But he had the gift of supreme confidence in himself and in his vision of the future for the Colony, which was inspired by an old-fashioned sense of duty to the Empire—the duty, quite simply, being to annex further territory on its behalf.

Kenya was always more fashionable among the aristocrats than Uganda or Tanganyika after the First World War. Uganda was a little too far from the sea, along the railway, and Tanganyika, until then, had been a German colony. The pick of the sites in the Kenyan White Highlands had an English air, almost like the rolling downs of Wiltshire, all on a supernatural scale and under such an immense sky, that when you are first exposed to it, you may be seized both with vertigo—from the sheer speed and height of the clouds—and *folie de grandeur*. Such grandiose surroundings were irresistible to the English settlers and often went to their heads.

In the earliest settler scheme, a million acres were given away on 999-year leases. The contract required a capital sum to be invested in the first five years and an annual rent to be paid to the Government. Failure to comply meant confiscation.

Delamere was granted the first plot, at Njoro, along the railway line north-west of Nakuru. It was at Njoro that he began the experiment that nearly ruined him, but that almost alone laid the base for Kenya's agricultural economy.

The distribution of the land was a chaotic process centred on the Land Office in Nairobi. In 1904, the year the Norfolk Hotel was built—soon to be known, from its guest list of English trophy hunters, as the "House of Lords"—the town still resembled a bleak and over-crowded transit camp, with its rows of identical huts and its makeshift roads which were either knee-deep in mud, or carpeted with the red dust which hung in a cloud over the town. Prospective settlers pitched their tents near the Land Office and waited, often for months, for their applications to be dealt with by the overwhelmed bureaucrats. The Whitehall plan became a full-scale frontier scramble—appalling fights broke out almost nightly at the Norfolk—and under pressure, the laws protecting traditional African land rights were often loosely observed. The nomadic grazing land of the Masai in the Rift Valley, for example, was considered unoccupied, and stretches of Kikuyu land were added to farms alongside the reserve—a costly political mistake.

The English settlers were often quaintly ignorant about Africa—its history, the tribal distinctions, the wild animals, which were believed to attack on sight and on principle. They would be amazed by the virulence of the diseases that affected crops and livestock—some settled on land that the Masai had known for generations to be bad for cattle—and angry at the difficulties that were bound to arise where Edwardian attitudes met with the more cosmic outlook of the Kikuyu or the Masai. There were simple misunderstandings. Patience and politeness were the very basis of the African disposition, especially towards strangers and guests. But Western forms of gratitude were alien to most of the tribes—there is no word for "thank you" in Kikuyu. On their side the shrieking memsahibs rapped out their commands in pidgin Swahili, with a fierce English accent that sounded grating and discourteous to African ears.

There were notable exceptions. The more feudally minded pioneers like Delamere managed to establish a relationship with the African population that allowed a genuine intimacy, a form of startled mutual respect that was not to be repeated in the next generation.

The European's greatest fears, however, were reserved for the equatorial sun itself, whose rays were believed to damage not only the spine (hence the boom for the London tropical outfitters in "spine pads"—a thick strip of cotton gauze that stretched from the neck to the buttocks, worn with intense discomfort), but were thought to attack the liver and the spleen as well. Lord Lugard advised the wearing of heavy flannel cummerbunds. Winston Churchill, who took an unofficial tour to Kenya as Under-Secretary of State for the Colonies, feared its effect on the nervous system, the brain and the heart. If it was necessary to remove the hat, even momentarily, he wrote, "it should be done under the shade of a thick tree." Some advised never removing it at all, even indoors, since corrugated iron, although a brilliant British invention and a memorable contribution to British colonial architecture, was not considered adequate against the rays. Out of this came the fashion of wearing the double terai, two wide-brimmed, floppy hats, one on top of the other. Removing all this armour was done standing on the bed, well away from the *siafu*, the safari ants who hunted their prey— anything up to a large antelope—in brilliantly executed pincer movements, travelling in columns often a mile long.

White nerves were not calmed by wearing the hottest uniforms in the high temperatures of Africa. And yet the lengths to which the settlers went to propitiate the sun suggest a more irrational fear than that of sunstroke. They seem to revive the Victorian shibboleth that exposure to the sun was improperly sensual and immodest, and certainly not something that could easily be shared with Africans on an equal basis. Thus taboos were raised against it, the most peculiar reserved for women, who were advised to line their dresses and headgear not with flannel, but with bright scarlet cloth.

Debility, irritability, even nervous breakdown, were

warned against, on account of the heat and the altitude, as well as unexpected mood swings from elation to depression. Small grievances would quickly become great ones. "Take plenty of wine after sunfall," Lord Cranworth prescribed, "more especially Burgundy and Port. These enrich the blood and are an excellent prophylactic."

The farming of this land was immensely difficult, a heart-rending process of trial and error which tested the very hardest pioneering temperament. Despite their privileged backgrounds, the early settlers turned out to be of the right calibre. Yet most of them were chronically undercapitalised, and without the lessons of Delamere's energetic experimenting, his ability to match disaster with more and more cash, hope might have died for many of these farmers. Delamere spent almost as much time advising his neighbours as he spent on his own sprawling interests. By 1906 he was farming 160,000 acres at Equator Ranch—all of it enclosed by 1,000 miles or so of barbed wire fencing. But by 1909 he was broke. The estates in Cheshire were drained and he was forced to sell up there and borrow against what remained of the family trust.

His predicament was typical, if more dramatic than most. He had tried sheep, cross-breeding local ewes with English rams, local rams with New Zealand ewes, and cattle, crossing Hereford and Shorthorn with the local Boran. They were variously struck down by rinderpest, which rots the flesh of a walking beast, pleuro-pneumonia and Texas fever, which claimed the Herefords; by sheep-pox, scabies, swine fever, foot and mouth, and by East Coast fever, the deadliest of all the viruses, borne through the herds by ticks.

Delamere would take his rifle and shoot a whole herd of zebra to prevent the spreading of the viruses. He would dip all his cattle each day, but to little effect. Then he discovered that the land was deficient in minerals, so he switched to barley and wheat, which was wiped out, again and again, by black stemrust. After the fungus came the locusts, and there was a drought which struck for three years from 1907. He moved his cattle and sheep to Soysambu, Elmenteita, the present headquarters of the Delamere estates on the floor of the Rift Valley near Lake Naivasha. There they began to prosper. He diversified, growing lucerne to improve the grass, and strawberries for the lotus eaters who were gathering in Nairobi. He even tried ostrich feathers, which soon went the way of all fashion, blown away by the motoring boom.

On top of all the problems, the bureaucratic obstruction of the Land Office, which insisted on petty and needless regulations, was intolerable to the farmers. (Written permission was needed, for example, to draw water from the stream that ran through your farm.) The simplest decisions were taken in London, where they were filed away for months. Delamere, as usual, led the fight against them, on one occasion, when his application was refused to build a flour mill on a chosen site, by stacking firewood under the Land Office itself and threatening to set fire to it. The Land Office quickly reversed its decision.

Delamere believed that if the settlers were prepared to take slender profits to open the country, they should not, at the same time, be choked with red tape. Out of these early conflicts a bitter hostility developed between the settlers and Government over the question of land, which was to dominate the Colony's history until independence.

By 1907 Delamere was an eccentric-looking figure, with his hair flowing around his shoulders as protection against the sun, surrounded by ochre-painted Masai chiefs, who gathered daily at his breakfast table and observed his morning ritual of playing his only record, "All Aboard for Margate," on his wind-up phonograph. He lived now almost as part of their tribe, admired them passionately and had learned their language. Yet he could never be accused of going native: he was much too grand for that.

The Masai had been the favoured tribe from the days when Delamere first met them, laughing with pleasure and cracking skulls with their long clubs. Only the feudally minded could make allies of them while they were still raiding cattle from Lake Victoria to the Indian Ocean, killing herdsmen and their women and children as a matter of pride. At first the Masai stole mercilessly from Delamere's herds, practising their belief that all the cattle under God belong exclusively to their tribe and that even Delamere's imported Hereford bull had been taken from them long ago. (Hence their withering looks when they came to watch the European cattle auctions.)

There is nothing more valuable to the Masai than cattle, and next to that, perhaps, their passion for physical adornment. Because they never ate meat and never slaughtered or sold their livestock, the Masai chiefs that Delamere befriended owned upwards of 50,000 cattle each, and by 1910 the tribe was estimated to own three million head. But they had consistently lost grazing land in the several treaties made with the white man since the setting up of the tribal reservations in 1905. No consideration was given, for example, to their traditional places of retreat in times of drought or pestilence, and by 1914 they were suffering from land hunger.

The Somalis were the fashionable servants, the top "boys" in any household in the early days. They were immensely proud and elegant, the essence of nomadic nobility, with their waistcoats and gold watch chains, their low, guttural voices and their strict Mohammedan ways. Many of them, like the Masai, were rich in cattle in their own country across Kenya's northern frontier. They were linked in fame and fortune with their employers and associated by name, Delamere with Hassan, Berkeley Cole with Jama, Denys Finch Hatton with Bilea, Karen Blixen with Farah. Blixen wrote that a house without a Somali was like a house without a lamp: "Wherever we went we were followed at a distance of five feet by these noble, mysterious and vigilant shadows."

The Kikuyu, whose land stretched from Nairobi to the slopes of Mount Kenya, who were later to outstrip all other tribes in political ambition, were hired as labourers and domestic servants. At the outbreak of the First World War, they were drafted, with the other tribes, into the King's African Rifles and the Carrier Corps as porters, and died in their thousands in one of the most shameful campaigns ever waged by a British Army, in which, at the start of hostilities, 250,000 British Empire troops were held down by 10,000 Germans under Count von Lettow-Vorbeck, who had to forage for supplies for the duration of the war. When it was over the British force had been reduced to 35,000 and the German force to only 1,300.

As the monuments were put up to the African soldiery, the usual sentiments were expressed. In this case the natives had "responded most loyally to the call by the Government for porters." In fact, of course, they had little choice. (One of the unremembered battles of that war was between draft-resisting Masai and the British forces themselves.) The Kikuyu, in particular, went unrewarded. After the war, a new scheme was devised to persuade ex-soldiers from Britain to settle in Kenya to swell the European population. The land this time was distributed by lottery. As this new wave of settlers invaded the highlands, more pressure was exerted on the Kikuyu. The farm wage was reduced, hut and poll taxes were levied, and identification cards issued, forcing their dependence on the white wage.

By the early 1920s the general areas of production were set up. Gilgil and Nakuru were the centres of the livestock business, Thika was coffee, Njoro was wheat, Naivasha was sheep and cattle and Londiani, in the west, was flax.

All the land schemes had clearly favoured the European at the expense of the African population. It was a short-sighted policy and the Kikuyu made their first organised protest in 1922, only two years after Kenya became an official Crown Colony.

The settlers now had their own parliament, the Legislative Council, but ultimate power rested with the Governor, who was answerable to London. Tension increased between the two sides. As politicians, the settlers were, to say the least, fractious and arrogant, and lacking in finesse. Their mood was further blackened by the devaluation of the rupee in 1921—which added a third to their overdrafts and ruined many of them, and the simultaneous failure of the flax market, which had been seen as the miracle crop. Their hope was for the same self-government that Rhodesia achieved in 1922. It was they who had made the country viable, they argued, and they who should run it, not meddlesome bureaucrats and young district officers newly arrived from London.

But they were not to achieve it. By now London had turned its attention to the unmentionable question of political rights for the rest of the population. There was pressure on the Government to allow immigration from India to Kenya, and to enfranchise the Asian population already there.

The Colonial Office under the Duke of Devonshire had also declared a policy for the Colony that would pursue ''the paramountcy of native interests'' over those of the other residents. The incredulous farmers set up a ''Vigilance Committee,'' headed by Delamere, to oppose the plan for Asian votes. Delamere took a team of settlers to London, installed them in a grand Mayfair house, and lobbied loudly for a change of plan. And at home the settlers began to arm themselves for a take-over, hatching a plan to capture the Governor—a keen fisherman—and isolate him at a remote trout stream until their demands were met. The eventual ''compromise'' must have pleased the settlers. The highlands were to remain exclusively white in perpetuity; there was to be no Indian immigration and only a very limited representation of Asians on the Legislative Council. Despite the ''paramountcy'' declaration, the Colonial Office invariably fell in with the settlers' suggestions for running the country from now on.

The 1920s, thus secured for the whites, were the beginning of a more flamboyant, expansive age. They began to replace their mud and wattle houses with grander designs. They built bungalow mansions in the "Surrey Tudor" style—a design peculiar to Kenya and its Indian builders, straining to imitate Edwin Lutyens—with tiled roofs instead of corrugated iron, with open stone hearths and large, comfortable sitting rooms, and with large verandas supported on brick pillars.

There was somehow a provincial tackiness about them that pervades the residential suburbs of Nairobi to this day—a style that journalist James Cameron once described as Equatorial Ealing. The effect is produced, in part, by the universal steel window frames, the smallness of the windows themselves, designed to keep out the dreaded sun, and the gloominess of the greyish-yellow stone, which the Indian craftsmen chipped out of the rock to make walls of formidable barrack-like solidity. In the rain, these buildings look particularly sad.

But the gardens were laid out magnificently. First the lawn was seeded and rolled, then the deep borders were dug, on a scale worthy of Sissinghurst Castle or Cranborne. The earth was rich, there was no dormant season, and the garden always looked at its best, with scarlet canna, frangipani, bougainvillaea mingling with the tender English roses, long-stemmed lilies and fuchsias, and as a backdrop, the avenues of jacaranda, Nandi flame and eucalyptus trees. In the air was the scent of jasmine and mimosa. The many garden boys watered and clipped all day, swinging pangas at the blades of thick kikuyu grass that provided the surface for lawns, tennis courts and croquet pitches.

The settlers had brought out the trappings of their civilisation—their silver, their family portraits and prints, their bits of good furniture, their china, whatever could be spared from the attics of the family houses they had left for good. Many commissioned Indian craftsmen to make quite passable imitations of Jacobean furniture.

With their large numbers of servants—to whom orders had to be issued daily—aristocrats and middle-class officials now became enslaved in the ordered rituals of the butlered existence. The table was laid—again and again —with the place mats of hunting scenes, the bowl of bougainvillaea petals, the bottle of piri-piri (an innovation from the Indian Raj), and the sherry, which was taken with soup. The astonishing African talent for cooking European food, in particular hot English puddings, provided undreamed-of comfort. For their part, the Africans were astonished at the number of meals required by Europeans every day, and the quantity of food consumed. Europeans seemed always to be eating.

At night the sounds of hoopoes and nightjars took over, of shrieking hyraxes and the musical tapping of ground hornbills, like three or four small Indian drums playing in perfect syncopation, and often as not, the cough and roar of lions.

The settlers went to considerable lengths to preserve the way of life of the English county families, substituting the jackal for the fox and the Indian pyjama for the dinner jacket. Their pleasures were formally organised and indulged in with legendary passion. They had their polo grounds, their racecourses, their country clubs, their gymkhanas and lunch parties, and always a limitless supply of champagne. (Despite the overdraft, Lord Delamere gave a dinner in 1926 for 250 people at which the guests drank 600 bottles among them.)

Large distances were covered visiting friends. The greatest excitement of all and often the greatest misery was negotiating the Rift Valley escarpment in the rains, with its precipice at the edge of the narrow road and the terrible mud. Bugattis, Hispano-Suizas, Model T Fords would get hopelessly stuck, often overnight, providing an opportunity for yet another impromptu party.

A leading "soldier-settler" to take up the post-war scheme was Lord Francis Scott, second son of the Duke of Buccleuch. Scott was to succeed Lord Delamere as the settlers' leader after Delamere's death in 1931.

His wife, Eileen, daughter of the Earl of Minto, kept a diary which illuminates, often with an ingenuous touch, the experience of the first days in the great landscape. She recorded, for example, a hunt near Nakuru: "Wonderful going, glorious grass and no holes. Ten couple of hounds, all very young but very fast, the Belvoir strain." (Belvoir is the family estate of the Dukes of Rutland.) She described a visit to their neighbours, soon after their arrival, fording rivers and climbing over boulders with great difficulty, until they found their small tent, beside which their friends were eating lunch from a Fortnum and Mason chop box. After a shooting safari, she wrote home:

I shall never be able to describe or forget the beauty of our last morning in the camp. The sun rises about six. I woke soon afterwards and lay and watched the changing loveliness from my bed. It was perfectly still, very thick dew glistening on the grass and a golden haze in the distance, like a fine September morning at home, our fire still alight and every now and then a puff of delicious smoke was wafted into our tent. The birds singing everywhere. The colourings of the butterflies and birds are amazing—brilliant greens and blues and crimsons. The smell of the blossom on the thorn trees is divine and there is a perpetual smell of mimosa in the air.

Lord Francis had set up a polo club and acquired a string of Somali ponies while he was still surveying his land from a tent and while Lady Francis's china—one set for the nursery and one for themselves—was piled in crates in the corner. They came amply supplied with household goods. In 1979 I was invited by their daughter, Pam, to the vast stone house they had built at Rongai in 1922. She gave me a linen towel marked with a coronet and the date "1916." I remarked that Lady Francis's linen had lasted extraordinarily well. "Most of it is still unpacked," said Miss Scott.

Many of the new arrivals, looked down on harshly by the pre-war generation, had money to spare and no great interest in making a profit, earning themselves the disparaging description of "veranda farmers." Among them was Jack Soames, an old Etonian who was thirty-two when he arrived in 1920. He bought many thousands of acres at Burgeret, near Nanyuki, at the foothills of the Aberdares, settled in for a wasted decade and quickly adopted the habit of offering visitors a pink gin whatever the time of day. His former Somali servant, now in his seventies but still preferring anonymity despite the passage of time, described in Swahili the life at Burgeret:

He had many servants and a great deal of money. There was, for example, one servant whose only job it was to make whiskies and soda, one to look after the dogs, one to start the generator, one for hunting buck, and so on. They earned between thirty and forty shillings a month. The Bwana could never stay alone in this enormous house and would always go to look for his friends, often driving for many miles. Because of that I went with him all over the place. Usually there were many guests. Each house guest was allotted his own servant and servants that the guests brought with them were not allowed near the house. Every day the guests came slowly down to breakfast and started drinking at one o'clock. Then they played tennis at about four o'clock and started drinking again and in the evening they danced until the early hours of the morning. Most evenings the Bwana played the piano and the violin . . .

Into this "community of English squires established on the Equator," as Evelyn Waugh described them, came other travellers from the glittering New Age. Largely through the hunting safaris that Denys Finch Hatton was among the first to organise, an expedition to Kenya became a romantic adventure for the rich. The added frisson of danger brought out the great adventuresses, too, like Vera, Lady Broughton, who was said to have eaten human flesh while investigating cannibal tribes in Borneo, and who had certainly shot many elephants.

A few socialite settlers—whose exclusive interest was the pursuit of pleasure, although there were a few veranda farmers among them—gathered in a prime area that was given the name of Happy Valley in the early 1920s. Anywhere between the Aberdares and the town of Gilgil on the plain might have qualified for Happy Valley. But its real centre was beside the Wanjohi River, which ran down from Kipipiri—the mountain that stood at its head—and which was joined to the Aberdare escarpment by a saddle-shaped cedar forest.

It was supremely beautiful landscape—the valley itself a wide grassy plain, the escarpment wooded and leafy with patches of rugged gorse. From the Wanjohi Valley you could look over the next mountain, the Kinangop, which was shaped like a long, narrow headland, into the Rift Valley beyond.

The great social events were the race weeks at Christmas and mid-summer, when the farmers came to Nairobi and turned the place upside down, staging rickshaw races, shooting out the street lights, brawling drunkenly in the bars—conspicuously led by Delamere himself, who would shoot at the bottles on the shelves—and pursuing whatever sexual liaisons had been simmering away in the previous months.

The settlers congregated in the few strongholds of luxury which existed in the late 1920s. The oldest established was the Norfolk Hotel, run by a formidable lady known as "Auntie." ("She practically runs the country," you would be told.) There was also Torr's Hotel, nicknamed "Tart's Hotel," built by Grogan in 1928, where *thés dansants* were held each afternoon in the circular Palm Court lounge.

Most exclusive of all was the Muthaiga Country Club. A young French visitor, Count Frédéric de Janzé, described the Muthaiga Club in *Vertical Land*, a book of "pen portraits and travel sketches":*

* Duckworth, 1928.

Why do we all belong to Muthaiga Club?
Why do we go out five miles for a cocktail?
Why do we have to fight for a room during Race Week?
Why do we have to put up with our things being stolen and our laundries mixed?
Why do we drink champagne at 35 shillings a bottle?
Why are we told to go to bed at one, like naughty boys?
Why do we stand boring food and draughty halls?
Why do we live in rooms without mosquito netting?
Why do we put up with our "boys" being ruined?
Why do we stand the Committee's smile?
Why does our money keep Muthaiga going?
That twice a year, swamping the "regular member" in our numbers, all together, once more delighted, hearts beating, throats drinking; from Moyale, from London, from Rhadjputna, from Queenstown, from New York and Tyrone. We can bang the bar, break the glasses and on the morrow in numberless "prairie oysters" repent—

The Muthaiga, with its golf course, squash courts, croquet lawns and ballroom, was an exclusively up-country farmers' club run along St. James's Street lines. Though women were allowed in of necessity, Jews were not: once the Club's piano was set alight with paraffin in protest against the suggestion, quickly withdrawn, that they might henceforth be admitted. The officials and tradesmen of Nairobi kept to themselves, as a separate class, in the Nairobi Club—and it was a strictly observed division, giving rise to much sneering and disapproval from the officials at the effete goings on in the other place.

The Club was built in true Kenya style, by Indian artisans, from large blocks of stone, covered with pinkish pebbledash with the usual steel windows and with small Doric columns to give it a glimmer of grandeur. The walls were cream and green like a well-upholstered nursing home, the floors were polished parquet. With its deep armchairs and loose chintz covers it gave out the atmosphere of Thames Valley gentility and Betjemania—of Ranelagh or Hurlingham.

Bachelors slept in the spartan "military wing" with cell-like bedrooms. The double rooms, with twin beds, were large and austere, in the colonial manner, the bathrooms luxurious.

All payments were transacted on chits of various colours—cash never changed hands. You could get a drink at any time of the day, but between six and eight in the evening the bar was reserved for men only, or "toughs," as Waugh described the members he encountered there. The Club was empty for days, then suddenly it would be impossible to get a table, unless you were in the favour of a powerful Somali called Ali—who ran the dining room and who was considered "a genius" at table-shuffling. Every year Lord Delamere gave a dinner for the Governors of Kenya, Uganda and Tanganyika, otherwise the evenings were mainly given over to bridge, backgammon and the many private parties, including the annual Eton Ball.

During race weeks the Club really came alive. The drinking started soon after midday with pink gins before lunch, followed by gin fizzes in the shade at teatime, cocktails (Bronxes, White Ladies, Trinities) for sundowners, whisky and champagne until the lights went out.

At the nightly balls, the guests might have been dressing for royalty, and women were required to wear a different dress each night. Later on, as impromptu Rugby games took over, the ballroom furniture would be wrecked in displays of unashamed public schooliganism. A popular attraction was a gentleman called Tich Miles, who would climb into the roof and hang from the beams like an ape. Another was Derek Fisher, a Happy Valley resident, who would order the servants to arrange the chairs in lines to resemble a train. He would push the chairs through the sitting rooms, hooting and puffing to the howling encouragement of his friends. That would turn into musical chairs and the chairs in turn would be hauled through the windows.

The dances usually ended around 6 a.m., four or five nights in a row at the height of the season. Squash and golf would take over immediately. No one liked going to bed. By lunchtime the following day, all had been patiently swept up, the fines presented for payment on the club chits, and serious offenders called in to the Secretary's office.

In all the descriptions of those heady nights, it is remarkable how little time was taken up with sleep as opposed to the sexual escapades for which the Club was famous. The altitude should have been tiring. Instead it seems to have worked as a stimulant, and as an irritant too. Wars and brawls broke out incessantly during race weeks, and terrible grievances took root in that libidinous, drunken atmosphere.

Edward, Prince of Wales, visited Kenya in 1928, and was immediately at home in the atmosphere of Muthaiga. Sir Derek Erskine, who was later Kenyatta's lone supporter among the Europeans before independence, remembered one of the nights when he was present:

Edward P. as we called him in those days, was a very likable person but already he showed signs of dissolute behaviour, though I must say he always kept himself extraordinarily fit. He insisted after a very vigorous day on dancing all night. Now we hadn't got a resident band at the Muthaiga Club. Syd Zeigler would come up with his band on Saturday nights. On other days we had to put on gramophone records, and one night Edward P. was dancing with my wife and he suddenly lost his temper with the records which he said were the wrong kind, and I very much regret to say that aided and assisted by my wife, they picked up all the gramophone records and threw them through all the windows of the old ballroom, which is probably the reason, some people say, why it fell down twenty years later. Well, I had to pay the bill for all those records, and I remember it well. Edward P. would then go to bed, at say four o'clock in the morning, and at half past six he would be down on the racecourse. I remember, quite clearly, Sonny Bompas who lived down on the racecourse and was training horses there, said to me, ''Do you mind cantering slowly round the course, because Edward P. wants to run round holding on to your stirrup leather?''

So the madness went on. This was 1928, one year before the great crash, which drastically thinned out the settler population. It was also the year in which Josslyn Hay's father died, and Josslyn became the Earl of Erroll and High Constable of Scotland. He had already been living in Kenya for four years, in the heart of Happy Valley.

2
HAPPY
VALLEY

Fu I loved the high cloud and the hill,
Alas, he died of alcohol.
EZRA POUND

1923: In the middle of June, close to midsummer, I met Josslyn
Hay. It was inevitable that he should be conscious of such wonderful good looks as he possessed, and with these he had an
arrogant manner and great sartorial elegance. His straight pale
gold hair was brushed up into wings on either side of his head.
He was the kind of young man that my father most disapproved
of, and his manner seemed to become even more cocky when
he was in my father's presence. He never called him "Sir," as
most of my young men did, and he always beat him at tennis.
Josslyn had a scornful way of looking at people—an oblique,
blue glance from under half-closed lids—and this impudent look
was even turned on my father.

There was a terrible row when my father discovered that I
sat out with him on the back stairs at dances. The morning after
this scene Josslyn sent me an enormous bunch of red roses. I
kept them hidden away in my bedroom basin until they died—
the first present of flowers I had ever received.

My father's disapproval of Josslyn only added to his fascination, and I was beginning to imagine myself in love with him
when he suddenly eloped with a married woman to Kenya.*

* Daphne Fielding, *Mercury Presides* (Eyre and Spottiswoode, 1954).

That year Josslyn Hay was twenty-two. At seventeen he had been sacked from Eton, or rather he had been "asked to leave." He would tell a funny story, by way of explanation, something to do with being sold a motorcycle by a Jewish boy, that always went down well, with his gift for mimicry.

He was certainly the most attractive boy in the school and when, many years later, a British peer was asked on a quiz show who, *had* he been homosexual, he would most like to have had an affair with, he mystified his audience by replying, "Josslyn Hay."

An Eton contemporary, Sacheverell Sitwell, confirmed this memory of Hay as an object of schoolboy adoration. He wrote to Connolly, "I suppose the time I am thinking of is the summer half of 1916. I saw him, more than once, followed down Keate's Lane by a whole mob of boys. And heard a lot of talk about him.

"A great friend of mine, Victor Perowne, who was eventually Ambassador to the Holy See—he's dead now —'took it'—'hook, line and sinker.' He even published several poems and prose pieces on 'Haystacks' (if you see the association, rather a clumsy one) in the *Eton Chronicle* —they must still be found there—of which the editor was sympathetic, and perhaps bitten, too. But I remember Josslyn myself indistinctly—and could never 'see it' as the phrase goes."

Hay's family was of immense antiquity and grandeur. The Earls of Erroll, as Hereditary Lord High Constables of Scotland since 1315, walked directly behind the Royals at coronations. The Jacobite Lord Kilmarnock dominated the family strain, but Josslyn's great-grandmother was a natural daughter of William IV (from whom there was no legitimate descent), thus, perhaps, adding Hanoverian stamina to Highland gallantry. There had been family seats at Slains, Aberdeen, and Rosenglass, Cumberland, but the Erroll fortune had been whittled away by the 19th Earl, who had been unable to economise or adjust the management of his estate after his return from the Crimea. Many of the family assets were sold by Josslyn's grandfather, the 20th Earl, who had commanded the Household Cavalry and was Lord-in-Waiting to Edward VII when the Empire was at its height. His father, Victor, Lord Kilmarnock, was godson to Queen Victoria and in 1919 went to Berlin as Chargé d'affaires, the first diplomat to be sent to Germany after the Armistice. He took Josslyn with him as honorary attaché—his only job after leaving Eton—on the grounds that some practical experience might be useful before the boy took his Foreign Office exams.

Josslyn returned to London in 1922, passed the Foreign Office exams, and began to exploit his remarkable sexual attraction in London society, while the older generation began to describe him as "spoilt." There was no question about that, but he was vulnerable, too.

The following year he fell in love with Lady Idina Gordon, the married woman with whom he eloped to Kenya. She was born Idina Sackville, the daughter of the 8th Earl De La Warr, and she had been married twice, first to Euan Wallace with whom she had two sons, and secondly to Charles Gordon, whom she divorced in 1923. Gordon did not defend the case.

Idina was apparently irresistible. She was already *mal vue* in society for her "fast" reputation. She had had many boyfriends during her first two marriages, including Oswald Mosley, who had presented her with a pearl-inlaid dressing table. "She could whistle a chap off a branch," said an old acquaintance. "She didn't pinch other people's men, but if they were left lying about, she'd pick them up." She had a perfect figure, slight and little girlish, for which she was famous, and much admired; always wore the chicest clothes and walked barefoot whenever possible "to show off her size three feet." Her face might have been beautiful were it not for the shotaway chin and, it is said, she was intelligent, well read, enlivening company.

Josslyn's liaison with Idina became high scandal. Not only was she twice divorced, she was soon to marry a mere boy, eight years younger than herself and the heir to an earldom. In addition she was seen, correctly, to have ended his chances of the Foreign Office career that in spite of the stigma of Josslyn's dismissal from Eton, his father had managed to secure for him. Even after their marriage in September 1923, it was hinted that Joss and Idina would have been "unwelcome at Ascot" had they stayed in England. Idina had already lived for a year in Kenya with her second husband, Charles Gordon, and now it seemed the obvious, indeed the only, place to go. Their departure in April 1924 launched the Colony's reputation as a place beyond the reach of society's official censure, and so beyond the pale, although this was tame compared to the scandals that followed. The couple set up house at Slains, a fairly modest bungalow on the slopes of the Aberdares, named after the castle sold by Joss's grandfather.

In 1925, they moved from Slains to a house in the valley called Clouds, a large, low thatched mansion with many guest bedrooms along each of its wings, facing on to a courtyard. Guests began to come out from England in large numbers, and it was often so wet on the escarpment, so difficult to negotiate by car, that it was hardly worth leaving for weeks on end. Idina would make it very difficult for her guests to leave at all.

She was not to come to the height of her powers for another ten years, but she quickly dominated what there was of the social life of that remote part of the White Highlands and it was there, under her influence, that the Happy Valley legend began.

Idina was only happy, according to the survivors of her house parties—and it was held as truth at Government House where she was on the blacklist—if *all* her guests had swapped partners, wives or husbands by nightfall, or certainly by the time the weekend or the invitation was over. She would organise, from time to time, after-dinner games of "blowing the feather" across a sheet held out by the guests around a table. It was a frantic game that was designed to create near hysteria; when the feather

landed all eyes would be on Idina, who, like a high priestess presiding over a sacred ritual, would divine and then
announce who was to sleep with whom.

The bedrooms were locked, and Idina had numbered
keys with duplicates which were laid out on a table so that
bedroom partners could be chosen by an alternative game
of chance, or what appeared to be so. "We always called
Idina's bed 'the battleground,' " said a survivor, "and we
all used to end up in it at various times of the day or
night."

Lady Altrincham (then Lady Grigg, wife of the Governor) put Idina on her blacklist. She remembers visiting
Clouds and being shocked to find Idina's clothes and pearls
scattered across the floor, the dogs unfed and the servants
gone. It was considered that Idina carried on shamelessly
in front of Africans and this—the setting of a bad example
—was inexcusable. Retrospectively, Idina is even thought
by some to have made a significant contribution to Mau
Mau and the end of British rule, through her scandalous
behaviour.

Lord Francis Scott frowned on young officers visiting
the Wanjohi, or frequenting Clouds. Eileen, who could
never forgive Idina's ability to assimilate this landscape
so effortlessly, may have had something to do with it.

She wrote in her diary, "Most of the women wear
shorts, a fashion inaugurated by Lady Idina who has done
a lot of harm in this country. It is very ugly and unnecessary."

"Unnecessary" was the key word. Sacrifice and toil
was the image of the settlers that Eileen wished to project
to her relations at home. Glamorous eccentricity trivialised
the frontier and made it look easy and enjoyable, or worse.
Idina was spoiling things. She infuriated Eileen, who believed deeply in the inherent superiority and virtue of those
born to rule. After a miserably inadequate lunch visiting
neighbours, Eileen wrote, "I wonder how Idina will enjoy trying to eat this type of food and washing out of a
cracked old tin basin . . . Everything is so intensely dry.

It splits the face and hair . . . All the women in this country, except Lady Idina, are burnt brick red, which is not
very becoming.'' Once they met at Nakuru races: ''Lady
Idina was there in an Ascot gown with a lovely brown
ostrich feather hat. Why she didn't die of sunstroke I can't
conceive.''

Idina's closest neighbours were Comte Frédéric de
Janzé and his young American bride, Alice. Frédéric,
twenty-six, elegant, laconic, aristocratic, had motor raced
at Le Mans, fought in the Rif mountains and moved in
the literary circle of Proust, Anna de Noailles and Maurice
Barrès.

De Janzé's *Vertical Land** includes anonymous pen
portraits of some of the Happy Valley residents, their names
pencilled in by the author in my own copy. This is how
he evoked Idina:

With her back to the fire, gold hair aflame, in red and gold kekoi,
she stands . . . Sunk in chairs, legs crossed on the floor, propped
up against the wall, all our eyes hang fascinated on that slight
figure . . . The flames flicker; her half-closed eyes waken to our
mute appeal. As ever, desire and the long drawn tobacco smoke
weave around her ankles, slowly entwining that slight frame;
around her neck it curls: a shudder, eyes close. Contentment!
Power! The figure in the golden kekoi.

He described Happy Valley as the ''Habitat of the
wild and free'':

In this décor live a restless crowd of humans, hardly colonists
—wanderers, perhaps, indefatigable amusement seekers weary
or cast out from many climes, many countries. Misfits, neuras-
thenics, of great breeding and charm, who lacked the courage
to grow old, the stamina to pull up and build anew in this land.

De Janzé described the principal cast of characters,
among them Fabian Wallis, a homosexual and a close

* Duckworth, 1928.

friend of Josslyn's; Michael Lafone, a fierce womaniser with an eyeglass, who was briefly and disastrously married in Kenya to Elizabeth Byng, daughter of the Earl of Strafford, and above all Raymond de Trafford, the epitome of the remittance man.

Raymond came from a grand English family from Lancashire, and had been in the Coldstream Guards before coming to Kenya. He was devilishly attractive, quick-witted, original, cultivated, hopelessly indiscreet, a heavy gambler and drinker. To women, he could be delightfully attentive when he felt like it, and a great relief to talk to. Evelyn Waugh called him a "fine desperado," took a great liking to him when he met him in Kenya in 1931, and kept up with him afterwards. "Something of a handful," he observed, "v. nice but so BAD and he fights and fucks and gambles and gets D.D. [disgustingly drunk] all the time." They stayed together with the Delameres at El-menteita. Waugh wrote of Trafford in his diary: "He got very drunk and brought a sluttish girl back to the house. He woke me up later to tell me he had just rogered her and her mama, too."*

There was a music-hall jingle that went the rounds in Nairobi:

> There was a young girl of the Mau
> Who said she didn't know how,
> She went for a cycle with Raymond and
>   Michael,
> She knows all there is to know now.

Along with the champagne, the drugs of the new age, cocaine and morphine, had found their way into Happy Valley. The chief dealer was Frank Greswolde Williams, who got his supplies from Port Said and who openly plied his trade in the Muthaiga Club. One of his best customers was the American Kiki Preston, a Whitney by birth, a

* Duckworth, 1931.

beauty who often stayed with Idina. She had had many lovers, including the two Valentinos, de Trafford and Lafone—and the late Duke of Kent.

When her supplies ran low, Kiki would send her aeroplane to Nairobi for a fresh consignment. Cockie Hoogterp was a close friend of Kiki and remembers her extraordinary performance with her silver syringe.

She was great fun and very witty and never made any bones about morphine. She always looked marvellous. She would be quite open about it, digging the needle into herself while we sat up drinking whisky. She never went to bed until 4 a.m. Next morning we were always hung over and sleeping: but she was up at 8 a.m. beautifully dressed, and looking lovely, as if nothing had happened.

"I'm sorry to say," said Sir Derek Erskine, whose wife had helped the Prince of Wales to destroy the Muthaiga Club dance records, "that drugs played a very large part in that period. Cocaine was taken like snuff in Happy Valley and certainly didn't do anybody any good." At another dinner party for the Prince of Wales in 1928, at Muthaiga, Erskine saw Greswolde Williams suddenly being manhandled out of the room by a white hunter called Archie Richie. When Erskine asked what had happened, he was told, "Well, there is a limit, even in Kenya, and when someone offers cocaine to the heir to the Throne, something has to be done about it, particularly when it is between courses at the dinner table."

JOSSLYN'S DAYS were mostly taken up with horseracing and polo—which was seen as a painful but bracing hangover cure. He had a farm at Nakuru, but paid little attention to it. Near Gilgil, on the plain below the Kinankop, four separate polo fields had been cut out and rolled, under the mountain, from the great orchard of green-black cactus trees and scrub—the sombre landscape that you still cross, on a few miles of dirt track, to reach them now. Josslyn would turn up here wearing tightly fitting shorts with wide corduroy stripes and, invariably, with a red-ochre Somali shawl flung over his shoulder.

Unlike Berkeley Cole and Denys Finch Hatton, who had adopted the Somali shawl as a somewhat romantic affectation, Josslyn carried off the fancy dress without a trace of self-consciousness, more in the spirit of the privileged boys of Pop at Eton, whose right it was to make flamboyant variations on the school uniform, wrapping themselves in bright flannel.

Josslyn's charm, and even his arrogance, brought him close to the males around him. His assumption of the leader's role was effortless. He had indeed inherited, like the sons of Mary, "that good part."

Petal Allen, daughter of Sir Derek Erskine, remembers Josslyn Hay as the first really elegant man she ever saw, as a child. He sat on a shooting stick at the racecourse, and held Petal on his knee. He wore a white tussore silk suit, a polka dot bow tie and a panama hat. In the Wanjohi he would often wear a kilt. His hair was still oiled down and brushed into wings on either side and there was a transcendent perfection about his looks. He was immensely popular with most of the colonial community for his friendliness and his quick wit—a striking figure who made a lasting impression on the people he met.

And yet extraordinarily little is known about his life in Kenya, beyond the Don Juan legend. He is poorly remembered by the few surviving colonists who knew him, and he rarely returned to England. Either the drink has sealed away the memory or possibly the summary style of colonial language, whose every word is final, has suppressed it. "Oh! *Tremendous* charm. *That* was the thing."

To press for detail is to introduce a tone of contradiction. But the judgments are often revealing. David Begg, a Scotsman known to the remaining whites around the Kinankop as "Bwana" Begg, knew Josslyn Hay well. He lives in a house of austere Highland décor, beside those same polo grounds at Gilgil which he owns, and which he cut out himself fifty years ago. He plays a skilful game, aged over seventy, and still speaks with a strong Scots accent. "He was a first-class fellow," he said. "He was like a lot of those who never had anything to do. Clever, always had a brain. He'd always an answer. I used to play polo with him quite a bit. I would give him a hand loading his horses and he was always ready to take advice. Good eye for a ball and a strong, hefty fellow."

"Tough," a voice barked in the Muthaiga bar, "but very attractive indeed. Exploited by women, to whom he was irresistible."

"He was very witty and pleasant to be with, a very good bridge player and a *wonderful* polo player," said another contemporary, "but he wanted conquests and had innumerable women. Of course, you could live extremely well, put up a tremendous show for £2,000 a year."

One of the few women who didn't see him as the epitome of sexual attraction was Dushka Repton, a Russian beauty married to a settler farmer, Guy Repton, who was insanely jealous of his wife and eventually died of drink. Only once did Mrs. Repton consider Josslyn "irresistible," when he appeared at a fancy dress ball at the Muthaiga Club, dressed in a black evening gown, sequins and pearls. The pearls belonged to Idina. She remembers Joss saying, "Pearls must be *worn*."

At Clouds the parties that Joss and Idina gave were magnificent, and famous for their excesses. Nina Drury, born in 1901, was the young bride of Jack Soames, and in the mid-1920s they often went over to Clouds for dinner. "The dramas that used to take place were unbelievable," she said. "It must have been the climate, I think."

The evenings would begin with a certain formality and ritual preparation. In addition to her permanent house party, Idina would summon her neighbours, too, and all her young men, accepting no refusals. She had a Somali chef famous for his cooking and many servants to lay the separate tables and fill the rooms with fresh flowers. Then, at the appointed hour, Idina would take her bath—which was in the centre of her large bathroom—and like some royal mistress, bathe and dress herself in front of all her guests, talking away, insisting on permanent company, summoning new arrivals.

The excitement of Idina's presence, of sharing her toilette, was heightened by a steady consumption of cocktails, and by the time dinner was served most of the guests were in a fair state of intoxication. One evening, Nina Drury remembers, a young woman, said in a loud voice that she had been making a list of all her lovers since she had been in Kenya. "Not very nice," said Josslyn, "when she was my mistress this afternoon."

A furious argument began between Raymond de Trafford and Frédéric de Janzé. Jack Soames told his young bride, "Now, my baby, there's going to be trouble and you must go to bed." Nina was very annoyed at being prevented from watching the drama. "But then," she said, "various people were led into my room, sobbing and crying and saying that there was going to be a duel and that they were going to kill each other." At the height of one of these evenings, Raymond de Trafford, maddened with drink, went outside and set fire to several of the African houses. His crime was settled like a gambling debt, and he was forced to pay up.

It seems that Josslyn was quite sober at these moments. His own recklessness was more methodical: he was more dedicated than most to the cause of seduction. But he would never question the right of his friends to act without restraint, whatever the burden on the African staff. Servants, by nature, were there to be inconvenienced. "Hay never paid his servants," said his former Somali houseboy, "but the Somalis said 'don't worry,' and when he eventually got round to it he gave the wages to the top Somali. Sometimes they waited six months to be paid, but they were fed and clothed and housed."

Paula Long, a famous beauty of the period, married

to "Boy" Long, a cattle rancher at Elmenteita, remembers Josslyn's unpleasantness towards the staff: "He was horrible to Africans, and swore at them in Swahili," she said. "He kept the staff up all night and was quite unscrupulous."

This cynical, bullying side of Josslyn's personality could also be seen within his own circle. The roaring jokes and the good company he provided redeemed him only up to a point, and he often antagonised people with his scathing tongue and his sexual arrogance. His innumerable women had one thing in common—they were all married. "To hell with husbands," he was fond of saying. And to cuckold a man carelessly, while slapping him on the back or borrowing a fiver, added to his pleasure.

Patricia Bowles lived through two marriages in Happy Valley as a close friend and neighbour of Idina, and, at times, a participator in her ceremonies. (She has since retired to Kilifi.) Though fond of Josslyn, she well remembers this vicious element in his nature.

"At the Norfolk Hotel one day he said to some child, 'Come to Daddy.' I thought, 'You bounder!' It stuck terribly in my mind that he could say something so awful to somebody, indirectly, who was within earshot. That was the sort of thing he'd think funny. And he could be very humiliating and crushing to women. He would say, 'What a revolting dress. God, how I hate mauve.' " The men's bar at Muthaiga was the perfect place to display this particular form of wit and to boast of his conquests. In these conversations with his male friends, women would be divided into three categories, "droopers, boopers and superboopers."

"He used to hold forth in the men's bar, telling dirty stories. He was a terrific gossip," said Patricia Bowles, "until he saw a pretty face through the hatch, when he would go and accost the stranger. He thought of nothing but women, liked them rich and broke up many marriages."

One of the first marriages to be threatened by Josslyn was that of Frédéric and Alice de Janzé.

3
THE FASTEST GUN IN THE GARE DU NORD

A L I C E fell in love with Joss the moment she saw him, on her first trip to Kenya with her husband in 1925. She was twenty-five. They had been married for three years and had two small daughters. Patricia Bowles, who became her closest friend, says of her affair with Joss, "It was on and off, on and off, I think on many and various occasions. It was never a sort of acknowledged affair. But I think she was always in love with him."

Alice was probably the most dangerous of his mistresses, perhaps the most fascinating and certainly, when she was in her twenties, before the excesses of Wanjohi got the better of her, the most exquisite-looking. Her face was pale and delicate, with high cheekbones and wide, calm eyes of deep violet colour. She had a lovely, slightly frail figure and short black hair bound tightly in the nape of her neck. She would invariably dress in corduroy trousers and bright, loose flannel shirts.

Alice was the only child of William Silverthorne of Chicago, a rich felt manufacturer of Scots descent, and through her mother she was an heiress to the Armour meat-packing fortune. She possessed all the attributes that Josslyn found irresistible: she was mysterious, she was married, and she was rich.

The danger came from Alice's waywardness and instability, heightened by the madness of the 1920s, with which she was fatally touched. She had been a wild teenager, the shock element at Chicago deb parties, and there was a disorder somewhere in her psyche, a lasting melancholy. Her mother had died of consumption when she was five years old and Alice herself was consumptive from birth. She was brought up mostly by a German governess, in large houses in New York. After a traumatic and unexplained incident involving her father, who was a drunk, she was made a ward of her uncle. But her father had often taken her to Europe, dressing her in lace and taking her to nightclubs while she was still in her early teens. Alice developed a liking for cocktails and a mania for animals and would be seen conspicuously walking her black panther, in its white collar, up and down the Promenade des Anglais in Nice.

She met the sensitive, literary Comte de Janzé, who came from an ancient Breton family, in a Paris antique shop when she was twenty-one. They were married in Chicago in 1922 and spent most of their short marriage, between the births of their two daughters, on a succession of safaris in Kenya.

The virtual absence of children in Happy Valley is something of a phenomenon. They would certainly have obstructed the grown-ups' leisurely programme, and it is a tribute to the residents of the Wanjohi that they managed to keep even accidental children from crossing the border. Joss and Idina did have a baby, called Diana, whom Nina Drury once saw asleep in the garage, dumped like the shopping on the back seat of their Hispano-Suiza. Alice's solution was simply to leave her two children behind, and later to dismiss them from her life altogether. They were brought up by Frédéric's sister at the family château in Normandy, and in Paris. "Alice knew that she would be a hopeless mother," said Patricia Bowles. "I admired her for her honesty."

Alice saw her children only occasionally on her rare

visits to Paris, when she would stay at the Hôtel de Bourgogne. One of her daughters, Nolwen, who is married to Lord Clark, recalls, remarkably, feeling no trace of resentment or *angoisse* at these meetings. Instead, she says, she was dazzled by the glamour of this mystery mother who lived in Africa. "I was very much in awe of her," she says, "and later, as I grew up, I appreciated her great virtues of courage and fortitude . . . However, it was the quality of her beauty, which was so delicate and transparent and her delicious grace and elegance—*that* was what made my heart turn over when I looked at her. And her hats, scarves, shoes had one enthralled. She dressed beyond perfection, with an instinctive and mysterious subtlety."

Alice made a great impression on Happy Valley, and on Idina herself, and seemed to inspire universal affection among her friends. She was always at the centre of things. She had a keen sense of the comic; she entertained them on her ukelele, singing in a low, broken voice. She was also intensely emotional, angrily bridling when her sense of justice was offended—especially when it came to the treatment of animals. Frédéric warned in *Vertical Land*, "No man will touch her exclusive soul, shadowy with memories, unstable, suicidal."

There is a telling, beautiful photograph of Alice, sitting in a wicker chair on her veranda, wearing her usual corduroy trousers and a wide felt hat of the period. On her lap is a lion cub, weighing at least forty pounds, evidently too grown-up to be a pet, with paws the size of her own hand, and its tail hanging down almost to her ankle. Alice is staring to one side with a distant look of an icon mother. She was often described as looking like a "wicked madonna," and the pose is perhaps self-parody. The lion cub, named Samson, was reared by Alice, who had a sizable menagerie on her farm. When it grew to be a lion, it required two zebras a week for its food. Alice n't face that, and sent it away.

The photograph powerfully evokes that period in Kenya, in mid-1926, when Alice was beginning her stormy romance with Raymond de Trafford. Her intermittent affair with Joss, which continued despite her new infatuation, had been conducted in some secrecy and for a time without Frédéric's knowledge. But with Raymond, who always extracted the maximum drama from any situation, that was impossible.

At first Alice had taken a violent dislike to Raymond, which made Frédéric suspect the beginning of yet another affair. As Alice told the story later, it was Joss who first discovered it. At a large party at Clouds he noticed that she and Raymond had slipped away. He crept into the adjoining bedroom, climbed up the wall partition, lay along the top of it, and heard the couple making plans to elope. "And what about poor Joss?" he interrupted. They did elope that night, but only as far as a cottage on Idina's estate.

Nina Drury remembers Idina's complaints the previous day about Joss's affair with Alice getting out of control. Now she said, "I do wish you'd find Alice for me."

Nina said, "But Idina, aren't you upset by her behaviour with Joss?"

Idina replied, "You seem to forget that Alice is my best friend."

There was a conference the following morning to decide how to get Alice back. Frédéric, the long-suffering husband, agreed to go, and found them in the cottage. Raymond had occupied the bed and Alice was sleeping on a chair. That was thought to be typical of Raymond. "I shall always remember her reception when she returned," said Nina Drury. "She was received like Royalty. All the men went down on one knee in front of her."

Frédéric took Alice home to Paris in an effort to save the marriage, but she returned to Kenya almost immediately to be with Raymond, then went back to Paris again to ask Frédéric for a divorce. On March 25th, 1927, Raymond came from London to Paris to tell Alice that his family, devout Roman Catholics, forbade him to marry her and had threatened to cut him off if he did so. A friend said, "Raymond could have written a letter, but he loved trouble and difficulty." He got considerably more than he bargained for. Before he left for London, he lunched with Alice in a *cabinet privé* at Lapérouse. Afterwards they went to a sporting equipment shop, where Alice had a small parcel wrapped at the far end of the counter and Raymond looked at the rifles. At the Gare du Nord, Alice climbed into the carriage of the train to see him off. She knelt in front of him, kissed him, pulled out a gun and fired, first at him and then at herself. Both were badly wounded, Raymond near the heart, and Alice in the stomach.

Alice had brought with her a friend's dog, a German Shepherd, which became hysterical and threatened to attack any of the attendants or policemen who tried to approach the wounded couple. Paula Long, the owner of the dog, said it was typical that Alice's only concern, as she was carried away bleeding on a stretcher, was to make sure the dog was returned to the right address, which she repeated several times. In the English hospital Alice told Paula with some relish of a nurse who looked into her room, clutching a dead baby in each arm, and who said, "Back in a tick."

Alice was charged with attempted murder. The scandal received enormous coverage, and she was released on probation from the Correctional Court on a wave of public sympathy. She was seen as the unhappy heroine of a true *crime passionel*, and the judge was seduced. "*Vous êtes une traîtresse, Madame,*" he told her before letting her off. It came out, during the hearing, that Alice had already made four attempts to kill herself. When the question of her having abandoned her children was mentioned, she said, somewhat ingenuously, "My only reply is that my action shows the strength of my love for the man for whose sake I made the sacrifice."

Early the following year, Alice was back in Kenya, but under orders from Government House to pack up and leave the country, as an undesirable alien. In the remaining weeks she took up her old affair with Josslyn. Karen Blixen, in a letter to her elder sister, described their arrival at her house at the end of February that year. She met Joss in Nairobi and invited him out to the farm for a ''bottle.'' He asked if he could bring Alice. That same day Karen Blixen was paid a surprise visit by Lady MacMillan (Northrop had been given an honorary knighthood) and three ''really huge and corpulent'' old American ladies, who had landed from a cruise ship for some sightseeing. They were hoping, above all, to see a lion. Blixen wrote,

They started to discuss all the dreadfully immoral people there were in Kenya, Americans too, unfortunately, and as the worst one of all mentioned Alice, and I, who of course knew that she was about to turn up, let them go into great detail about it. So when their car drove up and I went out to receive them, and came in and presented Lord Erroll and Comtesse de Janzé, I don't think that the devil himself could have a greater effect if he had walked in. It was undoubtedly better than the biggest lion and has given them much more to talk to their fellow passengers about.*

* Isak Dinesen, *Letters From Africa 1914–1931* (Weidenfeld & Nicolson, 1981); Karen Blixen also wrote under the name Isak Dinesen.

4

THE BONNY
EARL
OF ERROLL

IN 1928, JOSS'S FATHER had died and he
became the Earl of Erroll. His marriage to Idina was coming to an end, in a blaze of acrimony and bad debts which
he had run up in her name with the Indian merchants. Idina
might have approved of casual affairs, but not a serious
romance that would take him away for long periods and
disrupt her social programme.

Erroll had now fallen in love with Molly Ramsay-
Hill, another married heiress and a beauty, also older than
himself; a petite, slender, animated woman with auburn
hair. Her husband, Major Cyril Ramsay-Hill, was a rancher
who had built himself a huge whitewashed castle in the
Moroccan style on the edge of Lake Naivasha, with crenellated walls, a minaret and lawns sloping down to the
edge of the water. Oserian, as it was called, had been
known since Happy Valley days as the "Djinn Palace."
Compared with the sub-Lutyens gloom of most settler architecture, it is a house of haunting beauty, with a magnificent Art Deco bar outside the dining room.

There is a legend, still current in Nairobi, that Ramsay-Hill horsewhipped Erroll, for his seduction of Molly,
outside the Norfolk Hotel, "in front of a mixed audience
of Africans, Asians and Europeans." Erroll's own Somali
servant, who claims anonymity, witnessed the incident all
those years ago, and remembers it differently.

He had gone with Erroll to the Djinn Palace, where a house party had been arranged. One day he was ordered by Erroll to load up Major Ramsay-Hill's two Buicks for a safari into the Masai Reserve, towards Narok. The first Buick set off with Erroll and Mrs. Ramsay-Hill and the second followed with the luggage. When Major Ramsay-Hill discovered the absence of his wife and his Buicks, he sent his own Somali servant to look for her and then joined the hunt himself. It is not remembered precisely how many days this took but the search included a visit to the Norfolk Hotel in Nairobi, already a distance of some 100 miles and wildly off course. In fact, the Somali servants knew exactly where the party had gone but held back, apparently out of flawless discretion and because this was, after all, how the Bwanas chose to spend their time.

Ramsay-Hill finally found the couple in a tented camp at Narok. He had come with a rhino whip, with which he laid about Erroll as best he could, chasing him through the bush; then he got into one of his Buicks and went home to Oserian. In the divorce proceedings, Ramsay-Hill cited Erroll and won £3,000 damages to pay off the debts the couple had run up in his name, although Molly kept the Djinn Palace.

"It is obvious," said the judge, "that the co-respondent is a blackguard." As for Molly, it was obvious, that she too was a woman of very low character, though "that may be largely due to the influence of the co-respondent." Assessing the damages to Major Ramsay-Hill, he said, "I should have thought that he was very well rid of a bad woman, but he does not take that view. It is obvious that he had a great affection for her." In her own petition, meanwhile, Idina cited Molly and produced two enquiry agents to prove "misconduct" in a flat in Sloane Street, London, in April 1928.

In 1930, Erroll and Molly were married and moved into the Djinn Palace. The Scottish lord must have felt at home here, beside this beautiful lake, that had the look of a wild highland loch, encircled as it was by mountains and plains, its wide grassy shore bordering the water which, seen from the veranda of the Djinn Palace on a fine day, was a clear, cool blue pool. For decoration there were herons, black duck, chalk white egrets, and hippos rose and sank in the water among the floating islands of papyrus.

The bedroom doors of the house faced an inner courtyard with a tiled pool and a fountain in the centre. Thus entrances and exits were easily observed. There was a sunken marble bath lined with black and gold tiles in the main suite—to facilitate, so the story goes, the vomiting of overindulgent guests. The rooms and terraces were furnished with deep sofas and armchairs, loose-covered in flowered chintz. And Erroll's full-length portrait, in unpaid-for Coronation robes, hung at the top of the stairs. Once again, however, he was financially secure: Molly's estate produced an income of £8,000 a year.

Before long, out of boredom and an acute sense of his own abilities, the ruling instinct in Erroll began to assert itself and to bloom, encouraged by Lord Francis Scott, who recognised his natural talent for politics. The opportunities for power in that community were infinite: it was a tidy constituency and there was a marked absence of competition. The Premier Earl of Scotland was likely to be a figure of some weight, and he also expressed some forceful political sentiments. In 1934 he became a paid-up member of the British Union of Fascists.

Nellie Grant, Elspeth Huxley's mother, described Erroll's exploits on Oswald Mosley's behalf in her posthumously published book, *Letters from Africa*:

11th December 1934. Wednesday last was Joss Erroll's meeting at the (Muthaiga) Club to explain British fascism. There were 198 people there, no less, and a very good-tempered meeting, as everybody cheered to the echo what anyone said. British fascism simply means super loyalty to the Crown, no dictatorship, complete religious and social freedom, an "insulated Empire'' to trade with the dirty foreigner, higher wages and lower costs of living . . .

All questions and answers cheered to the roof . . . Whenever Joss said British fascism stands for complete freedom, you could hear Mary Countess [Molly] at the other end of the room saying that within five years, Joss will be dictator of Kenya.*

The following year Mussolini invaded Abyssinia, and Joss Erroll dropped his membership in the British Union of Fascists. Instead he was elected, aged thirty-four, to the Presidency of the Convention of Associations, the ''settlers' parliament''—a separate and unofficial rival to the Legislative Council. Eileen Scott, who described Erroll as ''much improved,'' was at the election.

To my surprise and delight, contrary to the expectations of most people, Joss Erroll was voted to the chair, largely outnumbering the Left Wing, and most of the executive are sound men too. It is a pity Joss hasn't had a year's more practice and experience; he has a brain like lightning, and it is difficult for him to listen patiently to this slow minded, if sound, community. However, it is a great step in the right direction, he is very able and a gentleman. Nearly everyone expected a Bolshie to be elected.

By now Erroll had begun to lose interest in his second Countess, and this, for Molly, signalled the beginning of a sad decline. She wanted desperately to produce a child and heir, and had many false pregnancies. Realising that she was losing Joss, she started to drink heavily and eventually to shoot morphine.

Erroll's absences were prolonged: ''He was very naughty with Molly,'' said Patricia Bowles. ''He gobbled up all her money and had walk-outs all the time.'' ''Bwana Hay told the servants,'' his own Somali servant recalls, '' 'I don't mind if she dies.' She got very drunk and had

* Elspeth Huxley, *Nellie: Letters from Africa* (Weidenfeld & Nicolson, 1980).

hidden the bottles. He said: 'Give the woman as much as she wants to drink. If she wants to die, let her have it. If she wants a drink, let her have one.' Then she died.'' The date was August 1939.

Dr. Joseph Gregory, the G.P. to the Muthaiga Club set, remembers that on his visits to Molly the house smelled of champagne and vomit. Molly's body was covered with heroin abscesses. Gregory remembered their last conversation:

She had been ill and lonely for a long time and she said to me, ''You will promise to come to my funeral, even if you're the only one?'' I said of course I would. She died that afternoon. After her death the flowers came pouring into the house, but while she was alive, not a daisy.

Molly's trustees stopped the flow of money, and Erroll temporarily closed down the house, although she had left it to him in her will. He moved to a bungalow in Muthaiga, near the entrance to the Club. He was broke now, living on credit. His father had left him an income of £300 a year. Otherwise he was down to Molly's pearls and his *droit de seigneur*.

By now, Erroll's taste for politics had turned him into a hard and conscientious worker. He had become secretary to Sir Ferdinand Cavendish Bentinck (later the Duke of Portland), at the Production and Settlement Board. ''He was rather a bounder,'' said Cavendish Bentinck. ''Very quick repartee, quite intelligent, very superficial. Bright, certainly, but not very profound. Too bright in that way really. Attractive chap.''

In 1939, Erroll was elected to the Legislative Council as the member for Kiambu. His political views had come round from those of fascist sympathiser to outright opposition to the appeasement policies of Neville Chamberlain (although most right-wingers in Britain were appeasers). Hitler had demanded the return of Germany's pre-war col-

onies. In his maiden speech in the House of Lords on a
brief visit to London the previous year, Erroll had argued
forcefully against the return of Tanganyika to Germany.

By 1940, Erroll, now thirty-nine, had become military
secretary for the Colony—he had joined the Kenya Regiment with the rank of Captain—and head of the Manpower Board. He was busy marshalling the East African
fighting force for the Abyssinian campaign, and his ad-
ministrative skill was widely praised. Sir Wilfred Have-
lock, who worked under Erroll, said, "I saw him as an
executive; he was a demanding man, brilliant at his job.
When he was working as head of Manpower, the records
of all the military personnel were destroyed by fire. Erroll
built them up again, completely out of his head."

In 1940, Erroll was also in the middle of a serious
love affair with a married woman from Happy Valley
whom I shall call Nancy Wirewater. She was unpopular
with the other women in that social set, who were bemused
by Erroll's infatuation with her. The lovers were forced
to meet mostly in the lunch hour: Erroll would have a
bottle of champagne put on ice each day in the billiard
room of the Norfolk Hotel, where he was once caught by
Auntie, the proprietress, having his way with Mrs. Wirewater on the billiard table.

Erroll never seemed to lose the affection, the devotion
even, of his discarded mistresses. One woman who held
a particular emotional claim on him, who had never quite
got over their brief affair, was Gwladys (pronounced
Gladys), Lady Delamere, widow of Hugh Delamere. In
1920, against the wishes of her friends, she had married
Sir Charles Markham, who was younger than herself and
considered a waster. The marriage lasted seven years with
some conspicuous unfaithfulness on both sides.

She married Hugh Delamere in 1928, three years before he died. That same year she had travelled out to Kenya
as the girlfriend of Edward, Prince of Wales on the first
of his safaris. She was considered very attractive, with her

pale skin and jet black hair, although not by Karen Blixen who described, in addition to her "odd" looks, a fierce streak of recklessness in her behaviour. She wrote to her sister,

Lady Delamere behaved scandalously at supper, I thought. She bombarded the Prince of Wales with big pieces of bread, and one of them hit me, sitting beside him, in the eye, so I have a black eye today, and finished up by rushing at him, overturning his chair and rolling him around on the floor. I do not find that kind of thing in the least amusing, and stupid to do at a club; as a whole I do not find her particularly likable, she looks so odd, exactly like a painted wooden doll.*

On the Prince's next safari, Gwladys was dropped from the entourage.

By 1940, Gwladys had become somewhat more unbalanced, partly, it was thought, from the effect of a serious bout of typhoid, and from unhappiness in love. She had lost her looks; her face had turned puffy with drink and she had taken to wearing elaborate headdresses. She had become exhibitionistic, touchy and unpredictable: loyal at one moment, she would cut you dead the next. At her birthday party at the Muthaiga Club, she threw a plate of bacon and eggs at another woman, and had to be removed. She was equally violent on the subject of race, publicly insulting a woman called Sybil Martineau for "having African blood" and leading the Muthaiga members to bar the Aga Khan—the spiritual head of the large Ismaili community in Kenya—from coming to the Club. Blunt, autocratic, perceptive, with a strident air and a sharp tongue, Gwladys, now the Mayor of Nairobi, had become the repository of "good advice," the breaker and maker of matches. Her feelings for Erroll were now expressed in matronly possessiveness. In general she found it difficult to tolerate younger and prettier women.

* Isak Dinesen, *Letters From Africa 1914–1931* (Weidenfeld & Nicolson, 1981).

Meanwhile, Alice had been allowed to return to Kenya and take up residence in the Wanjohi Valley. In 1932 she had made the mistake of marrying Raymond de Trafford five years after the shooting at the Gare du Nord. Barely three months after their marriage, at Neuilly, they were separated. Paula Long remembers their incessant fighting, and the final scene, enacted on a café terrace in Paris, over a dispute about the comparative gifts of two conductors. Alice was wearing a hat with a short veil. Raymond hurled his cocktail at her face, the maraschino cherry stuck to the veil, and he burst out laughing. They never saw each other again. In 1939, Raymond was jailed for three years for manslaughter—he had killed a pedestrian while driving in an advanced state of drunkenness. He was next in court in 1946, charged with bankruptcy. He gave his address as the Riviera Hotel, Maidenhead, Berkshire.

In the Wanjohi, Alice resumed her life of ease and her bouts of depression. She lived mostly alone with her pet eland—a buck of enormous size—and her precious Dachshund "Minnie." Patricia Bowles described her life:

She adored her dogs, she read a lot, played a hell of a lot of backgammon—we were new at it. We used to spend a considerable amount of time trying to decide where to have our S.N.S. [Saturday Night Souse]. We would drink as soon as she could persuade us to. She did a whisky sour with grenadine and fresh lime, which was delicious. She'd find very curious liqueurs from the duka [local store] and make the most wonderful cocktails, but the whisky sours sent you pretty quickly. Her house was all under one roof with no ceiling partitions between the rooms. So whatever was going on you could hear it and that often caused trouble. You might have thought it was off-putting, but it wasn't. It was quite encouraging.

By 1940, Alice had adopted a new friend, Julian "Lizzie" Lezard, who was already a celebrated figure in London society. Lezard was an inspired buffoon—untidy, unshaven, and hilariously funny. Forever gambling, always broke, he had been sent to Kenya not by his father, his regiment or his trustees, but by his wife. Men found him an exhausting joke. Women, with whom he was obsessed, found him "a tremendous relief at weekends full of twits." They remember, too, his vitality and his profound curiosity about them. There is a pen portrait of this incredible figure in Sir Charles Johnston's book of wartime Cairo, *Mo and Other Originals** (Lezard came to be known, for his exploits behind enemy lines in France, as "the man who broke his back at Monte Carlo"). Johnston describes Lezard greeting the news of his engagement in Cairo:

"You and Natasha are going places, Charlieboy," he said. "When I've nothing else to do, I like to lie in bed sizing people up, and that's the conclusion I've come to. Your life together's going to be like a really well run dinner party. You know, there are some dinners where everyone's drunk with the fish, and some where they're drunk with the meat. But in your life everyone will be drunk at midnight and not a minute before. Of course, my trouble," he added reminiscently, "was that I got drunk before dinner and had to go out and be sick during the soup."

"Lizzie" Lezard had been a gifted tennis player who had come from South Africa with the Davis Cup team. He was the privileged outsider, the victim of merciless teasing which he could turn to brilliant advantage. Deeply unsure of himself, he longed for affection and praise from the rich and aristocratic, and went to embarrassing lengths to secure it.

For some years Lezard was able to live in considerable style. He was taken up by and later married to Hilda Wardell, a lady of a certain age, and with plenty of money, who introduced him into the hunting world of Leicestershire. Tricked out in pink swallow-tails, his black curls escaping from one side of his top hat, Lezard rode with reckless bravery and little style with the Quorn and Pytchley, falling off and remounting like a circus clown. "It

* Hamish Hamilton, 1971.

was a strong Jewish urge of the period," a fellow guest at the Wardell house remembers, "the determination to martyr themselves on the hunting field. I suppose it was to do with keeping up with the philistines." Lezard always retained the jargon of the hunting field. His favourite motto was "Hit 'em and hold 'em."

After several years, Hilda Wardell could take no more. Perhaps she had had to bail Lezard out of a gambling debt once too often. They divorced amicably and she sent Lezard to Kenya without a penny. He was told that Alice de Trafford, now divorced from Raymond and living in Happy Valley, would look after him. Alice brought him back to the Wanjohi Valley in her box-body car. The Wanjohi road was at its worst, the car slewing to the edge of the escarpment and the rain beating at the windscreen in curtains. Lizzie Lezard turned to Alice and said, "Look, I think I'd rather be a shit in London than a pioneer in Kenya."

Erroll and Lezard were perfectly matched: the comedian and the Earl, both broke, both mad about women. Lezard was fascinated by Erroll, and the obvious place to stay, the very centre of social activity, was Erroll's house at Muthaiga.

5

A SPELL
IN
MASAI COUNTRY

Such rich men with absentee wives may be revived only
by a successful love affair. They are too grand to work
and too intelligent to play. Boredom stalks them, age
and bitterness follow. They find themselves in a prison
of the *déjà vu*, surrounded by good advice and
grey hair; within the spirit is as youthful as ever,
protesting "Can this be all?"
CYRIL CONNOLLY

The Delves Broughtons (pronounced "Brawton") began coming to Kenya on hunting safaris soon after the
Armistice. Sir Jock Delves Broughton's first wife, Vera,
was a mighty huntress and adventuress, and Broughton
had been told by his Harley Street doctor, Sir Farquhar
Buzzard, that a spell in Masai country would be the best
cure for his headaches and his excitable mental condition,
though Broughton claimed this to be the result of sunstroke, contracted at Portsmouth while his battalion was
loading up for France in 1914. In 1923 he had bought a
coffee plantation in Kenya. Now in 1940, aged fifty-seven,
he was returning with a new wife, this time looking for
refuge from another war.

Broughton was born into the protected, leisured world
of racing and into the big league of landowning families.

His father, the 10th Baronet, owned three houses: Doddington Park in Cheshire, Broughton Hall in Staffordshire and 6 Hill Street, in Mayfair, London. Doddington was the family seat—a fine if somewhat gloomy Samuel Wyatt house in an eighteenth-century setting of parkland and lakes. With the houses came some 34,000 acres: a vast estate mostly of prime Cheshire farmland, which would now be worth something over £70 million.

Broughton was born in 1883 (though *Who's Who*, for which he filled in the forms himself, gives the date as 1888). His mother died when he was two, and his father remarried. He could never get on with his stepbrother and stepsister, and hated his father, who kept him chronically short of money, instilling in him a lifelong sense of injury and disadvantage by comparison with his peers. There was a rumour at Eton, where he was thought both dim and overproud, that he had been forced to steal because of his tight allowance, and another that he had fits of ungovernable temper that kept his fellow pupils out of his way. After Eton he went to a crammer's for some force-fed tutoring and joined the Irish Guards in 1902.

In 1913 he married Vera Boscawen, who came from an impoverished branch of a good family. She was tall and blue-eyed, with outstanding good looks, and Broughton may have been in love with her—he was certainly proud of her glamour and the wonderful clothes she wore. A Cheshire neighbour said of Vera that she was hard as nails, loved nobody and was determined to get all she could out of life. She liked racing, bridge, canasta and mah-jongg—any game or sport that made conversation impossible and dull people tolerable. "She also enjoyed the adventure of killing huge, brilliant animals. She probably despised Jock but found his money comforting."

Broughton was thirty-one when his father died in 1914. Along with Valentine, Viscount Castlerosse, he was considered the best-looking officer in the Irish Guards. Having for years found it difficult to pay his bills at the officers' mess, he now had a princely income along with the houses and the acres.

Just then, on August 12th, 1914, the Irish Guards (including the future Field-Marshal Alexander) sailed for France. With one exception. Kipling, whose son was killed in the same regiment, wrote in *The Irish Guards in the Great-War*, ''Just before leaving, Captain Sir Delves Broughton, Bart, was taken ill and had to be left behind.''

Broughton was taken off the S.S. *Novara* by tender, and a telegram went off to headquarters, asking for Captain Hamilton Berners to take his place. The *Novara* cleared at 7 p.m. As dark fell, she passed H.M.S. *Formidable* off Ryde and exchanged signals with her. The battleship's last message to the battalion was to hope that they would get ''plenty of fighting.''

On the Aisne, exactly a month after his arrival, the replacement, Captain Hamilton Berners, was killed. So, too, was the Guards' Colonel, the Hon. George Morris, and two other officers. Lord Francis Scott became Delves Broughton's new Commanding Officer. Two more of the Guards' wounded officers were invalided home: Captain Vesey and 2nd Lt. Viscount Castlerosse, who joined Delves Broughton at the Depot at Warley.

What was the nature of his illness? It was described later as ''sunstroke'' brought on through long hours of loading, but it suggested more strongly some severe psychosomatic affliction. A survivor wrote,

I merely heard he had gone sick. The day had not been over-strenuous for a normal fit man and there can be no question of sunstroke. He was not a very bellicose gent and he was certainly never again in a service battalion.

Nevertheless, Broughton was treated in hospitals at Netley and Millbank, and retired from the army in 1919, with a 50 per cent disability pension. He now dragged his left foot as he walked; he had an arthritic right hand with a weak grip—the result of a motor accident in 1915—and was subject to bouts of confusion and amnesia.

Now began the twenty-year-long innings of the thirty-six-year-old Baronet, who started to spend heavily as if to make up for lost time, to gamble, to entertain on a large scale. Haunted by the fear that he would at any moment run short of cash, despite an income of £80,000, he liquidated a large part of the estate, some 15,000 acres, almost as soon as he had inherited it. He joined the Turf Club, kept a stable of thirty horses; and he sat on the Nantwich Bench as a Justice of the Peace. He had a passion for bridge and racing—although he was always "somewhere warm" for most of the steeplechasing season—and he was a tournament-class croquet player. Vera became a hunter of big game and in 1919–20 they made their first trip to Kenya. They went back again in 1923 and met Broughton's old school friend, Jack Soames, who had settled in Nanyuki. Broughton bought the Spring Valley coffee estate near Nairobi. In 1928, again in Kenya, he met the Earl of Erroll at Muthaiga, and stayed with Lord Delamere and his wife, Gwladys, at Soysambu.

At Doddington Broughton insisted that all the guest rooms were filled each weekend. He would hire the band from Ciro's to play the guests down to Cheshire on the train and would hold up the express at Crewe if his returning guests were late getting away to the station, with a telephone call and a brace of pheasants flung into the guard's van. Train tickets were sent round in advance to his London guests by the secretary at Hill Street. The weekend parties were often reported in the *Sketch* and the *Tatler*, the guests paraded on the gravel drive for photographs, the readers reminded that the Broughtons were an ancient family, "of consideration for centuries in the counties of Cheshire and Stafford."

For all his hospitality, Broughton, the sporting Baronet, was not popular among his contemporaries. Other men were suspicious of him—possibly because of his great wealth, or because he could only unbend with women. He was certainly vain, "with his high collars and his haw-haw voice" (the false entry in *Who's Who* hints at that); he was a name-dropper, and yet he could sulk for a week without giving a reason. He was distant, lonely, somewhat humourless. His guests at Doddington noticed his disconcerting habit of going into what appeared to be a trance for five minutes or more, especially at meals, staring blankly into the distance, unable to hear any remark addressed to him. "Sour!" was the adjective supplied by an elder statesman.

"You mean cynical?"

"No, worse than cynical. Sour."

"He looked as if there was always an unpleasant smell under his nose," said a Cheshire neighbour. "He liked scatological jokes."

"Not a nice man," said the Club servants, "arrogant, like the Blenheim lot. None of us liked him."*

"Dishonest, charmless, morose," was the Clubmen's view. "He was a coward, faked a sunstroke because he feared going to France." A woman described him as a sad, rather querulous man, who never smiled, and another as "vicious, cold and cruel in more ways than one."

Vera went racing with Lord Carnarvon, Lord Rosebery and Sir Brograve Beauchamp, but she was often away from home on her adventures to unreachable and forbidden places, and from the mid-1930s she spent more and more time on safaris or cruises with her great friend Walter Guinness, the third son of the Earl of Iveagh, who became Lord Moyne in 1932. There was certainly an imbalance in the marriage. Vera was energetic, curious, full of vitality. Broughton, by contrast or necessity, was afflicted increasingly with boredom and world weariness. They began to go their separate ways. The Earl of Antrim, who often visited Doddington, wrote to Cyril Connolly in 1969,

* Blenheim Palace belongs to the Dukes of Marlborough and the Spencer-Churchills.

Perhaps Jock was finding life tedious; he had no intellectual tastes
and although he went out hunting he never cut a dash. I believe
he craved sympathy and affection and most of all to be amused.
One could see how he lit up when he was enjoying himself.

Broughton's only son and heir, Sir Evelyn, the present
Baronet, was born in 1915. By the time he was nineteen
and a Cambridge undergraduate in 1934, Evelyn and his
father were more or less strangers, and Evelyn's description of his father is revealing of the man. What contact
there was occurred mostly out of doors, hunting and shooting. It appeared that Broughton was inflicting on his son
what he himself had suffered as a boy. He visited Evelyn
only once during his five-year career at Eton, and had
never been to see him at his prep school. "If there was
anything wrong," said Evelyn, "my mother came down."
    When the Fourth of June, the birthday of the bene-
factor George III, came around at Eton, and other parents arrived with their hampers, Evelyn asked leave of his
housemaster to go racing. (The Fourth of June sometimes
coincided with the Coronation Cup at Epsom.) Often his
father would be there, and they would meet in the grandstand, as if by chance.
    Later, Broughton could not understand how Evelyn
managed to take out girls, go to Paris for the weekend,
eat at fashionable restaurants, and so on, on the very small
allowance that he gave him. Though Evelyn kept two
hunters at Cambridge and subscribed to a fashionable
shooting syndicate, these were approved expenses paid
directly by his father.
    The truth was that Evelyn had another source of in-
come. He took large betting commissions from his father's
own stable employees, and he was usually lucky with his
own bets. One day at the racecourse, he put £700—£400
on an unbeaten horse called Windsor Lad, hoping to wipe
out a debt of several hundred pounds to a bookmaker. The
bookie wanted to refuse the bet. Evelyn pointed out his

father in the grandstand and said that Broughton had three runners that day, and that if something went wrong he would pay up.

"I'm sure he'll pay up, he's a gentleman," said the bookie. "I'll take your bet and good luck to you."

So I went up to the stand, and I saw my father and he said, "My boy, you're sweating a lot aren't you?" I said, "Am I, Daddy?" He said, "Well, I think Windsor Lad's a good thing. Here's five pounds. I don't often give you any money, but, look here, I'm going to give you a fiver." So I said, "All right, Daddy." So, I made all the motions. Went right the way down to the bookies' stands. Windsor Lad won. I crept back to the stands. He said, "What's wrong, my boy, you're completely relaxed. You're a different person." I said, "It's your fiver, Daddy."

Like all that generation, I think we were brought up to a considerable amount of self discipline. We were used to threats. If someone said you'd be horsewhipped, you'd be frightened. Nowadays we'd just walk out of the house.

I remember one acrimonious dinner party. I was sitting at one end of the table at Doddington, about thirty to dinner—and I'd been accused by my father from the other side of the dining room of leaving the stud gates open. Hadn't been near the stud all day. And I answered back, in front of all the guests. Frightful acrimony went on and finally he said, "You mustn't argue with your father," and he got up from the table with his napkin—he was a heavy man and I had no idea what he was going to do. Anyway he collapsed in the doorway. I, by that time, was half way up the stairs. He bruised himself and had to be picked up by the butler. And my mother roared with laughter. But you see, you'd not to answer back. Not in front of the guests.

One day in 1935, the tedium for Broughton was suddenly interrupted: at a weekend at Tadcaster, staying with his friend Jack Fielden, he met his fate, as Connolly put it: "His Green Hat, his Blue Angel, the woman who would renew his youth and bring him back into the world of feeling." Her name was Diana Caldwell; she was twenty-two, and she had been proposed to that very weekend by

Fielden himself, but had turned him down. Although not a classic beauty, she was very striking, with her pale blue eyes and mass of blonde hair; her way of radiating enjoyment and the quickness of her smile had touched off many an infatuation.

Connolly was fascinated by Diana and later described her as "one of those creamy ash blondes of the period with a passion for clothes and jewels, both worn to perfection, and for enjoying herself and bringing out enjoyment in others. Her large pale eyes would be called cold by those on whom they had not smiled, her mouth hard by those who had not kissed it."

She was already a talked-about social success: she danced in London, hunted in Warwickshire, flew her own plane to Le Touquet, Vienna and Budapest.

Her father, Seymour Caldwell, of the Red House, Hove, Sussex, had been a gambler and little else since leaving Eton. Her mother had been a beauty. Diana had been briefly married to a playboy musician called Vernon Motion, who played second piano to Carroll Gibbons and his Savoy Orpheans; who was much in demand at parties, but disowned by his family. Diana divorced him for adultery soon after the marriage. Her address was now 4 Duke Street, Manchester Square, London.

She had gravitated naturally to the racing world and to the Grafton Hunt in Warwickshire, where she kept a pony in stables and where she hunted most weekends in the season. Her grey pony could jump the highest hedges out of plough—twisting oddly in the air as it took off—and Diana was often asked to lead the field, thereby attracting many early admirers. In London she ran a cocktail club with her friend Betty Somerset, called the Blue Goose, in Bruton Mews, near Bond Street. She led a hectic social life, and used her aeroplane to pursue it across Europe. She flew with the famous aviatrix Amy Mollison. She fell in with an exclusive group of aviating aristocrats, one of whom was Prince Stahremberg, the Austrian Vice-Chancellor. They would meet in Budapest and the *Tatler* correspondent was somehow always there. The pair were photographed sitting in a rowing boat in swimsuits, Diana holding her shoes. Fashionably, she had put on a little weight.

Perhaps it was the bitter experience of that first marriage that led Diana to look for an older man. For his part, Broughton couldn't believe his luck. Now a lonely middle-aged man—Vera was rarely at home—he had one wish: to be loved for himself and, failing that, to be allowed to love someone who was delightful to look at and not boring. The very coolness of Diana Caldwell was part of her attraction. It was fashionable to be grown-up, sophisticated, bored—a reaction against the looseness of the 1920s. Yet in other women she provoked a suspicion and a deep jealousy which has lasted throughout her life. Her contemporaries remember her vividly, especially the peculiar "red" of her lipstick on the hunting field, which was thought a little "too much," and the danger she posed. She was punished for her success with men by the suggestion that she was tough, scheming and faintly "common"—that uniquely English insult that in the end has more to do with detecting origins within a narrow social group than with personal style. Diana's flaw, especially in the peculiarly intense snobbery of the 1930s, was that while she was winning the hearts of the most eligible young men there was nothing, to the relief of her competitors, you could look up in *Burke's*.

For social ambition she was compared to the two wives of Valentine, Viscount Castlerosse. She was said, for example, to have the same overriding passion for jewellery as his first wife, Doris Delavigne, who was known as "Mrs. Goldsmith and Silversmith" and who would make the sign of the cross as she muttered to herself, "Tiara, brooch, clip, clip." "She had cold, cruel eyes like Enid Kenmare" (his second wife), said a contemporary in 1968. Diana's own models might have been

Carole Lombard and Constance Bennett in Hollywood, and from the English aristocracy, Diana Mosley, the most beautiful of the Mitford sisters. To her aristocratic rivals, who considered her *arriviste*, Jean Harlow was more to the point.

Diana was much photographed. She had a wistful picture taken in 1937 by Lenare and published in the *Sketch*, her lovely neck still innocent of pearls, when she was to be a bridesmaid to Lady Patricia McKay. A *Tatler* photograph in 1939 shows her with a perm and a large trilby hat at Leopardstown races in Ireland. She was often photographed in the company of a handsome young lieutenant called Hugh Dickinson. Indeed, Dickinson was never far away from Diana, and he was a frequent guest at Doddington.

Broughton now saw himself as Diana's chief "suitor," and began to refer to her as "my blonde." They were not, apparently, a possessive couple, and he raised no objections to the nightly dances, the driving, the aviation, and the many suitors. He even encouraged them. He would stay at Doddington alone while Diana, in London, went off to the 400 Club in Leicester Square.

A member of the 400, then aged twenty-one, remembers Diana there with Broughton one night, in about 1938.

He seemed much older than the other men, who thought him rather odd, a little sad because the 400 was very racy and glamorous then. To me she seemed older, too, even with the small difference in age between us. I didn't see her as a great beauty. She was rather Aldershot, with slightly heavy features. She wasn't particularly slim or tall. She had a mass of blonde hair, and wore her make-up to give the "natural look."

Diana Caldwell was roughly the same age as Broughton's children, and as the relationship with Broughton developed it led to increasing difficulties with them and with Vera. Consequently the house parties at Doddington began to dwindle.

A constant friend of Broughton's in these pre-war years—I will call her "Harriet"—remembers Broughton's increasing loneliness in this period and the Gatsbyish air that took over his existence at Doddington. Harriet, the life-loving young divorcee, had first met Broughton at Highclere with Lord Carnarvon in the late 1930s. She had found him charming, but also devious and unscrupulous —a weary man of pleasure with his houses and stables and rather exaggerated sense of position. At dinner Harriet told him she would like to spend a million pounds a year.

"You couldn't," he said.

"What's the most you've ever spent?" she asked.

Broughton replied, "In a good year—1926 I think— I spent £120,000. The first eighty was quite easy, but unless you gamble, the rest is sheer extravagance."

They became friends, and Broughton invited Harriet to Doddington. He rang up to say it would not be a house party, only his "blonde" would be there. Harriet, a self-confessed snob, already disliked Diana intensely. She couldn't come, she told him, "because I didn't want to have to be polite to someone in one place whom I would cut in another." Her father told her not to be rude on the telephone: just to say she wasn't able to go.

Broughton promised that Diana would not be there for the weekend after all and Harriet was persuaded to change her mind.

When she arrived she was taken up to the long gallery and offered champagne (Broughton then disapproved of cocktails). Diana Caldwell was standing by the fire. Harriet said, "I think I should take the next train back to London." "Don't fuss, darlin'," she remembers Broughton saying, "there's no need. She's going on it." Diana had been there on Friday to hunt and had already planned to return to London. Nevertheless, if she was aware of it this was an unforgettable slight. When Diana had left for Crewe station, Harriet asked Broughton what he had said to her. "I more or less told her what you said," Broughton replied. "I said, 'How awful,' " Harriet reported, "and you know, I really think he didn't care."

Harriet concludes that money was Broughton's first love and that he never really liked women. He would show some sexual interest, but—in her case at least—accept a refusal instantly. These late-night entrances, she thinks, were more signs of loneliness and the need for sympathy and affection—a need also perceived in Broughton by the Earl of Antrim. Perhaps there was a streak of masochism in his choice of women, especially of Vera and Diana— both somewhat commanding figures—a legacy of his unhappy childhood.

In 1938 Broughton and Vera made a final public appearance together at the marriage of their daughter Rosamund to Lord Lovat. The following year Broughton sold another 15,000 acres of land, leaving Doddington with an estate of less than 4,000 acres. Broughton House in Staffordshire had gone already, and rumours had begun to circulate that he was heavily in debt, that he had made some catastrophic mistakes in his investments. Although he claimed that his racing cost him nothing, there may have been betting losses too. There was no other way to explain the disintegration of the family fortunes. "Sheer extravagance" couldn't really account for it, since the estate was legally in the hands of the trustees.

That year Broughton reported two robberies, and collected the insurance on both. In the summer the Broughton pearls, insured for £17,000, were stolen from the glove compartment of Miss Caldwell's car outside a fashionable restaurant on the Côte d'Azur, where she was dining with, among others, Rory More O'Ferrall, Mark Pilkington and her old friend, Hugh Dickinson. Broughton was in England. As Dickinson remarked, "It was a damn silly place to leave them." In October, a thief broke into Doddington while Broughton was in London and cut three family portraits from their frames, including two Romneys; these, too, had been heavily and recently insured. The thief had got in through an open window on the first floor after a messy attempt to cut through a ground floor window pane with a diamond.

Harriet remembers a conversation with Broughton about a friend of his who had collected the insurance on three burned houses. Broughton thought this ''very successful.''

''Do you know what you are saying?'' said Harriet. ''You're implying that he set fire to three houses to collect the money.''

''I only meant that everything had gone well for him,'' replied Broughton. ''But if he needed the money, well, why not?''

IN 1939 LORD MOYNE'S wife died and Vera, who hoped to marry him, began divorce proceedings against Broughton. This surprised Broughton and hurt him deeply. He had tolerated Vera's affair, but to lose her was a severe blow to his vanity, and he would miss the familiar habits of twenty-five years, hard and distant though they had been. In August he wrote to Harriet telling her of his despair, saying that he felt his life was falling apart, and that it had been entirely his own fault that Vera had left him. She remembered him saying that Vera was the only woman he had ever loved. This stood out in her mind because she had always found him such a cynical man.

Broughton's response was to propose marriage to Diana, and to make plans to emigrate to Kenya. He had his properties there to look after, and he could imagine that by contributing to feeding the mass of troops gathering in Kenya, he was helping the war effort. And there was another good reason for leaving, apart from the debts: the situation in England might soon prove very unpleasant; it was as bad a place to be in 1940 as to be away from in 1914. Diana was eager to accept the proposal, for what also seemed to be negative reasons. Her father had recently died. Her mother had always been feckless and inattentive. All her close friends had disappeared to the war or into marriage, and she felt that her life, too, was falling apart. Not everyone thought the marriage a good idea, and Harriet saw it as a disaster.

They went out by boat via South Africa. They discovered that because of the shortage of accommodation in Nairobi, a permit was needed to enter Kenya. While they waited, news came through of the divorce decree granted to Vera in London. Broughton's marriage to Diana did not follow immediately. Cockie Hoogterp, then the Baroness Blixen (Bror Blixen's second wife after Isak Dinesen) met the couple in Johannesburg a few weeks before the ceremony finally took place and detected some uncertainty on Diana's part. Cockie made a dinner date with Broughton, and then, when her husband arrived unexpectedly from war duties, she proposed that they go out as a foursome. "Jock said we'd better make it another time," she said. "When I saw him later and said that I thought it would have made a *partie carrée*, he said, 'Oh, Diana and I never go out together. I always go out separately.' " Driving with Broughton to the Country Club, Cockie asked him if he was serious about marrying Diana. "There's many a slip," was his reply.

Cockie began to wonder about the happiness of her old friend. "Jock asked me not to write to anybody in Kenya about Diana. He had already asked for an entry permit, and had given the impression that the Lady Broughton he was bringing would be Vera." Nevertheless she did write—to Lord Francis Scott. "He asked me what I'd written and I told him that he was with an extremely glamorous girl, but I thought she had a heart of steel and that she was a gold digger. He said, 'You're quite wrong, she's not like that at all.' Perhaps I was wrong in the end.

"When I met Diana, Jock asked me if she would like Nairobi. I said she would adore Nairobi, but did he realise that every man there was going to fall flat for her. He said, 'Oh, that's all right. I'm not the least bit jealous.' I thought, that's very lucky for you."

Six weeks before the marriage, Broughton entered into

a peculiar contract with Diana which was quite separate from their marriage vows. If Diana fell in love with a younger man, and wanted a divorce, Broughton, in view of the difference in their ages, agreed not to stand in her way, and to provide her with a gross income of her own of £5,000 a year for at least seven years after divorce. It was a generous deal which made no demands on Diana and seemed to expect remarkably little of the marriage.

The ceremony took place in a Durban register office on November 5th, 1940.

6
SUNDOWNERS
TO
SUNRISE

THE NEWLY WED couple arrived by boat in Mombasa on November 12th, 1940, where they met up briefly with Hugh Dickinson, who was now a Lieutenant in the Signal Corps, and had been posted to Kenya. In fact Dickinson, although married, had organised his transfer to be near Diana, and had arrived only five days previously. That same day, with their new white lady's maid, Dorothy Wilks, the Broughtons flew to Nairobi.

On the same flight was a sadistic, satanic character called John Carberry, whose exploits any new arrival in Kenya would quickly hear about. His wife, June, was at Nairobi airport to meet him. She and Diana struck up an instant alliance and were soon to become "best friends."

Somewhere along the way, probably at public school, Carberry, who was born John Evans-Freke and had become the 10th Baron and 3rd Baronet Carbery at the age of six in 1898 (the barony, as opposed to the family name, was spelt with one r), developed a violent dislike for his native England, which he now called "Johnny Bull," and an equal passion for America. He had been educated at Harrow and Trinity College, Cambridge, in Switzerland and at Leipzig; and had served during the First World War in the Royal Naval Air Service. In 1919 he had taken out American naturalisation papers, which were withdrawn because of his involvement in bootlegging, and in 1920 in Kenya had changed his name by deed poll to John Evans Carberry, dropping his title. Carberry had even acquired an American accent, addressing Beryl Markham, the celebrated Kenyan aviatrix, for example, as "Burrrll." His first wife divorced him for cruelty in 1919. His second wife was Maia Anderson, another flier, who died piloting her plane in 1928. In her daughter Juanita's view, this was suicide provoked by the bullying and cruelty of her husband.

Carberry had by now become a Nazi sympathiser out of pure anti-English sentiment. Earlier that year, 1940, at a wedding party at the White Rhino Hotel at Nyeri, he had proposed the toast: "Long Live Germany. To hell with England." He was reported to the police but it was thought best to let the matter lie.

Recalling Carberry forty years later, a woman who knew him then retained a vivid image of his magnetism. "He was not only tall and handsome, but the way he swung along the beach at Malindi was . . . captivating." He had a house at Malindi, an airstrip—he was a trophy-winning pilot—and a bar called the Eden Roc, where the drink measures contained marbles. He owned another house and a ranch at Nyeri called Seremai (a Masai word meaning "Place of Death"), an historical scene of bloodshed between the Kikuyu and the Masai. There Carberry ran his liquor still with his partner, Maxwell Trench, whose Jamaican parents had taught him the art of distilling cane. They made cheap gin, Jamaican rum, crème de menthe and eau de cologne.

In 1930 Carberry was married for the third time, to June Mosley, the only woman who proved able to stand up to his monstrous behaviour. Dushka Repton remembers meeting the couple in Paris that year:

At seventeen she couldn't put two words together, and she was common as hell. J.C. introduced her as his "baby." "That's my dumb baby," he said, in a broad American accent. Some *baby*. We went out for dinner. She had this ghastly outfit. She wore a scarlet jersey dress and a burgundy red hat and it really looked twopence halfpenny. I think she had brown shoes. I said, "Where the hell did you get that outfit?" But she was very pretty. Huge, rather *à fleur de tête* eyes, long lashes, long hair and very painted lips. She looked like a very pretty chorus girl. When she married Carberry she said, "I refuse to have any presents," and she was rather careful with his money. Carberry took her up in a plane, soon after he met her, and asked her whether she would like him to do some stunts. "Now, baby, wanna do some stunts?" She undid her safety belt to show she wasn't a coward. Luckily all the stunts were perfect, and that's how she won his heart.

Later she was described as a "terrifyingly unnatural blonde. Deep bass voice. Tough as boots. But a wonderful person, warm hearted and totally unjealous. Cut her in half, you'd find mostly gin."

June's drink in fact was brandy and soda, and she drank it all day, as she chain-smoked. Carberry drank too, but never after dinner. The couple used terrible language to each other and they had violent rows, but Carberry adored his wife, and admired her tenacity. She had many affairs and Carberry usually didn't mind. Once when June went off with Derek Fisher on a trip to Meru while Carberry was away, he came back unexpectedly. When he discovered his wife gone, he took off again and caught up with the couple driving across Cole's plains. He had loaded the plane with medium sized rocks, with which he bombarded their car from the air.

His servants called Carberry by the Masai name, "Msharisha"—the long whip with which oxen are driven—because he was tall, and because he used to lash them on the slightest pretext. His attitude to the African race is best described by Lady Altrincham. "I took a great dislike to him. Once, when some petrol had gone missing, he said, 'Blame it on the boy.' I said, 'But he didn't do it.' 'That doesn't matter,' said Carberry."

Animals as well as humans were subjected to Carberry's distinctive brand of sadism. Once, for example, he took a particular dislike to a hen which June had adopted and which had a privileged position in the Carberry household simply because June, who loved animals, had taken a fancy to it. It had even been allowed to lay its eggs on the sofa. This was too much for Carberry. The hen, he declared, must be subjected to a test of worthiness. He bet the manager of the Seremai estate that it would fly if he dropped it from his aeroplane, or, at least, fly well enough to survive. The guests at Seremai that day remember the hen dropping out of Carberry's aeroplane like a stone. It was at first presumed dead, but some hours later it was found limping lopsidedly through the coffee shamba. Only then was it allowed to resume its privileges.

A table for three had been booked for lunch on the day of the Broughtons' arrival (November 12th) at the Muthaiga Club, where they would stay while they looked for a suitable house. Their guest was Gwladys Delamere, the Mayor of Nairobi. Broughton had known her well during her first marriage in England and considered her a close friend. Gwladys was the Tsarina of Nairobi social life, and Broughton was wise to pay his first respects exclusively to her. Perhaps Gwladys, too, thought he would be arriving with Vera. Diana would require her approval.

WALKING PAST the porter's lodge and into the chintzy sitting rooms of the Club, Broughton, after thirteen years of absence, must have found it somewhat shorn of its former grandeur. The Club then had usually been almost empty on weekdays; now it was humming with activity, with officers up from South Africa, or shuttling between England and Cairo. Nairobi and the Muthaiga had become recreation centres for troops on leave.

Gwladys claimed the honeymooning couple for dinner as well as lunch that day, and added another guest, Broughton's contemporary, Jack Soames, who came in from his farm at Nanyuki. There was much to talk about: Britain

under the blackout, the difficulties of keeping an estate
running during the war, Turf Club gossip. They ordered
Bronxes before dinner, and champagne. The subject came
up of why Broughton had wanted to leave England. He
made a reply about a man his age not being able to find
any proper war work in England. Furthermore, he thought
a new life deserved a new background and he was looking
forward to showing Diana this country.

Almost immediately the couple set off on an up-country
journey to introduce Diana to Broughton's old friends.
They visited Lord Francis Scott, Mervyn Ridley, Soames,
and "Boy" and Paula Long. It was the Longs' first glimpse
of Diana and they were surprised that the new bride should
say in front of her husband and her hosts, "I'm not sharing
a room with *that* dirty old man. I insist on having a room
to myself." This, it seemed, was the unwritten part of the
pact. The couple never did share a room, either before or
after the marriage. Broughton appeared to be besotted by
Diana, but she had clearly already begun to find the relationship unbearable after the years of semi-freedom, of
flying and dancing and escaping with her beaux to the 400
Club.

Diana's impressions of Old Etonians abroad cannot
have been improved by their visit to "Commander" Soames
at Bergeret. At school he had been a contemporary of
Broughton, and they had travelled on the long journey out
to Kenya together in 1923—Broughton for the first time.
Soames had divorced Nina Drury some ten years before
the Broughtons' arrival. But even then, although she never
suffered directly from his peculiar habits and compulsions
—all acted on surreptitiously—she was keenly aware of
them. "He could be so charming to people that they were
often never aware of the other side of it," she said. Soames
had developed a sinister and morbid imagination, and had
become a voyeur with an alarming style. He would drill
holes in the roof above the guest bedrooms and peer down
at them.

"It was all becoming rather paramount even before I

married him," said Nina Drury, "and people had started to become wary of him."

He had also become bad-tempered and tyrannical towards his servants. On one occasion a guest complained that the houseboy had "buggered up the bath" by omitting to fit the plug properly and thus draining the supply of hot water. Soames picked up a gun and hunted the terrified houseboy all through the property, swearing to kill him. When Gloria, his mistress, and later his wife, told the servant who brought the tea to take the remainder of the chocolate cake for himself, Soames said, "You're not going to give the cake to those baboons, are you?"

One morning when there was nothing better to entertain his guests, Soames suggested target practice. No one needed reminding that there was a war on. Broughton was all in favour: it was essential, he felt, that Diana should learn how to defend herself with a revolver. A target was set up. Broughton, Diana and Soames, watched by other members of the house party, shot fifty or sixty rounds into the undergrowth. Diana usually hit the target, but most of Broughton's shots went wide.

BROUGHTON AND DIANA returned to Nairobi around November 25th. Broughton left again almost immediately to visit the farm in which he had an interest, on Lake Naivasha. He was away for the Caledonian Ball at the Muthaiga Club on November 30th. That was the night that Joss Erroll and Diana met for the first time.

Diana had been upstairs in her room writing letters before dinner. As she came down the staircase she saw three men sitting on the sofa, all laughing, one of them dressed in a kilt. When their eyes met, as she recalled later, "I had the extraordinary feeling, if you can understand it, that I was suddenly from that moment the most important thing in his life." Erroll asked her to dine with him. She asked how many people would be there. She knew it would be impossible for them to meet alone without showing her own feelings. She had, after all, been married for less than one month. Erroll, on the other hand, was free. His marriages were in the past, and his current affair with Mrs. Wirewater was conducted now by correspondence between Nairobi and Cape Town, where she had gone to install her children in school.

When they did find themselves alone for the first time, and even before the first embrace, before, as Diana described it, "there had been anything in any shape or form," let alone a declaration of love on either side, Erroll said to her, "Well, who's going to tell Jock? You or I?" It was in fact almost six weeks before Erroll and Broughton met to discuss the topic. In the meantime, Diana had fallen in love for the first time in her life.

When Broughton returned to Nairobi two days later, he and Diana settled in to what appeared to be a rhythm of lunches and dinners at the Muthaiga Club, of croquet games, bridge, backgammon and tea parties. Erroll was now constantly in the Club. The military headquarters, where he worked, was near by, and his house only a few hundred yards away. Broughton, who had known him slightly from previous visits, struck up a friendship with him. By the beginning of December, Broughton and Diana rarely had a meal without sharing their table with Erroll. Even when Diana had other plans, Broughton and Erroll usually lunched together.*

What did Broughton think of Erroll? He described him as an "out and outer," but also "one of the most amusing men I have ever met," and above all Broughton wanted to be amused. He was also flattered by the atten-

---

* In the descriptions that follow, Broughton's quoted speech, and that of others, such as Gwladys Delamere, is taken from the shorthand notes of the trial, at which these succeeding days and moments were examined in great detail. Most of the factual information comes from that source, although I have added some material from my own interviews, in particular the conversations between Erroll and Diana.

tions of a younger man—it revived his self-image as one of the most glamorous officers in the Irish Guards.

"If you can make a great friend in two months," he said in court, "then Joss Erroll I should describe as a great friend." These were happy meals. Broughton could dazzle his new friend with his stories of the Liverpool Cup, the London seasons, the peculiar cases he had heard as Chairman of the Nantwich Bench, the affairs of his closest friends, and sample, in return, Erroll's caustic wit and flashes of unashamed self-revelation.

Meanwhile, Diana had acquired two constant companions—her old friend Hugh Dickinson and a new one, Major Richard (Dickie) Pembroke, who had arrived in the course of duty. In fact, Pembroke had fallen in love with the wife of a brother officer in the Coldstream Guards, and regimental etiquette had demanded that he apply for a transfer. The lady did not follow Major Pembroke, however, and he was, in the jargon of the day, something of an "extra man." Occasionally he played bezique with Broughton. And he, too, fell in love with Diana. She thought him the dullest man she had ever met, and after their first dinner together she remembers asking him to remind her what his name was. "Dickie," came the answer, "Dickie Pembroke."

There was nothing astonishing to Broughton about these "sorties" of Diana's. He had made a pact: she was allowed to enjoy herself. And yet he seemed to work his side of the bargain with a fastidiousness that was more than passivity; he seemed almost eager to concede his first claim.

Then, on December 5th, the Broughtons moved from the Club into their house at Karen, the Nairobi suburb named after Baroness Blixen. It was a solid Sunningdale Tudor structure, with twenty-two acres of grounds. Fifteen servants were engaged and put in the charge of Wilks and the head boy, Abdullah bin Ahmed, who was a "catch" from the Muthaiga Club. Broughton approached Sir Fer-

dinand Cavendish Bentinck, Chairman of the Production
and Settlement Board, and an old acquaintance, for a job.
They seemed all set for the duration.

       ON DECEMBER 18th, Broughton suddenly went
to stay with Erroll in his house at Muthaiga, near to the
Club, leaving Diana at home for four nights. They were
reunited on December 22nd, when Gwladys Delamere held
a joint birthday party for herself and Diana at the Club
with forty-four guests. There was dancing ''from sundowners to sunrise,'' at what turned out to be one of the
last soirées of the *ancien régime*. The guest list must have
included many of Erroll's former girlfriends, including
Gwladys herself and Alice de Janzé, and possibly Idina.
Paula Long described Diana and Joss dancing ''as if they
were glued together.'' When two people find each other
supremely desirable, as Broughton said later, there is nothing to be done except give in or run away. It was wartime
and there was nowhere to run to.

     Over Christmas the love affair crystallised. Most of
their friends noticed that by early January the new couple
were inseparable—particularly Diana's other ''licensed''
escorts, like Dickie Pembroke, who said, ''Anyone who
saw them at that time would have thought they were in
love.'' Some acted as accomplices, particularly June Carberry, who was to become a kind of handmaid to the
romance. But Broughton's awareness only came slowly
—at least so it appeared, and so he behaved.

     By January 3rd, the deception of Broughton had be-
gun. Diana and Erroll went to June's house at Nyeri for
the weekend, June having discreetly disappeared to Malindi, on the coast. On Monday 6th they returned to Nairobi. Broughton picked up an anonymous note from his
rack at the Muthaiga Club which read:

You seemed like a cat on hot bricks at the club last night. What
about the eternal triangle? What are you going to do about it?

He showed it to Diana at the Club that night and said, "What do you think of this?" They all laughed. And yet Broughton knew what was happening. He had tackled Diana on the subject of their trip to Ceylon, planned for that month, and received the excuse that the décor at the Karen house would not be ready and needed her supervision.

Broughton was forced to confront the problem when he and Diana gave a dinner party at Karen on January 12th. Around the table sat Gerald Portman, Richard Pembroke, a Miss Lampson, Erroll, the Broughtons and Gwladys. Much of the energy that evening was generated by the Mayor of Nairobi, who picked a fight early on with Major Portman about the relative contributions of Britain and the colonies to the war effort. The shouting match was unstoppable. A glass candlestick was broken by someone hammering on the table.

"Did that improve matters?" Portman was asked later.

"Not at all," he replied. "It was a particularly heated argument. It was so heated that I think there must have been something personal."

The Mayor at one stage commented that if Mr. Portman felt as he did, why the hell had he come out here?

"It was a very unpleasant dinner to start with," Broughton recalled. "Lady Delamere [Gwladys] and Mr. Portman had a most frightful row and abused each other like pickpockets, which is always embarrassing for a host. We then went into the room where we dance and where the piano is. Not content with their fight in the dining room, they began all over again, which, I must say, annoyed me very much indeed. The next thing I recall is that Lady Delamere and my wife went upstairs to my wife's bedroom where they remained about half an hour. The men downstairs were very bored as they had nobody to dance with."

The gramophone was now playing, but Gwladys, having turned her sights away from Mr. Portman and the war effort to a more pressing topic, had effectively cleared the dance floor. First Lord Erroll had taken her aside, after dinner, in a small room on the ground floor. "He told me he was fond of Lady Broughton. Very fond," said Glwadys, "that he would do anything for her and that he was determined to marry her; that he had never been so happy, and did I like her. He asked my advice and I advised him to make a clean breast of it to Sir Delves." What did he say to that? "He said, 'You are often right. I will think about it and let you know.' "

Then Diana approached her, or it may have been Gwladys herself who took Diana into the sitting room, and asked, "Do you know Joss is very much in love with you?"

Diana replied, "Yes."

"What are you going to do about it?" enquired the Mayor. That was one of Gwladys's favourite phrases.

Diana offered to show Gwladys around the newly decorated house and the conversation continued in her bedroom. "Does he want to marry you?" asked Gwladys. Diana replied that he did. Gwladys told Diana how fond she was of Erroll and that she would like to see him happy; that he had been unhappy with his first wife and that his second wife, Molly, had been too old for him. She suggested that this new love was Joss's first chance of real happiness. Diana said she was fond of Broughton and didn't want to hurt him.

"Yes," said Gwladys, "but he is an old man and has had his life. Take your happiness where you can find it. There is a *war* on."

Finally, Gwladys gave Diana the same advice she had given Erroll—to make a clean breast of it. "He will never give you up," she said. "It's the best thing you can do." Joss had tried to persuade Diana that the marriage pact should now be invoked—Broughton had given his word, and it should be taken seriously. Diana, nevertheless, was wavering; she felt she couldn't go through with it. It was

Gwladys's official approval that finally persuaded her to go ahead.

Gwladys seemed to be promoting the affair under the veil of "sound advice." Erroll had already told her that he was prepared to elope, and she said, "Don't have any farewell scenes. Write a note and leave it on his pillow." (She denied this later.) Now, after her conversation with the two lovers, she turned on Broughton and delivered the bad news.

Broughton had come upstairs to complain that the men below were very bored and had no one to dance with. "They came down," said Broughton, "and Lady Delamere came and sat next to me. She was watching Lord Erroll and my wife dancing . . . I was sitting by her also watching them dancing. Lady Delamere said to me, 'Do you know that Joss is wildly in love with Diana?' and I'm afraid that gave me a great deal of food for thought and I became rather distrait and I did neglect my duties as a host in not being as attentive to Lady Delamere as I should have been. It confirmed my worst suspicions and I was very absent-minded afterwards."

Despite the shock of discovering that his wife's affair was public, Broughton now invited Erroll to stay the night. Such passivity, exaggerated friendliness, the concealing of his true feelings, was to become typical of Broughton's behaviour; and Erroll's lack of restraint was typical of his professional contempt for husbands. The two men even went riding together early the following morning, with Diana, in the Kikuyu Reserve.

Later that morning Broughton talked to Diana about the situation. ("I think you are going out rather too much with Joss.") They lunched at Muthaiga with Erroll, then the parties split up. In the afternoon, Diana left Nairobi by train to stay with June Carberry at Malindi, in a house full of air force personnel. No one knew that Erroll was joining the train at Athi station, just outside Nairobi, with his man, Waiweru, and his portable drinks cabinet. Hugh Dickinson would be staying there too.

"Only a very few people knew officially that they were in love," said Dickinson. "I was stationed at Malindi at the time, but in pretty uncomfortable conditions. I was in charge of a small working party, so I left the sergeant in charge, and moved into the Carberrys' house. When Diana and Joss arrived they told me they were in love. They actually told me they wanted me to be the first to know."

Dickinson took one of the very few photographs of them together, on the Kilifi ferry: Erroll in uniform and shorts, Diana in tight slacks and dark glasses, standing beside an army car.

Broughton, meanwhile, had gone on January 13th to seek refuge with his old friend Jack Soames, at Nanyuki. When he arrived he was quite normal, but then, according to Soames, his behaviour changed. "We had a whisky and soda at six o'clock," said Soames, "turned on the wireless at 6:45; had two more whiskies and sodas and he passed out completely."

Broughton, who had been drinking heavily for the past week, had gone to Soames for advice. He was worried that Erroll, a much younger man, was taking Diana away from him; using racing jargon to make his point, he told his friend, "he had the better of me in the weights to the extent of fourteen pounds." Soames delivered his advice: Broughton should see Erroll and ask him whether he was in love with Diana. "If he says no, tell him to buzz off. If they are in love with each other, cut your losses. Pack your boxes and get off back to England."

As the drinking, and the effect it had on Broughton, became more extreme, Soames began to worry about his friend. Broughton told him that since his discovery of the affair he had taken to whisky and gin, and that this always sent him to sleep, although it made him depressed and maudlin too; that he wasn't used to drinking quantities of spirits. He said that he had nevertheless begun to take whisky as a nightcap, "perhaps two or three," since he had been in Kenya. Soames still didn't think Broughton was sleeping well, apparently, since he introduced him to Medinal—a form of morphine—during their four ponderous, depressed days together. Broughton took the bottle back to Nairobi with him and began to use the drug regularly.

He returned there on Saturday, January 18th. Diana and Erroll had already been back in Nairobi for four nights, staying together at Erroll's house. June had returned on the 17th.

By now Erroll had telephoned Gwladys Delamere and told her, "Gwladys, we have taken your advice." June Carberry was listening in to the call and heard him continue: "There will be no farewell scenes, and we are not going to leave a note."

That same day, Broughton received his second anonymous letter in the Muthaiga rack. It read: "Do you know your wife and Lord Erroll have been staying alone at the Carberrys' house at Nyeri together?" Broughton destroyed the note, and this time did not show it to Diana.

It seemed that nothing could get in the way of a Muthaiga lunch—for Broughton it always signified a truce—but at that particular meal on the 18th, as the four of them, including June, sat down together, the mounting tensions were beginning to show, particularly on Diana. *"It was quite pleasant,"* said Broughton later, "but my wife was frightfully upset and in a state of nerves." She told Broughton that she wanted to speak to him later, and he must have guessed what was coming.

When they got back to Karen that afternoon, Diana told him that she was in love with Erroll. Broughton suggested, or so he said later in court, that she come to Ceylon with him for three months to find out if the affair was serious. Then he rang Erroll at his office: "Don't you think you ought to see me, Joss?" They met within the hour at Erroll's house. Broughton was early, strolled into the house, back on to the veranda and demanded a whisky and soda from Waiweru.

The confrontation between the two men was recorded by Waiweru and Erroll's garden boy, who was cutting the grass. ("Erroll's face changed like a person who has received bad news so as to annoy his heart; Broughton was speaking loudly and in heated tones, striking the chair with his fist, and Erroll was quietly listening in sympathy.") Broughton maintained that the conversation was emphatic but unheated—a business discussion.

The conversation, as it was presented in court, began: "Diana tells me she is in love with you." Erroll replied, "Well, she has never told me that but I am frightfully in love with her." Broughton told Erroll that he should try to persuade her to go away with Broughton to Ceylon, "as we have been so frightfully happy," and suggested that Erroll go away as well.

On the surface, at least, Broughton had "cut his losses" ("as a racing man I'm used to it"), and was keeping to the marriage pact. For this reason, he claimed to have been unperturbed when Erroll refused to go away. Erroll himself was as familiar with this situation as an old dance step, and kept calm. He could not go away, he said, he was terribly sorry, there was a *war* on. (Broughton said later that Erroll had repeated this observation three times in the course of their conversation.) He tried to discover Erroll's financial position, but got nowhere.

Was that all? "He did say he felt miserably unhappy about the whole thing," said Broughton, "as we had been such great friends. Both of us were as dispassionate as possible."

For appearances' sake, Broughton wanted Diana to stay in the Karen house at least until he went to Ceylon. He even hoped that she might stay there for the next three months, while he was away, and not go to live with Erroll.

The discussion was ended by the arrival of Diana and June across the lawn. Broughton walked away with June and told her that since neither Diana nor Joss would go away, he felt he was intruding and "rather in the way."

Perhaps he ought to get out. The way he put it, June thought he was talking about suicide, and Broughton later admitted that he might have been hinting at it. It was six o'clock now, and Erroll had gone into the house to make Diana a cocktail. He then drove Broughton the half mile to the Club.

From there, Broughton went home alone with his driver. Erroll, Diana and June stayed on and were seen laughing and celebrating together. Later, Erroll ordered a table for eight. Broughton dined alone at Karen, for the first time.

Then, unable to sleep, Broughton waited up for his wife and June Carberry to return from Muthaiga. When they came back at 3:30 a.m., Diana, to his evident astonishment, was wearing a new set of pearls. June Carberry said later that she shared Diana's bed that night because she was frightened of "creaks in the house." But she began to laugh when she saw Broughton looking at them through a crack in the door and she delivered an unbearable taunt: "I told him it reminded me of a play—*Love From a Stranger*," a drama based on an Agatha Christie story of murder within a triangular romance, which had recently been performed in London.

Broughton had only one thing to discuss at that late hour. Diana told him that the three strings of pearls around her neck had been given to her by Erroll. Broughton reminded her of another valuable piece of jewellery—also a set of pearls—for which Diana had paid half in England, and Broughton had promised to pay the other half. "I asked her if she would like to pay the remaining half and take over the jewellery, or whether she would like me to pay the whole lot and take it over myself." Broughton was saying, in effect, that he wanted the other pearls back. He wasn't prepared to give up quite so easily.

Diana was still wearing Erroll's pearls as she breakfasted in bed the following morning, the 19th. According to Broughton, they had a "very pleasant" Sunday lunch that day. The whole of Derek Erskine's family rode eight miles across country to Karen for the occasion, with the

Broughtons and Gwladys, June and Erroll. His young daughter, Petal Allen, remembered the afternoon clearly. "We did a lot of cavorting about in the pool. Diana said to her maid, 'Give Petal any bathing suit she wants!' She had about forty. There were lots of piggybacks and shoulder rides. I remember Broughton drinking too much and being angry. Diana and Joss were obviously very attracted to each other, and making no effort to hide it. There was a lot of flicking towels and horsing about." Her brother, Francis Erskine, was learning to dive that day. He remembers looking up at the house and seeing Broughton frowning and glowering from the window, and being frightened of him.

Afterwards, June announced that she was going to Nyeri. Diana, at the last moment, said she couldn't stay at Karen with her husband, given the situation, and wanted to go with her. Instead, they decided to go to Erroll's house at Muthaiga à deux, and Diana was seen dancing with Erroll at Torr's Hotel in Nairobi by Mrs. Phyllis Barkas, an upright and ever-vigilant member of the Muthaiga Club, on the 21st. Mrs. Barkas also overheard Broughton telephoning Erroll that day from the Muthaiga Club and saying, "Is that Lord Erroll? Is that you, Joss?" and later, "You understand, Joss. You quite understand." It sounded like an ultimatum.

While Diana was away, Broughton told his personal servants, Mohammed and Alfred, that two revolvers, a silver cigarette case and a small amount of money (a five-shilling note which he always kept in his address book) had been taken from the living room. He repeated this to the police, who found no clues except a broken climbing rose. He told them, "I think access was gained to the room by means of a door on the veranda which leads to the room, and which I think may possibly have been left unlocked." There was a bell under the carpet which an intruder would certainly have stepped on, and which sounded in the servants' rooms, but nobody had heard it.

On the 21st, too, Broughton and Erroll went to their

lawyers about divorce; Broughton, who had cancelled a proposed trip with Diana to Ceylon some days earlier, now rebooked his passage and wrote to Soames, telling him of the burglary and admitting defeat:

I have taken your advice. I put the position to Erroll and Diana. They say they are in love with each other and mean to get married. It is a hopeless position and I'm going to cut my losses. I think I'll go to Ceylon. There's nothing for me to live in Kenya for.

A third anonymous letter appeared in Broughton's rack at the Club:

There's no fool like an old fool. What are you going to do about it?

But on the morning of the 23rd, Broughton was wavering. Erroll told his friend Julian Lezard that Broughton was being "very difficult." "He won't make up his mind what he's going to do." Nevertheless, another lunch at Muthaiga was arranged and the usual foursome sat down to what June Carberry described as a "success . . . an ordinary, cheerful affair."

Lunch, as so often in the past, had improved Broughton's mood. "Lizzie" Lezard was summoned to Erroll's office that afternoon and told, "Jock could not have been nicer. He has agreed to go away. As a matter of fact, he has been so nice it smells bad."

Erroll told Diana that he couldn't believe that Broughton was giving up so easily. A celebration dinner had been arranged for that evening with Broughton's enthusiastic consent, and Erroll planned to take Diana dancing. Lezard recalled Erroll saying, "The old boy insists that I have her back by three o'clock because she is tired, and I must not be later than that. It suits me because I am tired too and have to get to work, and work hard tomorrow morning." Diana had spent only five nights at the house in Karen with her husband since the beginning of January.

Broughton had taken Diana on to the veranda after the meal and told her that she had nothing to worry about: he was prepared to go away to Ceylon and he would give her the Karen house. Two months later he would return to England. But he hoped she would at least stay at home until he left. Diana said, ''I am sorry it has happened so soon.'' Broughton made no reply.

Because the party had only been arranged at lunch-time, Broughton had to return to Karen to get his dinner jacket and a dress for Diana, who was to change in Erroll's house. He wanted to be back at the Club by 5 p.m. for a golf croquet game with Mrs. Barkas, but it was drizzling when he got there and they went inside and played back-gammon instead. He told her during the game that he was going to a party that night, that he was going to dance and he was looking forward to it.

Between six and seven, Erroll drove up with Diana and June Carberry, who went into the Club. Broughton was in the driveway getting something out of his car. As Erroll was on the point of getting out of his own car, Broughton said, ''I want a word with you, Joss,'' and sat beside him. ''How is Diana?'' Broughton asked, and continued, ''She was in a dreadful state at lunch, but I talked to her afterwards and I think I got her quite all right.'' Erroll replied, ''She is grand now.'' Broughton sat with Erroll in the Buick for two minutes, and then both men joined the ladies.

Broughton played bridge with Mrs. Barkas until eight o'clock, when the drinking began. ''Mostly champagne cocktails and one or two others, perhaps Bronxes,'' said Broughton, and ''quite a few'' of them.

Now the foursome sat down to this odd celebration, and ordered more champagne. Suddenly, during the meal, and to the astonishment of the other guests, Broughton raised his glass and proposed a toast, all possession and jealousy apparently forgotten, all losses cut, the champagne roaring in his blood. ''I wish them every happiness,'' he said, ''and may their union be blessed with an heir. To Diana and Joss." Later he said, "It was the most extreme gesture I could make." In the presence of this euphoric couple, mad with love for each other, relieved and grateful for Broughton's blessing, there was no room for Broughton's own hurt feelings. He had chosen to be part of it; to have stayed away would have added humiliation to his loneliness. The toast was perhaps the measure of his pain.

When the dinner party ended after two hours, at 10:15, Joss and Diana left the Club and went dancing at the Claremont Road House near by, leaving Broughton and June in the Club. Broughton had by now been drinking heavily for some days, for the first time in his life. He and June began drinking liqueur brandy, and Jock asked her if she wanted to go dancing. "I was not feeling particularly well," she said afterwards, "and I suggested we stay at the Club for a little while."

At about 10:30, Broughton passed Richard Pembroke in the hall and asked him when he would come and play bezique again. Pembroke made some polite reply. And then for about an hour, Broughton and June Carberry were alone, unobserved apparently, at the Club. Around 11:30, as they sat by the bar in the lounge, Broughton became "suddenly rather cross and peevish," according to June. She said that he began to raise his voice, but by then other guests had noticed the couple and had overheard Jock talking about his wife. June reported Broughton as saying, "I'm not going to give her £5,000 a year or the Karen house," and that she could bloody well go and live with Joss—that they had only been married for three months and look how it was for him. She tried to quieten him. Phyllis Barkas overheard him saying, "To think that a woman would treat me like this after being married two months." Another guest had it differently: "Juney, it's all very well, but we've only been married two months, and she does this."

Mrs. Barkas and Captain Llewellin, "Jacko" Heath and Gerald Portman were having a supper of bacon and eggs, and invited Broughton and June Carberry to join them. Broughton, according to June, complained endlessly that he was ''very tired,'' and begged to go home.

Despite his state of drunkenness, June Carberry thought that the party she had dragged him off to might cheer him up. When she finally agreed to leave at 1:30, they were driven home by Broughton's chauffeur, arriving at Karen at around 2 a.m.

Wilks was still up and she opened the door to them; June Carberry helped the old man up the stairs and at the top of the staircase they said goodnight to each other. June went into her room and asked Wilks for quinine for an attack of malaria. Wilks brought it to her room and stayed talking to June for some minutes. June said later that Broughton came to her door ten minutes later, asked if she was all right, and said good-night, but neither Broughton nor Wilks had any recollection of this.

Diana and Joss had left the Claremont Road House around midnight for his house at Muthaiga. Here they stayed an hour—and finally, talking and laughing and, according to the servants, ''looking very happy,'' drove to Karen with her three suitcases, the accumulation of her travels in the recent weeks. Once again the front door was opened by the ever-attentive Wilks, who took the suitcases upstairs. It was now somewhere between 2:15 and 2:25 a.m.

June Carberry said she heard the sound of laughter in the hall, and then the slamming of a car door, and the car driving away. Diana came upstairs, went to her room, put her dog inside, and walked back along the corridor to talk to June. June said Diana stayed talking to her for half an hour, perhaps more. Wilks, who had been darting in and out of June's room, was now going to bed. June said that Broughton paid a second call on her at 3:30 ''to ask me if I was all right,'' but afterwards Broughton couldn't remember the call, just as he couldn't remember the first one. June heard Diana's dachshund bark, either just before or just after his visit.

7

THE BODY
IN
THE BUICK

A R O U N D 3 a.m. on that morning (January 24th),
two African dairy workers—known as milk boys—were
driving their truck up to the intersection of the Karen and
Ngong roads. The heavy rainstorm that night had turned
to a light summer drizzle. They turned into the main
Nairobi–Ngong road, and saw the lights of a car blazing
in the darkness, pointing away from them towards Nairobi,
illuminating the dense grass and scrub on the right-hand
verge, 150 yards ahead of the intersection. Then they saw
the Buick lying at a steep angle, almost tipped over into
a deep murram trench.

The car had plunged into the grass on the wrong side
of the road, and when they looked through the window
they saw the body of a European in army uniform, crouched
on all fours under the dashboard, hands clasped in front
of the head. They turned the truck around on the grass,
and headed back to the Karen police post, where their horn
woke Third-grade Constable Luali, who was sleeping in
his hut. Luali alerted the corporal, who left with three
constables to investigate the accident.

Luali, the corporal and the three askaris must have
had a very long debate at the scene of the accident, without
even opening the door of the car—one that lasted at least
forty minutes. They were still there, having taken no further action, when Leslie Condon, a European dairy farmer

on his way to Nairobi, was flagged down by one of them at 4 a.m. (Condon had already passed the site at 2:40, or so he estimated, and had seen nothing on the road.) When he looked at the body he saw a wound behind the left ear which he was sure was a bullet wound. He drove to Kilimani police station, and reported what he had seen.

Now, some time after 4 a.m., Luali bicycled to the house of Assistant-Superintendent Anstis Bewes, a company director who had been drafted as a policeman, and who lived at Karen. Bewes had little police training, but that night he managed better than most.

He arrived at the road junction at about 4:50 a.m., and saw the wound behind the left ear. It had congealed since Condon had seen it, and he didn't recognise it as a bullet wound. He made the following notes:

Some blood on the nearside front seat. Car at an angle of 40 degrees precariously perched on edge of 18-inch drain. Askari opened nearside front door using handkerchief over handle, to enable closer observation. Strong smell of scent pervaded car. Headlights full on. Clock going. Left to report to police H.Q. from Karen police post. Fifteen minutes' delay in getting through.
Returned to scene. Lights left on. Nothing touched lest evidence be destroyed. Unable to identify body in view of its position. Heavy rain earlier had made car tracks plainly visible including a set of wide tracks from front of Buick towards Nairobi.

Bewes had called Inspector Fentum, and by 6 a.m. there were six white officers and at least five African Constables walking over the site, plainly believing that they were dealing with an ordinary road accident. But Bewes had noticed some other details: there were white pipeclay marks on the rear seat and a carpet on the floor in the rear, which was crumpled; both the armstraps had been wrenched away, and the ignition had been switched off.

Superintendent Arthur Poppy, the head of the Nairobi Criminal Investigation Department, had been told of the incident by telephone and had ordered photographs to be taken. At 8 a.m. the Government pathologist, Geoffrey Timms, who also lived at Karen, passed by on his usual journey to work. By this time, the rain and the policemen's boots had removed any trace of footprints or tyre marks. Timms noticed that the hands and face of the dead man were cold, the body under the clothing still warm; the head and neck were a blue, congested colour, and rigor mortis was beginning to set in. Timms, for some reason, ordered that the body be removed from the car and put on to a stretcher so that he could have a better look—an action he later felt he would never live down. It was only then that the body was recognised as that of Lord Erroll.

Superintendent Poppy was called to the mortuary at 10 a.m. When he first looked at the body he thought that the knobless spike of the headlight switch had been driven into Erroll's head as he had been thrown forward and sideways. There was also a bruise on his head which made it look as if he had hit the steering wheel. It was only when the wound was washed, revealing the scorchmarks of the gunpowder, that Poppy knew Erroll had been shot. The bullet that was extracted from his head had travelled into the medulla of the brain, in a straight line from ear to ear.

The car had been towed away too, and repair work already started. A second bullet was found near the accelerator pedal. It had first struck the central door pillar on the driver's side. And other items were discovered: a blood-soaked Player's cigarette, a bloodstained hairpin in the front of the car, and bloodstains on the windscreen on the passenger side.

Poppy informed Government House that the funeral would have to be delayed, and asked that the fact of the murder be kept quiet for twenty-four hours.

BROUGHTON WAS already awake when Alfred, the room boy, brought him his tea at 7 a.m. He put on a

sports jacket and grey flannels and set out for his usual
morning walk. On his return, feeling the hangover now,
he undressed and went back to bed. He called the boy for
more tea. By 8:30 he was up and breakfasted, and at nine
Gerald Portman rang from his office to say that Joss Erroll
had had a motor accident and had broken his neck.

June Carberry took the call. She called Broughton to
her room. He said "Good God," so she remembered, and
sat down on the bed.

Within a few minutes, Inspectors Swayne and Fentum
arrived from the road junction and took a short statement
from Broughton. Nairobi was, and still is, a small town,
and as soon as they had identified the body in the car,
they knew where to begin their enquiries. When they came
up the drive at Karen, Broughton said, "Is he all right?
Is he all right?" "Is who all right?" one of them asked.
"Lord Erroll," replied Broughton.

Diana was in a state of hysteria, and the policemen,
who could see her peering at them through the window,
decided to leave her alone. In a later statement Broughton
said, "My wife could not believe that Lord Erroll was
dead and she said to me, 'Do go and see if it is him.' I
said I would. I asked her, I think, if she had anything
personal, belonging to her, that she would like to put on
his body. She gave me a handkerchief. From my recollection I think I rang up the police and asked where I could
find Lord Erroll's body and they told me some hospital at
the top of the hill. I went there and it was not there and
they told me to go to some other hospital; it was not there.
I then went to the police station at Nairobi and I saw
Inspector May and he told me it was in the town mortuary.
I asked him whether I could put a handkerchief belonging
to my wife on Lord Erroll's body as he had been a very
dear friend of hers."

Broughton began his search soon after Fentum and
Swayne had left, driving past the scene of the accident,
where he stopped to look at the ditch. He was shaking

with nerves when he arrived at the station and showed the handkerchief to Swayne with both hands. Swayne remembered Broughton saying in explanation, "My wife was very much in love with Lord Erroll."

Alice de Trafford and Gwladys Delamere were already at the mortuary when Broughton arrived. Alice had put a small branch of a tree on the body; Gwladys, the Mayor of Nairobi, had asked for Erroll's identity disc. Broughton was not allowed inside the building, but persuaded a policeman to take the handkerchief and place it on Erroll's breast. Alice told Broughton that Erroll suffered from heart trouble, and that this might have been the cause of his death.

From there Broughton drove into Nairobi, and went straight to the Union Castle steamer agent. Some days previously he had, once again, cancelled his passage to Ceylon. Now he rebooked it. He returned home around 12:30.

June Carberry, who had made a lightning visit to Erroll's house, arrived carrying a small jewel case. And there were two other guests for lunch: Juanita Carberry, June's fifteen-year-old stepdaughter, and her governess, Isabel Rutt.

Three days beforehand, Abdullah bin Ahmed, Broughton's head boy, had been told to get petrol from the *dhobi* and put it in Broughton's bedroom. Now Broughton asked for it, and Abdullah watched him sprinkle petrol over a bonfire in the rubbish pit. As he was about to strike a match, Abdullah jumped back, afraid of being burned. Broughton then ordered him to produce the lunch, but before they went in to eat, seeing the fire spreading out of the pit, he told Abdullah to put it out.

Before the other guests had finished their lunch, Broughton asked Juanita if she would like to see the stables. Juanita was fond of Broughton. Unlike her parents or her governess, he was kind to her, and they both liked horses. As they went out, Juanita was surprised to see a pair of gym shoes lying in the bonfire. You never burned even a worn out pair of gym shoes in Kenya. You gave them to your houseboy.

They came back indoors for coffee and brandy. June began talking about the tragedy. Broughton had his hand up to his face and was crying.

That afternoon Diana, June, Juanita and Isabel Rutt travelled together to the Carberrys' house at Nyeri, leaving Broughton at Karen. (It was his suggestion that he be left alone.)

Broughton spoke to Gwladys three times that day by telephone. He described the dinner party the night before; how he had drunk the health of Diana and Joss. "I gave them my blessing," he said. In the evening he rang Gwladys and told her that Diana wanted a note dropped into Erroll's grave. He asked if she would do this for him at the funeral the following day. Gwladys refused.

The mourners were already leaving the churchyard the following day, the 25th, when Broughton made a late appearance. He was flustered and distressed. He told Gwladys that his car had broken down. Later, to the police, he said that he thought the funeral was half an hour later.

He asked Gwladys what he should do with Diana's note.

She pointed over her shoulder. "The grave is behind," she snapped, "I should take it there yourself," and walked on. Broughton threw the letter on to the coffin.

At the Muthaiga Club afterwards, Broughton asked Gwladys if he could join her for lunch. She said yes, "provided it is a quick lunch." Gwladys was to say later that Broughton abused Diana at the lunch—that he "blew hot and cold about her," bitterly regretting the break with his first wife, Vera, and his children. They discussed Diana's request, made to Broughton before lunch the previous day, that he take her to Ceylon. Gwladys had the feeling that Broughton would do anything not to be left alone. From the Club, Broughton sent a cable to John

Carberry, who was at Nyeri, asking if June could come
with him and Diana to Ceylon. He explained, "Diana has
nervous breakdown."

In the afternoon, Broughton made his first detailed
statement to Poppy at Karen. He described the final dinner.
"It was a very cheery evening," he said. "It was one of
the better nights."

Afterwards the two men walked in the garden, past
the rubbish pit which was still burning. Poppy was surprised to discover that Broughton had set the pit alight
himself, using aviation fuel, and that the blaze had been
strong enough to burn the surrounding grass. He decided
to put a guard over the pit the next day. Broughton showed
some anxiety about the results of the post mortem. He
asked Poppy several times why the inquest had been delayed.

It began two days later. As soon as murder was established, Broughton drove to Nyeri to break the news to
Diana. He found the house empty, except for Juanita, and
this upset him. He hadn't thought that his wife would be
in a fit state to go out visiting. He spent the afternoon with
Juanita, who had been left behind. Again they went to
look at horses together. Juanita kept a book of the likes
and dislikes of her friends and now she paid Broughton
the compliment of asking him to write in it. Broughton
wrote under the respective headings, "all animals" and
"loneliness."

June and Diana arrived two hours later than expected.
Diana hadn't eaten for four days—ever since Gerry Portman's call—and was still hysterical. At one point she
shouted abuse, including angry and direct accusations of
murder, at her husband, who suffered the attacks in silence.

Broughton was told that the police had been there the
previous day. He asked June what she had told them; had
she said that he was cross and peevish on the night of the
murder, while they were drinking brandy—June and he

—in the Muthaiga bar? She reminded him that he had knocked on her door, later on. He couldn't remember it. She told him that he had been drunk. She also said that she wanted to go to South Africa. She couldn't do that, Broughton said, because the inquest would continue and she would be a principal witness. Broughton recognised that by now he was a prime suspect.

The day before Diana had also made her first statement to the police. They asked her what she thought had happened to Erroll. She told them that Erroll was a very fast driver and she thought he must have lost control and crashed.

Broughton went over the ground for Poppy again on the 29th in a yet more detailed statement: the theft of the revolvers on the 21st; the marriage pact with Diana; the agreement with Erroll that he should take her over; his movements on the night of 23rd–24th; the note in the grave; the burning of the rubbish pit. The following day Poppy ordered a search of the house and grounds. On the rubbish pit where the fire had been the charred remains of a golf stocking was found, with blood stains still clearly visible. Poppy didn't seem to be looking any further than Broughton for a suspect now, and when he brought off what he considered his smartest piece of detection, he was convinced that he was on the right track.

From his spies in the Broughton household Poppy had heard soon after the murder about the revolver practice on Soames's farm, and on February 2nd he sent two detectives to Nanyuki to talk to Soames. They set up the targets in the same positions and fired away, then raked through the ground, and found, as they had expected, spent bullets, cartridge cases and live rounds from a .32 revolver. The spent bullets were taken to the Government chemist for comparison with the murder bullets—a process that was to take six weeks.

On February 6th Broughton made his final statement, and handed over the firearms certificate on which the Colt .32—stolen in January—was registered.

Then, later in February, less than three weeks after the murder, Broughton and Diana set off, incredibly, on a full-scale shooting safari, into the Southern Masai Reserve along the Mara River. They were accompanied by the famous white hunter, John Hunter, and Hugh Dickinson, whom they hadn't seen since the end of January. He had been in hospital in Mombasa at the time of the murder, his left foot poisoned by cactus. The infection had been serious, and his foot had almost been amputated, yet by now he was fit enough, apparently, to walk long distances after game.

The safari lasted eight days, and the party travelled by truck, open car, and on foot. It was already clear that Diana was deeply suspicious of her husband and their relations were severely strained. It seems astonishing that such a trip should have been contemplated in the circumstances, and without Dickinson's company it might well have been disastrous. Eight days in the bush can break the closest of friendships and Broughton, at the best of times, had been known to make terrible scenes on hunting trips with Vera, on one occasion overturning all the tables in the camp, and then kicking Vera until her shins bled. But as at Muthaiga, where lunch could never be suspended merely for reasons of bad feeling, so the ritual task of shooting lion and buffalo took precedence over personal crises, and provided its own therapeutic bloodletting.

Diana had recovered enough of her composure to shoot the first lion. She even took three photographs of her trophy before taking aim. Broughton claimed a lion and a small antelope, and Dickinson two lions.

It was an energetic safari. Broughton shot with a double-barrelled rifle weighing eleven pounds, and helped haul the carcass of a 450-pound lion into the truck. One day he walked for seven miles, in the heat of the day, after buffalo.

8
ONE VISIT
TOO MANY

I hope I have never looked like a murderer. I think all
my friends know it is not exactly my line of country.
However, in a strange country, God knows what will
happen.
SIR JOCK DELVES BROUGHTON

Like most of his colleagues, Superintendent Poppy
was already convinced of Broughton's guilt, even before
he had uncovered what he considered his two most important strands of evidence. A tall man, with an unhurried,
friendly manner and keen eyes, Poppy was a mixture of
benign predator and paragon of British fair play. He had
been with Scotland Yard for ten years, where he was a
member of the Flying Squad before being sent to Kenya
in 1935 to organise the fingerprint department. By 1940
he was Chief of Police in Kenya and head of the Criminal
Investigation Department.

When Connolly and I met Poppy in 1969, twenty-
eight years after the murder, he remembered finding
Broughton outwardly pleasant and confident and without
affectation, but inwardly he had judged him to be cold,
vindictive and vain; the sort of man who always wanted
a return for his money, who never forgot an injury and
would eventually look for his revenge. But Poppy got on

well with him, found him always friendly and hospitable on his many visits to the house even though, he said, Broughton must have known where his thinking was leading. He saw him as a proud man, very pleased with his position, and felt he would have been a nasty customer if he didn't like you.

In general Poppy disapproved of this new crowd. They were different from the older settlers like Francis Scott, Grogan and Delamere, who got drunk like gentlemen. He thought this group ruthless, like Broughton himself, rather than passionate. June Carberry, who called him "Popski," he considered feckless; she had manners but no morals. Furthermore, she drank too much brandy and soda and couldn't be relied on for accuracy. Poppy had already put her husband in jail for eighteen months for currency offences, and had no use for him, either. As for Diana, Poppy found her hard and haughty, and acquisitive. In his opinion Erroll would let her down sooner or later. Poppy found Dickinson very agreeable, but characteristically he also regarded him with suspicion. He was too smooth, a little too obsequious, too clever by half.

He had perhaps more sympathy for Wilks, "a typical lady's maid"; he called her "Miss Wilks," which pleased her. She was having "the change" and had a fierce crush on Broughton. She even told Poppy that she had spent the night with him, and when Poppy challenged Broughton with this he lost his temper—a rare lapse in his otherwise calm composure. Wilks, with no prompting from Poppy, became a police spy from the start, and was especially helpful with information on Diana. She was the only one who volunteered statements, of which she made about six. But Poppy didn't need a spy: he had planted the house with informers among the servants early on in his investigations.

This was how he discovered, among other things, that there had been shooting practice at the Soames farm. Did the Bwana use his guns? No, but he had done so once at Bwana Soames's.

When Poppy wanted to look at the note that Broughton had dropped into Erroll's grave, Walter Harragin, the Attorney-General, refused permission to exhume the body, on the grounds that it would involve immense problems of red tape. "Nothing, I suppose, to prevent me planting a rose tree," said Poppy, "anywhere I like?" "No," said Harragin. "Even if I dig rather deep?" At midnight he took six convicts from the jail to the cemetery at Limuru. They dug down to the coffin and found the note which had slipped down to one side. It had been written at the Muthaiga Club, from Diana to Erroll, and read, "I love you desperately." Erroll had written on the back "and I love you for ever." Poppy returned the note to Diana.

Harragin had told Poppy that he must give the Governor, Sir Henry "Monkey" Moore, at least forty-eight hours' notice before arresting Delves Broughton, "so that Lord Moyne could be informed." This made Poppy deeply suspicious that the process of law would somehow be tampered with. (Lord Moyne was not only Vera's companion, he was also Secretary of State for the Colonies.)

Finally Poppy was ready, and on the afternoon of March 10th, armed with a warrant from the Resident Magistrate, he drove to Karen. He arrived at 6 p.m., found Broughton in the garden, touched him on the shoulder and arrested him for murder. Broughton said, "You've made a big mistake." That afternoon he and Diana had been out riding. They had begun to argue once again about jewellery, and had split up, Broughton arriving home first. When Diana appeared and saw her husband surrounded by policemen, she apologised to him for the row. Broughton said to Poppy, "Do you mind if I have a whisky?" Poppy brought out his own hip flask and handed it to Broughton. By seven o'clock, Broughton was in a cell at Nairobi police station, and his lawyer was on his way to see him.

The arrest took Broughton by surprise, even though Lazarus Kaplan, his lawyer, had been warning him for some time to expect it. He was to remain in jail for almost three months before coming to trial. June and Diana, who was now desperate to help her husband, came to visit him nearly every day; Alice de Trafford came almost as frequently. Despite the shock to his system of being suddenly at the mercy of turnkeys, the oppressive prison routine and a small cell, Broughton was a model prisoner—calm, fastidiously polite, gentlemanly. Only occasionally did he show signs of depression and claustrophobia. Otherwise he seemed almost relieved to be in jail.

At the time Broughton was arrested there were only six Europeans among the 1,200 prisoners in Nairobi jail and three European warders out of a total of 150. Broughton's jailer, the Chief Warder, was Victor de Vere Allen. He was an intelligent, considerate man who had been retired for thirteen years when I met him in Nairobi in 1969. He remembered above all how well Broughton stood up to the prison routine, but he touched on Poppy's theme, too, that Broughton was hiding a growing desperation under the calm exterior.

"He was a very nice, very fine man," said Allen, "and a very good talker. A man who'd had a lot of interesting experiences. He was never any trouble. He was charming to all the other prisoners—listened to all their tales. They'd laugh at the old man. He'd look a bit out of place, reduced to the level of criminal, locked in his cell. Always immaculately dressed. He'd always crack a joke back and he never put anyone's back up.

"June Carberry and Diana came to see him two or three times a week. They were a pretty hard crowd."

"We talked continually," Allen went on. "My two sisters in Australia, by coincidence, had been to school with two of the wives of the Rajah of Kooch Bahar. His brother was a great pal of mine, and we talked about the people we knew. We had been shooting around the same lake in Kashmir, with butts in the middle of the water, where the duck were driven over."

Broughton's ordeal was mitigated by special privileges. Though Europeans were expected to clean their own cells, his own was swept out for him by another prisoner. He claimed he was unable to do it himself. Nor, because of his crippled hand, could he put on his high collar and tie without assistance. Because he was a prisoner awaiting trial, he could have food sent in, as well as chocolates, cigars and other luxuries from Torr's Hotel. "He knew how to get what he wanted," said Allen. "Ten shillings to a warder earning thirty-eight shillings a month was a lot of money in those days . . ."

Each evening, Broughton and Allen would go outside the jail for exercise, a half-hour walk of a mile or so. "He got a bit depressed at times. He'd get bouts of claustrophobia and used to look forward to the walk quite anxiously," said Allen. "A man would feel the walls closing in.

"He told me he would commit suicide if his people at home wouldn't accept him. It seemed that in the crowd he mixed with, once you were a part of a public scandal, you were sort of washed out."

Broughton wrote from jail at the end of April 1941 to an old friend, Mrs. Marie Woodhouse, a Cheshire neighbour and wife of the local doctor, with whom Broughton had developed a close platonic relationship after Vera's departure with Lord Moyne. They had once travelled to Madeira together on holiday. His handwriting, usually small and neat, had degenerated to an expansive scrawl, unsteady and vexed. Though it contains no new information, the letter is reproduced here for its interesting presentation of the case against him. As Broughton well knew, the first person to read it would be Poppy himself.

Nairobi Jail

29-4-41

My darling Marie,
    Very much touched by your cable which I thought the nicest of all that I have received. I do hope you and Jimmy are well

and prosperous. I wish I had never come out to this b . . . y country. I seemed to have paid it one visit too many. My case comes on May 26th. I can tell you the old saying neck or nothing is very much brought home to me. I will give you a very brief outline of the case. If it is censored you will know what has happened. On the night of June 23rd Lord Erroll [sic], Mrs. Carberry, my wife and myself dined at Muthaiga Club, Nairobi. After dinner Lord Erroll and my wife went on to dance at a road house. Mrs. Carberry and myself stayed up talking and drinking with friends till 1:30 a.m. We then went home in my car and got to my house at Karen at 2 a.m. Ten minutes afterwards Lord Erroll and my wife arrived back. He stayed 10 minutes and left in his car and was found shot through the head 2½ miles away in a murram pit just off the road. Four days previously I had my 2 revolvers, a cigarette case and some money stolen and Lord Erroll was shot by a bullet which came out of one of my revolvers which were stolen. He was also involved with my wife. The police took a long time making up their minds and arrested me 7 weeks after the murder. Their grounds were 1) Motive jealousy 2) that he was killed by a bullet fired from one of the revolvers that were stolen 3) the robbery was faked. These and certain conversations they have twisted round and the fact that I had a bonfire the day after the murder make their case . . . However my friends have been too extraordinarily nice and thoughtful to me. Wish me luck darling. I think wistfully of Madeira now. My fondest love to both of you.

Jock

Poppy, meanwhile, visited ''the ladies'' at Karen, who had begun to tease him. ''What? You here again, Popski?'' said June Carberry. ''Diana went on rubbing the hair from her legs with an emery board,'' Poppy recalled. ''They said, 'Once a week, it's something all we girls have to do,' or words to that effect. They served a particularly strong home-brewed Pimms.''

The murder made the headlines in London. Erroll's daughter, Diana, who was called Dinan, had come to England to live with her aunt, Lady Avice Spicer, in Wiltshire, when Erroll married Molly Ramsay-Hill. Now fourteen, she first learned of her father's death at the village shop, where she saw the news on the front page. She went home expecting an explanation, but never received one. When the newspapers were delivered each morning, she would steal downstairs before breakfast and read the almost daily news items about her father. Weeks later she would read about the trial of Broughton before slipping back upstairs to her room. When she returned to the dining room for breakfast, she would find the papers had been clipped. Though she had not been informed of it, she was now the Countess of Erroll. The circumstances of her father's death were never described to her.

9

THE ANGEL
OF
DEATH

I F B R O U G H T O N was found guilty of the murder,
and he now began seriously to worry about his chances,
it was likely that he would be hanged. "In a strange country, God knows what will happen," he had written to Mrs.
Woodhouse. "There are no counsels out here . . ." As a
colony, Kenya had the same system of jury trial as in
England, yet Broughton, the former magistrate, had asked
Poppy in one of their talks, "Are Europeans hanged for
murder in this country?" Three weeks before the trial he
was still without a defence counsel. It was impossible to
get a barrister to come from England in wartime, and there
was none to be had in Nairobi.

In the end it was Diana who rescued the situation.
Feeling responsible in part for what had happened, she
had decided to throw all her weight behind Broughton's
defence. She flew alone to Johannesburg, on her own
initiative, to hire the most gifted barrister in the South,
Harry Morris K.C.—a man already notorious for his flamboyant and aggressive style of advocacy, and for some
famous acquittals. Morris accepted the case immediately,
sensing the crowning achievement of his career, if he could
win it. He demanded a fee of £5,000, to which Diana
agreed.

The trial opened at Nairobi's Central Court on May

26th. The opening ceremony presented an extraordinary spectacle. Under the glass dome, in a panelled room of Edwardian neoclassical sombreness, the entire colonial community seemed to have crushed its way in to watch the show. The public galleries overflowed and the spectators, many of the men in uniform, all the women dressed in their garden party best, were two rows deep along the walls. It was a gaudy spectacle of prurient anticipation; all the champagne and exhibitionism would now be accounted for, and possibly punished by the death sentence. The decent and sanctimonious contingent was opposed by the Muthaiga and Happy Valley crowd, who had rallied in support of their cause, many of them waiting in the wings to give evidence. It was a major social event that had been preceded by four months of furious pre-publicity. In that period it had been a burning topic throughout the Colony, and with little in the way of hard facts to go on, strange rumours and outlandish versions of the story had come to be accepted as the truth.

There were many reporters filing for newspapers overseas, including a woman who had travelled from Chicago to provide her paper with daily exclusives. (Broughton smiled at her one day, on his way up from the cells, and said, "As long as you're here, my head feels safe on my shoulders.")

The courtroom crackled with old class divisions. Diana, especially, the symbol of privilege and wealth, the object of sexual conjecture, was a strong target for those who felt the Colony had been shamed when the war demanded public sacrifice. She attended court every day, returning each evening to her suite in the New Stanley Hotel. On that first day, she made a spectacular entrance as the crowd twisted round to see her. To their amazement she had come dressed as a widow, in a little black hat with a black face veil, and covered in diamonds. Diana's wardrobe was one of the wonders of the trial—it was said that she never wore the same costume twice. She took her place at the front of the court, a few feet from the Attorney-General. Then Broughton appeared from the cells, looking a little waxy, having lost some weight in jail. He shuffled to the dock, his right foot dragging, to hear the charge of murder from the Lord Chief Justice, Sir Joseph Sheridan.

Harragin, a tall, pale man with greying hair, began his opening address by saying that the case had "created a profound and painful impression on the minds of everyone in this Colony. There can be few of you who have not discussed and possibly come to some conclusion either on the case or on the various details which have been reported . . ."

What then followed for three weeks is recorded in detail in the 600 closely typewritten pages of the court record—a document of absorbing interest and a striking portrait of a confident oligarchy in the last years of its reign.

Broughton was asked at one point, "I think Mrs. Barkas has told us how you spent the succeeding days. You played golf croquet, bridge and backgammon at the Club."

A: "Yes, each day."

Lunches, dinners and sundowners intervene.

Mrs. Barkas was asked, "Do you recall other topics of conversation [with Broughton] that day?"

"We were hoping it would get fine and we could play croquet."

"It is a very mild outdoor game, is it not?"

"I think so."

"Just pushing a ball through the hoop with a light mallet?"

"It is not light to me," said Mrs. Barkas.

African servants and askari policemen pass through the pages and are asked the routine question, "Can you tell the time? What time is it now by the court clock?" After each reply to this question the stenographer added the word "correct" in brackets. One African witness, Mutiso Wa Thathi, was asked, "Did you have a watch with you that night or is it just what you think?'' He replied, ''I had a watch with me but mine was fast because I kept it fast. It was 1½ hours ahead.''

There are the ''experts''—doctors, chemists, ballistic scientists—alternating on the stand with the socialites, including the group of young officers: Portman, Pembroke, Dickinson, Llewellin, Lezard; and above all there is the remarkable performance of Broughton himself, who elected to give evidence and held the floor for several days.

The transcript vividly records a great defence barrister at work. Harry Morris, later immortalised in a biography called *Genius for the Defence*, was described by a lawyer on the opposing team as ''bluff, rough and impassioned, contemptuous . . . prone to descend to burlesque, abuse, even insolence.'' From a reading of this case, that description is unfairly pejorative. Morris would never insult a witness gratuitously, although he often managed to provoke one into angry retaliation. His style in court was aggressive, and sometimes abrasive. It relied upon a rich sense of humour, a sharp wit, and a degree of sarcasm. Morris also displayed an exceptional memory and a prodigious grasp of detail which he used to greatest effect in reducing expert witnesses for the prosecution, whenever possible, to the level of confused amateurs, tangling them up in petty contradictions.

It was in his talent for manipulation and mystification that Morris truly shone as a barrister. He believed that expert witnesses, forensic scientists and the like, with their carefully prepared evidence and their professional sureness and self-esteem, were the easiest prey for a good defence counsel. Furthermore, Morris was a leading lay authority on ballistic science—the knowledge of guns and bullets, especially the microscopic markings found on spent bullets that could identify them with the barrel of a particular gun. On his arrival in Nairobi he told both Broughton and Kaplan that he could defeat the Crown case on one simple point of ballistics alone.

In fact Morris was perplexed that the Crown case had

left him such a "simple answer" to give to the jury, namely to disprove the Crown's contention that the murder weapon was that same Colt .32 that Broughton had used for shooting practice at Nanyuki and which had subsequently been "stolen" from his house three days before the murder. But he gave no clue about his simple answer, even to his clients.

Linking the murder bullet to Broughton's Colt formed the main plank of the prosecution's somewhat flimsy case. They also maintained that live cartridges had been found in the undergrowth where Broughton and Diana were shooting, and that these were charged with black powder, which had not been manufactured since the outbreak of the First World War. There were marks of this same powder surrounding the wound on Erroll's head.

It was a carefully premeditated murder, claimed the Crown, the first step of which had been Broughton's faking the theft of the revolvers. He had begun to plan it on January 18th, when Erroll had refused to go away and give up Diana. Broughton's subsequent actions—his magnanimous renunciation of his wife, his honouring of the marriage pact with such fastidiousness, his drunkenness on the night of the murder, his forgetfulness of details afterwards, were all an act, according to the prosecution. Instead, when Broughton saw that his marriage was threatened by Erroll, his real nature showed itself: his exceptional jealousy, his anger, his deviousness and finally his desire to kill his rival. It was Broughton's character that was to be put on trial.

The Crown would show that Broughton had the opportunity to do the deed, yet Harragin could never explain how Broughton got out of the house undetected by Wilks or June Carberry, so he showed that it was possible to leave by the drainpipe, or walk soundlessly down the stairs. (Poppy had masterminded both experiments, although the drainpipe climbing he had merely supervised. Hugh Dickinson, who happened to be at Karen that day, had volunteered for the task.) Neither was he able to reveal exactly how the accused had acted when he left the house. Had he hidden in the car and shot Erroll just before the junction? Or had he walked to the junction and waited for him? The Crown could only guess at Broughton's actions. The leading evidence against Broughton came from the policemen, the African servants and the scientists. Dr. Francis Vint believed that the shots were fired by someone standing on the running board of the car, shooting through the open window, or sitting in the seat beside Erroll. From the scorchmarks on the skin, Vint concluded that the gun could not have been more than eighteen inches from Erroll's head when it was fired. The second bullet travelled straight across the top of the spinal column from ear to ear. (The first bullet went wide, striking the metal partition between the doors.)

The bruises on Erroll's forehead suggested that he had hit his head on the steering wheel as he ducked when he first saw the gun. The second shot killed him instantly. At some point, said Vint, the body must have fallen sideways—there were bloodstains exactly where the wounded side of Erroll's head would have touched the passenger seat. Vint also noticed that there was blood on Erroll's right trouser leg, below the knee, which suggested that Erroll had been upright at the wheel long enough for the blood to drip downwards—but nothing was made of this, although it might well have had some bearing on how the body arrived in that position in the footwell of the car, the knees tucked under the body, and the hands clasped in front of the head. There were smears of blood on both hands, particularly on the left one.

After many experiments, Poppy and Vint concluded that the body must have been manipulated into the footwell to get it free of the wheel and the pedals, that it would never have fallen that way naturally: the steering wheel itself would have prevented it from falling into the footwell on the car's impact with the ditch.

Poppy believed that Broughton had moved the body from the driving seat in order to be able to steer the car off the road. The ignition had clearly been switched off by hand; the lights were still on but because the knob was missing from the light switch it required a pair of pliers to turn them off—and a pair was found in the car.

To shoot from the running board while the car was moving would have required some agility, said Vint, but to shoot from the seat beside Erroll would have been relatively easy, if the murderer turned his back to his own door. He didn't suggest that the best position—if the car was stationary—was with the door open and the murderer stepping out backwards. Evidence was also given that the armslings in the car—which Mrs. Carberry, who always used them, said had been definitely in place the day before the murder—had not been wrenched off, but unscrewed and removed.

Harragin then tried to show that Broughton's behaviour both before and after the murder reeked of suspicion, especially his second call on June Carberry at 3:30 a.m., after Erroll had been shot—surely a blatant attempt at establishing an alibi. Wasn't it suspicious, too, that at Nyeri he had asked June Carberry if she had told the police that he had been bad-tempered and peevish in the Club that night, and had told her that she couldn't go away because she would be "his" main witness (June couldn't remember if he had said "his" or "a" main witness); and that he had asked the police, when they came to question him, what were the chances of finding a gun "buried somewhere in Africa"; and that he had asked at another moment whether a man would be hanged if he shot his wife's lover, having caught them *in flagrante delicto?* After Soames had told him that the police had been to his farm to look for bullets, didn't Broughton show an unnatural interest in ballistics, comparison microscopes and so on, especially in a conversation with Carberry at Karen after the murder?

Then there was Broughton's hasty lighting of the bonfire, on which police discovered a burnt golf stocking stained with blood (and his obsessive need to tell Poppy in such detail about the lighting of the bonfire); his trip to the police station with the handkerchief, shaking with nerves, incredulous, according to the police, that Erroll's death was being treated as a motor accident, and his impatience to know the result of the post mortem. Didn't Broughton say to June Carberry in the Club, "I won't give her the Karen house and £5,000, and she can damn well go and live with Joss," and "To think I've only been married three months, and she treats me like this"? Was this the attitude of a man who had gracefully conceded? And what of Broughton's visit to the Union Castle agent to rebook the passage to Ceylon on the same morning that the death of Erroll was announced?

Harragin showed, too, that, far from being physically disabled, Broughton was quite capable of sustaining long walks on hunting safaris and toting heavy rifles, and that he was therefore equally capable of having pushed Erroll's body from the seat into the footwell to enable him to drive the car; and then of walking the 2.4 miles back to Karen in the blackout in time to call on June, despite his protestations of lameness and night blindness. None of this constituted hard proof, but Harragin was trying to forge links between each piece of evidence to build up what was ever more clearly a difficult case for the Crown to prove beyond a reasonable doubt.

Apart from Poppy and the ballistics experts, Harragin's own main witnesses were June Carberry and Gwladys Delamere. June turned out to be of more use to the defence. She provided Broughton's only alibi; she alone gave the times of their leaving the Club together and returning to Karen, and she is the only source for what took place at the house after their return, since neither Wilks nor Diana gave evidence. Could they indeed have got back home much sooner than 2:00—which is June's estimation?

June's evidence was never really challenged, and Broughton himself explained his lapses of memory by claiming that he was too drunk to remember anything. June fully supported this. She even had to help him up the stairs, she said, with her arm around his waist. She was sure that Broughton at this stage was far beyond feeling any "emotion"—an ironic comment from a heavy drinker like June, unless she was claiming that Broughton was actually unconscious. But then she said that at 2:10 a.m. Broughton was in his dressing gown, bidding her good night with a knock on her door. At about 2:25 Diana arrived—also June's estimate—and from 2:40 Diana stayed in June's room for about half an hour. Broughton then paid a second visit to her at 3:30, twenty minutes after Diana had left to go to her own room, "to make sure she was all right."

"Did anything else attract your attention that night?" she was asked. "Yes, after that [Diana's retirement] Jock Broughton came along."

"About how long afterwards?"

"About ten or twenty minutes. It is difficult to judge the time."

"Had you no way of judging the time?"

"No."

"Did anything else happen in the house about that time to attract your attention?"

"Diana's dog was barking."

"Loudly?"

"Yes, quite loudly."

"What happened when Sir Delves came to your room?"

"He just knocked on the door and asked if I was sure I was all right."

The only damaging evidence June gave against Broughton was her description of his tirade against Diana after the lovers left the Muthaiga Club, though this had been overheard by other witnesses. To set against that was her favourable account of Broughton's character—his cheerfulness, his even mood, his sense of humour, his fundamental lack of jealousy, or even bitterness. June was very sure of herself in the witness box and as she stepped down, Harragin's secretary heard her say, "Well, I've left his head safer on his shoulders."

Gwladys Delamere was the only really hostile witness, and her responses to Morris's questions were brittle.

Q: Lord Erroll was a man of thirty-nine or thereabouts?
A: Yes.
Q: A man of some common sense?
A: Sense. I don't know whether it was common sense.
Q: Was there any reason why he should have called you aside at the dinner party at Karen to tell you those things, as distinct from other people?
A: I suppose he thought I had sense or common sense.
Q: What was your interest in the matter, Lady Delamere?
A: The tragic circumstances of it all. I wanted to make quite sure that both were definite about it.
Q: What had it got to do with you?
A: Purely that I was a good friend for many years of Lord Erroll.
Q: So you wanted to know because you were a friend of his?
A: I anticipated trouble and difficulty.
Q: Then why did you poke your nose into it if you anticipated trouble and difficulty?
A: Because Lord Erroll seemed to consult his friends about these matters.
Q: Did you say *these* matters?
A: I may have.

(Here Morris scored the point that Erroll had other enemies than Broughton.)

She described Broughton's expression as he watched his wife and Joss Erroll dancing. "It registered many things: anger, misery, rage, brooding, intense irritation and restlessness."

"Restlessness on his face?"

"Yes."

Gwladys denied that she had said to him, "Do you

know that Joss is wildly in love with Diana?'' and that this remark may have been the reason for his troubled expression.

The foreman of the jury asked, ''When you described the accused's disposition as morose, do you mean habitually so?''

''Yes, I have always thought so.''

''It may be,'' said the foreman, ''that he was only morose towards you?''

''If so,'' said Gwladys, ''he must have been morose for twenty years.''

Later, when Broughton was in the witness box, he was asked, ''Why do you suggest she should have turned against you?''

''Only by her evidence,'' he answered. ''She said I had a morose disposition when she knows full well I have not, and her evidence as to my distress when I was sitting next to her watching the dancing was entirely fabricated and also her saying my face registered every emotion of hate against my wife in the Muthaiga Club. Nobody was more suprised than I was at her evidence.''

Two key witnesses were not called: Diana and Wilks. Diana could not be compelled to give evidence against her husband, though she had, of course, made a statement to the police before she was told how Erroll had died, in which she may have let slip that her dog had begun barking loudly at 3:30. Did the dog bark because it heard Broughton re-entering the house? Diana left the court only once, when Erroll's ear, by now a ballistics exhibit, was handed round in a jar of spirits. She said, ''This is really *too* much. Poor Joss.'' When Broughton's disabilities were being illustrated by Morris, she was overheard to say, ''He's not nearly such an old crock as he's making out.''

The prosecution's neglect of Wilks, who would have been able to confirm or deny June's evidence, is more surprising. They gave as their reason that Broughton's servant would not be believed; but this had not prevented them from calling his other servants, or Erroll's Leporello, Waiweru, or his Somali chauffeur. It seems that Wilks had made several conflicting statements, and was not to be trusted in the witness box by either side.

      MORRIS CALLED only eight witnesses, including Broughton and the loyal Major Pembroke, against the prosecution's twenty. The eight were quite enough: he had already turned several of the prosecution witnesses into his own, all, except for Gwladys, testifying with impeccable politeness to Broughton's amiability and tolerance, to his lack of temper and to what Broughton called the "unimpaired friendship" with Erroll all through the crisis. (The Crown saw this as Broughton setting a trap for Erroll; a ploy to have him always close at hand and under observation.) Among his witnesses Morris also put up his own ballistics expert, Captain Thomas Overton, to contradict the prosecution experts, although Morris had already damaged the prosecution's ballistics case by then in cross-examination.

    It was in his brilliant handling of the ballistics evidence that Morris's expertise had been revealed. The technical battle that raged for days around a series of microscopic markings on a set of bullets was often confusing and difficult for a lay jury to follow. At moments, lawyers and experts were arguing only—as it seemed—for each other's benefit. Yet Morris always made sure the jury knew when he had scored a point, and the ballistics evidence on which the Crown case rested provided some of the most dramatic moments in the trial.

    Briefly, Morris had two propositions to attack. The first was the contention that the bullets fired at Soames's farm (the "Nanyuki" bullets) and the murder bullets came from the same gun. If these two sets of bullets could not be matched, then, Harragin said, "The case for the Crown falls away like a pack of cards." The second proposition was that the gun that fired all these bullets was a Colt .32 that belonged to Broughton and which he had arranged to be stolen (with another weapon which is not relevant) from the house at Karen. This Colt .32 was registered on Broughton's firearms certificate.

Morris proved that, given the markings on the bullets, none of them could have been shot by any Colt pistol ever manufactured—that was his "one point" on which he hoped to defeat the Crown case. The Crown, however, might reply that Broughton had another .32 hidden away, possibly a Smith & Wesson. To counter this Morris—using pedantry mixed with semi-terror tactics and the judicious use of ballistics textbooks—attempted to put grave doubts in the mind of the jury about the methods the prosecution experts had used in producing their conclusion that the two sets of bullets matched. There was no trace of doubt in the minds of these experts. But if the jury were at all uncertain, Broughton would have to be acquitted.

Morris dealt with the last point first. Until he began his cross-examination, the close similarities between the two sets of bullets, as demonstrated by the Government scientists, Ernest Harwich and Maurice Fox, seemed unanswerable. Fox, the chief Government chemist, had spent almost two months in the laboratory with a comparison microscope, photographing and analysing the bullets and carefully cataloguing these similarities.

A bullet passing through a barrel will pick up, in reverse, the impression of the rifling—the lands (ridges), grooves and striations, or thin lines, caused by irregularities in the barrel. Fox had photographed these features in each bullet for comparison, but through bad marking and classification, the large pile of pictures—as Morris showed—turned out to be almost useless, hopelessly confusing to a jury. Morris suggested that Fox had wasted his two months in the laboratory. From the start Fox had been defensive and pigheaded, resisting all Morris's definitions, and quibbling with his questions. (When Morris mentioned a work by a Major Burrard called *Identification of Firearms and Forensic Ballistics*, Fox said, "It is not a book on ballistics." "What title would you give it then?" Morris asked. "I would not like to give a title to another man's book," answered Fox.)

Fox spent seven hours in the witness box for the Crown. Morris questioned him for a further fourteen hours, with many interventions from the judge when the two men seemed to be coming to blows. Their mutual antipathy brought comic relief to the court which had become bored and muddled by Morris's minute examination of lands, grooves and striations. Morris asked at one point what the letters "S" and "W" signified on a cartridge.

"That the cartridge is suitable for a Smith & Wesson," replied Fox.

"Where did you get that from?" Morris asked.

"My mother told me," said Fox.

"Are you trying to be insolent or impertinent, Mr. Fox?"

"No."

"Well, you are succeeding."

The similarities were one thing, argued Morris, but what about the *differences*? Morris knew that there were always minute differences between two bullets fired from the same gun. He now discussed every chink and scratch visible on the bullets as if they had equal value with the Crown's universal similarities. He went into great detail, producing anarchy out of order to a jury already bemused by ballistic science. And could the comparison between different bullets really be conclusive without the firearm itself, which the Crown would never be able to produce? Under his own tireless assault from Morris, Harwich had already agreed that the identification of a bullet by its markings was "a very complex proposition" without the actual firearm. Having got both Harwich and Fox to qualify, accept, concede certain points, Morris would then ask (turning to the jury with a look of weary exasperation),

"And you *still* maintain that the bullets are from the same weapon?"

And now Morris moved in for the kill. It had been argued, he said, that all the bullets came from a revolver whose barrel had five grooves in the rifling, which twisted along the barrel in a right-handed or clockwise direction.

MORRIS: In all these bullets, was the direction uniform?
HARWICH: Yes, it is right hand in all the bullets.
MORRIS: Is the direction in a Colt revolver right or left?
HARWICH: Left in the barrel.
MORRIS: Can you say what kind of a gun the bullets came from?
HARWICH: I can say they came from a revolver.
LORD CHIEF JUSTICE: But not a Colt.
HARWICH: As far as my experience goes, all Colt revolvers have six grooves and a left-hand twist.

It was a heavy point for the defence, and the mystery remains of why, with all its ballistic experts to hand, with Fox working on the case for two months before the trial, the Crown should have ignored this flaw in its case.

There was still the problem of Soames's memory of the gun Broughton had used for target practice. He had said in evidence that he thought Broughton had shot with a Colt on his farm, although he wasn't certain. He thought, too, that it was a revolver that was hinged, in which the breech is broken—a characteristic of Colts.

Morris took the weight out of that with another question: "If Sir Delves tells his Lordship and the Jury that his gun was not a gun that broke, but one in which the cylinder fell out, you would not dispute that?"

"I would believe him," said Soames.

The similarity between the two sets of bullets—which nobody, not even Morris, disputed in the end—remained one of the most tantalising elements of the mystery. There was the added similarity of the black powder marks on Erroll's wound, and the live bullets found at Nanyuki, also charged with black powder, which was extremely rare at the time of the events under discussion, but widely available before 1914.

HARRAGIN: When did you tell us you bought these revolvers?
BROUGHTON: I cannot remember the date—12 or 15 years ago.
Q: Do you remember where you bought them?
A: I go to many gunsmiths and I cannot remember but I should think probably the Army and Navy Stores.
Q: Did you buy them together or separately?
A: I bought them at the same time.
Q: Can you remember why you should have suddenly bought two revolvers?
A: I cannot remember after 15 years but you never want a revolver in England and I should think I had it in mind that I might require them if I went abroad.
Q: Did you buy ammunition at the same time?
A: I think at the same time I bought a packet of ammunition for the .32. I rather think I had some old .45 ammunition at home and I don't think I bought any .45 ammunition.
Q: In any event you never used them in England?
A: No.
Q: And in fact you never used them until you went to Soames's farm where I think you used only one?
A: Yes.
Q: Did you use the same ammunition that you bought 12 or 15 years ago?
A: Yes, it was the only ammunition I had.
Q: How many rounds had you?
A: It was an unbroken box of, I think, fifty.
Q: How many rounds were shot?
A: About 40. I think I fired about 20 or 25 and she [Diana] 15. I fired more than she.
Q: And will you agree that if any live rounds of .32 ammunition were found there the probability is that they were yours?
A: There could not have been any of my ammunition found there.
[Why not? It is extraordinary that this reply was left unchallenged.]
Q: Were you firing with black powder ammunition?
A: I have no idea but if you go to a good gunmaker I think it is very unlikely that you would obtain black powder even 15

years ago. It is a very old-fashioned type of powder. When I was a boy I used black powder but I think it went out before the last war. I should have thought it very unusual to find it in revolver ammunition.

Q: Can you give any reason why there were black powder cartridges there, not necessarily yours?

A: I cannot give any explanation.

Broughton showed a remarkable composure in his twenty hours of testimony. Imperturbable, urbane, almost insouciant—an aristocrat before the guillotine couldn't have done better. And yet at one time Broughton's impassivity suggested Camus's *L'Etranger*. The witness was Dr. Joseph Gregory:

Q: Assuming a man is charged with murder, if you noticed his extreme calm and that he was apparently quite satisfied with the position or not interested in caring, would that indicate to you any condition of the brain?

A: No, sir.

Q: If he appears to be quite indifferent to the surroundings of the prison or the court, you would say that that was quite normal?

A: I would say it would indicate he is what one normally calls a philosopher.

Q: Or a man with a clear conscience?

A: Yes, either.

Morris was of course taking a calculated risk in putting his client into the witness box. Many a prosecution case in criminal history has been defeated by a good defence counsel, only to be lost in the end by a slip of the tongue from the accused, who has elected to give evidence. In his defence, Broughton claimed that he had honoured the pact, and this entirely explained the ease with which he conceded to Erroll. Broughton said he realised that it was all over when he saw Diana lying in bed with June Carberry wearing Erroll's pearls.

Why had he stayed away from the dinner on the 18th?

Broughton replied that he was "very upset." Diana had told him that if she couldn't get a divorce soon, she would wait a lifetime, or a number of years, he forgot which. He explained, "I had always visualised the possibility of my wife falling in love with somebody else, but it had come sooner than I expected. It was silly really because a woman may fall in love with somebody else in two months or ten years. I have always been devoted to my wife. I am devoted to her still. I realised that she had all her young life to live while I haven't and therefore the only thing to do was to cut my losses and go away to Ceylon. I was going there for three months and I had hoped that when I came back to Kenya she might be no longer in love with him and would want to come back to me. I certainly had not abandoned hope of that." He told Diana, he said, that he hoped she would stay on at Karen for appearances' sake, until he went away, "as nobody knew anything about it, as far as I know."

Morris had asked him, ". . . As an old racing man you realised that Lord Erroll had the advantage in the weights, and you were leaving the course to him?"

"Yes," replied Broughton, falling in with the jargon, "eighteen pounds."

Harragin put it another way: "You realised that in ten years' time you would be sixty-seven and she thirty-seven?"

"That is not very young for a woman."

"It is rather old for a man."

"It depends on the man."

"But a man with 40 per cent disability?"

"From which he has completely recovered."

Earlier on the 18th, he had intimated to Mrs. Carberry, as they walked in the garden of Erroll's house, that he would commit suicide.

Q: How do you reconcile that state of mind with the fact that you had just had a perfectly amicable conversation with Lord Erroll and that in view of the pact you were resigned to your wife leaving you?

A: You do not show your feelings to a man whereas you very often show them to a woman, especially if she is a great friend. I still felt very upset about it even at the end of the discussion. I would not demean myself by showing these sort of feelings to Lord Erroll.

Why, after his suspicions were aroused, was it necessary to have lunch with Erroll every day?

"Why not?" replied Broughton. "You cannot stop a thing like that in a small community like Muthaiga. How could I avoid it? My wife and I went to Muthaiga Club every day. Unless I had told him I did not want to see him, how could I stop him? We all lunched at the Club every day."

Why had he invited Erroll to stay the night, when he already knew what was happening between Diana and Joss? If Diana asked him, would he object?

"She could ask whom she liked," said Broughton. "I should not have tried to stop her in any event. I see no point in it. We met every day at the Club and I cannot see it makes any difference if a man comes to stay the night. It would be extremely bad strategy. In my experience of life if you try and stop a woman doing anything she wants to do it all the more. With a young wife the only thing to do is to keep her amused."

Harragin then asked about Broughton's jealousy, reminding him in effect that he had been cuckolded two months after his marriage.

Q: Can you explain to us why you took so placidly this robbery that was taking place under your very nose?

A: What is the use of having a pact if you do not honour it? I maintain between a man of my age and a girl of my wife's it is not very unnatural.

Q: I am putting it that your wife was your dearest possession and having asked you about such things as land I ask you now here is your dearest possession being taken from under your nose and you take it placidly because you had made a pact?

A: Yes, otherwise there would be no point in the pact.

Q: You also went further I think and said that you thought it was very flattering for a man to fall in love with your wife?

A: I think it is.

Q: Flattering to you?

A: Yes, I think one always likes one's possessions admired. I did not mind a bit so long as she did not respond.

Q: Is it flattering to have one's wife loved by people of the opposite sex with all that that connotes?

A: I had got very used to it in the last three years. I think we all like to have our possessions admired.

Q: Much in the same way as if you have a beautiful picture?

A: Exactly.

Q: But does it not become a different thing when your friend instead of merely looking at and admiring your picture proceeds to remove it from your wall and take it away with him?

A: As I have said so many times I had my pact and therefore had no right to object.

Q: And not even your pride was hurt at the thought of your wife being taken away?

A: No. She was taken away by a much younger man, a very intelligent man, a very attractive man and a man of very high social position.

Q: Would that fact make it any more pleasant?

A: It would soften the blow.

Q: And even your sense of property was not outraged?

A: I never thought of classing my wife as property.

Q: But the fact of losing your wife as a precious possession?

A: It comes back to the same thing. Of course I minded but I was tied down by the pact.

As to the financial part of the pact, was it not galling for Broughton that his wife and her lover would be provided for, for some years, at his expense? Broughton replied that he never imagined that Diana would actually exercise her legal rights to the £5,000 a year.

Q: What reason have you for saying "never"?

A: Implicit faith in my wife. I have known her for a very long time and she is the straightest person about money I have ever met . . . It is a question of knowing the woman. I knew she would not take it.''

And what of the champagne toast on the night of the murder?

Broughton said, ''It was a very intimate party between the three principals and a very great friend of the three principals and I think on those occasions you say things you would never dream of saying at any other time.''

Q: Was that a sincere toast on your part?
A: Certainly it was. The whole party was very happy and everybody on the top of their form. I was resigned to losing my wife and I had cut my loss.

Later, in re-examination, Broughton replied to Morris, ''I accepted the situation and I thought it showed my entire resignation to the situation. I think I had in mind that it was the most extreme gesture I could make.''

Later on the evening of the final dinner, after more champagne and liqueur brandy, on top of the champagne cocktails, Broughton described himself as ''very drunk,'' and said he remembered little of what happened. He did remember complaining to June Carberry and saying about Diana, ''We have only been married three months and look what she does to me.'' But he did not recall saying that he wouldn't give her the £5,000.

Having decided to hand Diana over to Erroll, why did Broughton insist on her being back at Karen by 3 a.m., considering that she had only spent five nights there since January 1st?

Broughton answered, ''I was still fond of her and she was still my wife, and likely to remain my wife for some years and old habits are rather difficult to get out of. I was always worried about her staying up too late.''

Harragin could never shake him: ''You do not agree that it would be quite ridiculous for a man to be seen carrying a lady's handkerchief in his two hands, the one admittedly quivering, and saying he wished to put that on the corpse?''

''I went to the police station and had a handkerchief in my pocket and I don't think I produced the handkerchief till one of the police officers told me he would place it on Lord Erroll's body as I could not get into the mortuary.''

''And do you not think it was an equally ridiculous request from a policeman's point of view?''

''Not if a man had any sentiment. I suppose I ought to have realised that policemen are not sentimental.''

''WHAT WAS your reaction to the news of Erroll's death?'' Harragin asked later.

''I was dumbfounded.''

''Wasn't it a very satisfactory solution to your domestic troubles?''

''Not at all; no solution.''

''What do you mean by no solution?''

''I do not think the average man would have relished resuming married life with one who had been madly in love with another man and was still.''

The bonfire, so hastily lit by Broughton was, he said, a habit from his childhood days at Doddington. Asked what enjoyment he got out of it, Broughton replied, ''You might just as well ask what pleasure there is in eating and drinking.''

Harragin then fired his last shot: ''Did you say at dinner one night to your wife when she was going off to the Claremont Club, 'Shall I throw the champagne in your face, or would you rather I threw the bottle at your head?' And did she try to soothe you down by saying, 'There, there, try and eat something'?''

Broughton replied, ''I think somebody has been pulling your leg.'' The mild, the unreproachful, the perfect response.

Broughton emerged quite unscathed. The most telling point against him was his lapse of memory whenever he was asked anything too near the bone. He forgot that he had not gone to France in 1914 (when the sunstroke kept him back). He forgot innumerable conversations or disagreements. He forgot that he had rebooked the passage to Ceylon on the day of the murder, directly after his visit to the mortuary with Diana's handkerchief. He had no recollection of visiting June Carberry twice at 2:10 and 3:30 a.m. (June's estimated times), or of the barking of Diana's dog, though he did remember voices downstairs and Erroll's car driving away.

Finally, what of the reported theft of Broughton's revolvers? Why did he bring them downstairs and put them on the mantelpiece, when his intention, apparently, was to put them in the safe?

Q: If Abdullah had the key, why did you not hand him the guns to go and put them in the gun room?
A: Why should I? I always put the guns away myself. I do not leave them to natives.

Why did he change the description of the stolen items three times in minor detail (a five-shilling note, two five shilling notes, a ten-shilling note and a pound note, etc.)? Was he becoming confused with his own story, forgetting the all-important detail?

The robbery itself presents a quandary. If Broughton intended to use his own gun, why, three days before the murder, would he invent the theft, thus announcing to the police that he had possessed two guns and forcing him to show them his firearms certificate? Was the answer that because other people in the house knew that he had two guns, Broughton would have had to explain the disappearance of one of them—the murder weapon? If it was as simple as that, it seemed a clumsy and suspicious move.

Or was it a masterstroke of deviousness, because Broughton knew that the firearms certificate was false and could never match the murder weapon? He had to arrange the "theft" to put the certificate in the hands of the police, who would conclude that it could not have been Broughton's gun that did the deed. The problem here is that Broughton would have thrown the gun away anyway, to ensure that the murder bullet would not be traceable to a particular gun.

Broughton couldn't have known in advance about the discovery of the Nanyuki bullets. Did he know enough about ballistics to realise that the murder bullet that he did fire would clearly be seen not to have come from the registered Colt—thus letting him off? At one point, to explain his detailed conversations with friends and policemen about guns and ballistics after the murder, Broughton said, "I have done a great deal of rifle shooting all my life. I had always heard you could identify bullets fired out of the same gun." Even so, it seems an impossibly sophisticated act of premeditation. Or was the revolver theft a genuine coincidence? If Broughton had a third gun—the one used at Nanyuki—why would he have to dispose of the others?

In his autobiography, Morris made the following summary of his case for the defence:

1. Erroll was shot with a five groove gun. No such weapon was traced to Broughton.
2. There was nothing to show that the bullets found at Soames's farm at Nanyuki were fired while he was there.
3. The expert photographs were so bewildering that they had to be abandoned.
4. There was no eyewitness. No one saw Broughton enter or leave the house.
5. There were three women in the house and a number of native servants; none of them heard a shot.
6. The motive was worthless. There were many others who had a motive for shooting Erroll.
7. Broughton was not physically strong enough to have moved the body in the car.
8. If he suffered from night blindness, he could not have driven

the car with its cut-down headlights, in the blackout—he was a notoriously bad driver. And he could never have found his way in the darkness, across the bush, back to his house.

9. Broughton's right arm was injured, his foot dragged. He would not have been able to let himself down a drainpipe or climb down—or up—a balcony. He would have had to return to his room by a creaking staircase. No one claimed to have heard him.

Morris shook hands with each member of the jury after his closing speech, then left for Johannesburg without hearing the verdict, which was delivered at 9:15 p.m. on July 1st.

As he returned from their deliberation, the foreman of the jury winked at Broughton, and gave him the "thumbs up" sign. Broughton described the moment later in a letter to a friend in England:

It was really very sensational when the Verdict of the Jury was delivered after a discussion of 3 hours and 25 minutes. I had been walking up and down outside the court with various friends and was beginning for the first time to feel the "strain," and although I never at any time visualised a "conviction" at the last moment one gets doubts and I feared the Jury might disagree, and there would be a fresh trial because all twelve of them have to be unanimous, and it is always possible that even one might think me guilty. Luckily they all were unanimous.

The Foreman, in a very clear voice said, "Not Guilty" and a loud sob of relief came from all over the court and a good deal of clapping. One could almost feel the Angel of Death, who had been hovering over me, flying out of that court disgruntled.

When I got outside there was a great rush of about 200 people, headed mostly by the police, to shake me by the hand. People have been extraordinarily kind and I have had 146 cables of congratulations and countless letters from all over the world, lots of them from people I've never heard of.

The letters Broughton wrote after the trial express elation and hope. He claims to have recovered at once;

never to have felt happier, and writes of Diana's loyalty and affection. Within a few days they were on their way from Mombasa to Ceylon together, on the long-postponed trip to look over Broughton's investments. There was time to spare before returning to Kenya, and they crossed to India to look up two old friends, the Nawab of Bhopal and the Maharajah of Jodhpur. Broughton was deeply grateful to be swathed in luxury once again (''we have six huge rooms and 4 servants to look after us''), and to find that nothing had changed since the 1920s. ''This place,'' he said, ''might be a million miles away from any war.''

But there was a nagging worry in the back of his mind. How had his friends reacted to the case? His private life had been broadcast in detail for the scrutiny of all his fellow clubmen. Would he be able to resume his life in England as it was before the war? He began to fear that he was irretrievably disgraced.

PART TWO

THE QUEST

10
THE VOICE
ON THE
ESCARPMENT

I N M I D - 1 9 6 9 , when I started work with Cyril Connolly on the Erroll story, I was twenty-four years old and employed as a feature writer on the *Sunday Times* Magazine in London. Before that I had served my apprenticeship on a provincial evening newspaper and for two years had travelled in Africa, as a reporter for various newspapers, including the *Daily Nation* in Nairobi, soon after Kenya's independence.

Connolly was then sixty-five, and his elegant prose had adorned the literary pages of the *Sunday Times* for fifteen years or more. As the author of *Enemies of Promise* and *The Unquiet Grave* and wartime editor of *Horizon*, he was a revered luminary of the world of letters.

Connolly's personality and the preoccupations which infused his writings were almost as renowned as the work he produced. There was his love of pleasure, for which the historian and writer Peter Quennell likened him to an eighteenth-century Man of Pleasure, later shortened to "Man of P"; his passion for beautiful objects; his sloth, which never dimmed his brilliance or his exacting standards, and his sense of regret at his own unrealised promise. Connolly traded in guilt and remorse, and he was beset with troublesome insecurities.

He was rarely seen by the reporters in the Gray's Inn

Road, where the *Sunday Times* has its offices. He lived with his family in a large Victorian house in suburban Eastbourne, Sussex. There he looked after his library—now at the University of Tulsa—gloated over his first editions and his collection of china, and cultivated his rare plants. He travelled to London on Wednesdays to deliver his copy and correct proofs. If one caught sight of him, getting in or out of a taxi, his unathletic frame was usually clothed in the smartest Savile Row suit of charcoal grey and he would be wearing a black homburg on his head. The dandy of the early 1920s had turned into some merchant banker of the 1960s, although the disguise was not perfect. One imagined he was making his way to White's in St. James's Street—whose rituals he observed with great seriousness—or to a carefully chosen rendezvous where he could feast on some longed-for pleasure. "Above all, the Dublin Bay prawn" is a phrase I remember at the end of a Connolly paragraph. It was in a piece written, I think, from a West African hotel where he had been subjected both to loneliness and to what he called "the torture of the table d'hôte." Later I imagined him repeating it, his soft voice reverential and quivering with ecstasy. His friend Peter Quennell has since told me of the elaborate stratagems, necessary or unnecessary, that accompanied these weekly visits to London, and of Connolly's sense of excitement as his train approached Victoria Station.

I held Connolly in some awe, not only for his great reputation. I had also seen how fearsome he could be if he was bored or irritated. I knew him slightly from the Sussex coast, where my parents had bought a house in the village of Firle, near Lewes. Before moving to Eastbourne, Connolly had rented a house on the Firle estate of Viscount Gage. From time to time he would come to dinner with my parents; often, in the early days of their acquaintance, an uneasy occasion since Connolly's reputation in the neighbourhood as an intellectual isolated among the gentry, who labelled him "distinguished and erudite," was also that of a difficult and unreliable guest.

On a bad night Connolly could play his part with cruel certainty. His famous love of pleasure was catered for to the best of my parents' ability, as it was by our other neighbours who befriended him. He would sometimes leave the carefully chosen vintage untouched, and the food as well, to sulk in so conspicuous a silence that the evening would begin to die around him. Neither was this behaviour always confined to his country neighbours. Quennell wrote in a tribute in 1952, when Connolly's idiosyncrasies were already a matter of history,

. . . if his pleasure makes itself felt, so does the opposite and complementary mood. His strength of will is positively royal; and Queen Victoria's "We are not amused," was scarcely more to be dreaded than Cyril Connolly's "I am not pleased," or rather the subtle change of expression, the indefinable lengthening of the features with which this alarming message is swiftly, surely rammed home. The temperature drops; candles flicker; the wine begins to taste corked.

In our neighbourhood, after Connolly had been to dinner, friends would ask, "How did it go?"

Towards the end of his life, Connolly made close friends with a local stockbroker, Tim Jones—himself a great lover of wine and food. Late one evening, after they had shared a particularly poor dinner at a neighbour's house, Connolly telephoned and said, "Tim, I just want to ask you one thing. What did you have to eat when you got home?"

Yet on a good night, depending on the company, and especially towards the end of the 1960s, the legendary wit and erudition would pour forth. There was almost nothing Connolly seemed unable to talk about in detail, and he had a lethal gift for verbal parody. I had always liked him; I had secretly relished the uncompromising silences and the awkward moments as much as the verbal brilliance, and he was invariably friendly and attentive to anyone under twenty-five.

In this period the *Sunday Times* Magazine, which operated separately from the body of the paper, had a certain literary distinction of its own. Much of this originated with the author and critic, Francis Wyndham, one of its senior editors, a tireless encourager and seeker-out of talent, who by his reputation could persuade almost anybody, it seemed, to write for us. Wyndham was a long-standing admirer of Connolly and had always wanted him to write for the Magazine. The problem seemed to be finding a subject that would entice him into action, to write at the greater length the Magazine required, although the reputation for inertia was exaggerated.

From time to time Connolly would be seized by obsessions—what he called his "dualogues" with a current craze. When these attacks came on they completely took him over: he blazed with mental energy, storing and retrieving detail with startling powers of recall, and closely interrogating any of his friends who had more than a scrap of knowledge of the subject. Burgess and Maclean was an example, but that had passed by 1969. More recently there had been "Who wrote Shakespeare?", the unaccounted for years in the life of Christ, and always in the background his passion for genealogy, porcelain and silver, in which he seemed to be pursuing somewhat neurotically the vanished grandeur of his Irish ancestry.

In May 1969, Connolly and his wife, Deirdre, came again to visit my parents. I hadn't seen him since before my African tour, and he had recently returned from one of his East African safaris, writing on travel and wildlife for the *Sunday Times*. He began asking me what I knew, from my time in Nairobi, about the Erroll murder. I thought I knew something about it. At one time it had been a hot topic in the newsroom of the *Daily Nation*, where I worked.

The paper had run a series on the story which had been stopped mid-way. The editor, George Githii, a graduate of Balliol College, Oxford, was a protégé of Jomo Kenyatta. He thus had a measure of political autonomy as editor, and could even publish the occasional piece attacking Kenyatta's own ministers, but when it came to the Erroll story, the pressure, to his great surprise, was sudden and swift and unlike any he had known in the normal course of politics. This had intrigued me at the time, and I had read up all the cuttings on the case in the library. Connolly then declared that the story had been a long-standing obsession with him, and from the way he told it, with its twists and its ironies and its echoes of Somerset Maugham, one could see why. Indeed, Connolly said that Maugham had wanted to write the story as fiction, but had decided that he was too old to attempt it.

Connolly already seemed to know a great deal, to have narrowed down his list of suspects from a real knowledge of the affair. Whenever he had travelled to Kenya, he said, he had brought the subject up in conversation, always with good results, and had many notes in his diaries. I told him that Francis Wyndham had always been keen for him to write for the *Sunday Times* Magazine. Would he write about Erroll? Connolly was flattered and interested. The following week Wyndham, after some discussion with Connolly, arranged the commission and I was assigned to work alongside him.

We worked together on the story for the next six months, first when our other commitments allowed it, and then full time. We did an immense amount of investigation—Connolly himself interviewed more than fifty people, some of them jointly with me, and the article came out in the Christmas issue of that year. On the cover was an oval colour-tinted picture of Diana; some artwork had been applied to the original Lenare photograph, and a caption underneath read "Cyril Connolly traces an obsession."

He contributed barely four thousand words towards the 6,000-word article—there was a limit on space—but they were distilled from a monumental store of notes and documents. His densely written, spiral-bound exercise books, covered with blue-black ink in every corner of each page, are the real evidence of his obsession, and also of his methods of investigation. They continue to record fresh discoveries almost until his death. He wrote towards the deadline at great speed, in longhand, with hardly a correction on his one and only draft. He generously insisted that we divide up the final act of writing into our special areas of interest, with each succeeding section headed with our separate by-lines.

His copy began with a thread of memory that led back to 1938, and a chance meeting with one of the main characters in the story.

One morning, in the last summer of peace, I was lying in the sun at Eden Roc. I used to swim out to the rocks of the Villa Eilen, across the water and then recuperate on my mattress, hired for the season with its coffin sized slab of limestone. Round the corner, invisible, were other slabs and mattresses, each with their locataire, regulars from the villas or the Cap d'Antibes or the hotel.

A woman's voice floated over the escarpment, one of those never-to-be-forgotten voices, husky, yet metallic, almost strident, a voice of the period, a touch of Tallulah, or, if anyone remembers her, of Brenda Dean Paul. "My God I hate men," she was saying, "I'd trust my dog more than any man. I'd tell my dogs things I'd never tell a man."

I was so impressed by this outburst, which came, I discovered, from a small and wiry dark-haired woman (since described as blonde, but there are blondes and blondes) that, as she left, I asked the beach captain her name. "That is Madame Carberry, but she is really Milady Carberry: they come from Nairobi."— Was it every year? I thought of "Carberry's hundred isles," Swift's poem, Somerville and Ross's stories, that lovely corner of southern Ireland where Castle Freke, the old home of the family stands in its woods.

That was in 1938. I was not to hear the name again until 1941 when the English papers reported the trial of Sir Jock Delves Broughton for the murder of the Earl of Erroll. June Carberry was the principal witness. I put the case from my mind (Sir Jock was acquitted) until 20 years later, I found in my bedroom in the house near Malaga where I was staying, Rupert Furneaux's book, *The Murder of Lord Erroll* [Stevens, 1961], which carried me through the small hours. The obsession was now formed: the poisons of curiosity and speculation united to form a morbid mental growth. I was hooked.

Furneaux's book was a slim volume in a crime documentary series, a useful textbook which gave a readable, dramatised account of the trial, but little more.

There were at least two main strands to Connolly's obsession with the case, which came out clearly in the article. The first was the pure fascination of an unsolved murder mystery.

Broughton had occupied the limelight, and yet there were too many missing links in the chain to believe that the police had been right to arrest him. Who else, of that gallery of characters, was at the crossroads that night? Or was Erroll dead long before he got to the crossroads? Was it certain that he even came back to the house at Karen with Diana? The alibis of all four characters in the house depended on each other; only two of them were called, June Carberry and Broughton, and Broughton remembered, so he said, little of the evening. Was there a conspiracy between them? Was there a hired killer? Why were the armstraps lying on the seat of the car, when they had clearly been in place the previous day? What of the hairpin, the bloodstained cigarette end, the marks of shoe-white on the back seat? Who could have written the anonymous notes? There were so many unexplained details.

Connolly's first reference to the Erroll case in print was in a review in the *Sunday Times* in 1960 of Julian Symons's *A Reasonable Doubt*—a collection of unsolved murder cases. Connolly wrote,

Does it appeal to our vanity, the notion that logic or intuition or knowledge of the human heart can jump to the conclusion which has escaped all the experts and baffled the police? Or is it the fear that injustice has been done and the wrong person convicted? Or that a murderer may still be at large? I believe those old teamsters, vanity and curiosity, play the strongest part, and that we all feel we can complete these jigsaws with human pieces.

The other strand lay deeper, and was much older. 1938, the year June Carberry's voice came floating over the escarpment at Eden Roc, was also the year that *Enemies of Promise* was published. Its later section deals with Eton and its teachings and the upper-class glamour that fascinated Connolly and also repelled him.

Even in College, among the seventy "scholars," "sapping" [swotting] was discredited and we were infected by the fashion from without, behind which lay the English distrust of the intellect and prejudice in favour of the amateur. A child in Ireland, a boy at St. Wulfric's, a scholar at Eton, I had learned the same lesson. To be "highbrow" was to be different, to be set apart and so excluded from the ruling class of which one was either a potential enemy or a potential servant. Intelligence was a deformity which must be concealed: a public school taught one to conceal it like a good tailor hides a paunch or a hump. As opposed to ability it was a handicap in life.*

Arriving at Eton from a faded Irish family on one side, middle-class on the other, very clever but thinking himself ugly and "set apart," Connolly was overwhelmed by the peculiar aura of the English upper-class. He looked feverishly into his own Irish progeny. ("Such were these early excesses that today I cannot listen to any discussion of titles, or open a peerage without feeling sick . . . I shall never be able to breathe again until they are abolished.")

The male characters in the Erroll drama were "all from the old school list." Connolly suggested this at the time of our article. He wrote,

* Cyril Connolly, *Enemies of Promise* (Routledge, 1938).

I arrived in College at Eton in 1918. Oddly enough my earliest friend was another new boy, Randall Delves Broughton, a cousin of the Baronet's family. Eton publishes a list of all the boys with their home addresses and the names of their parents or guardians, and these we used to study with fascination as the assemblies in School Yard, to be called over, brought out all the boys, athletes in their splendid plumage, scholars in their gowns, new boys in their short jackets.

Although we were supposed not to be snobs, except about those who were good at games, some of these addresses were unforgettable: "c/o H. M. King of the Belgians"; "Duke of Hamilton, The Palace, Hamilton"; "Sirdar Charanjit, Singh of Kapurthala, Charanjit Castle, Jullundur City, India" . . . and several people from our story were there too: "Hay, Hon. J. V., absent"; "Cholmondeley, Hon. T. P. H."; "Portman, G. W. B."—the future Lords Erroll, Delamere and Portman.

Connolly became as serious about his election to Pop, the self-electing oligarchy of Eton prefects which he had lobbied for so carefully, as about his membership of White's later on. White's was a place where the writers among its members might justifiably have felt uneasy, and Connolly had a phobia about the place. He once told me that he had the impression that everyone stopped talking the moment he came through the door, and he was sometimes seized with the fear, according to Peter Quennell, that he might have to submit to a ritual "debagging" there: the thought of being trouserless at White's reviving his early terrors at Eton, before he was saved by his Pop election. The passionate love-hate for athletes and philistines had pursued him throughout his life. At Oxford he had been proud of his wild friends. There were many reckless fauns in Happy Valley, like Waugh's friend, Raymond de Trafford.

Diana Caldwell was for Connolly the perfect complement to the males in that longed-for and detested world of upper-class glamour. There was a bloom on her, something to do with her looks, her figure and her clothes, that fascinated him. She was unlike most of the women who surrounded Connolly, but she had a certain appeal, a sexuality that attracted and impressed him.

Diana loved jewels, for example, and might go to considerable lengths to get them. He was intrigued by the fact that this woman, who had been jealously described as a "chorus girl," had turned herself into exactly what is required of an "English lady," and he thought her bold and admirable.

There was a hint of passion and even a voyeuristic streak in his quest. The possibility that he could never know the truth about Diana drove Connolly mad with curiosity. He was like the German Prince in Marlowe's *Dr. Faustus* who asks Faustus, now in league with the devil, to summon up Alexander the Great's concubine so that he can satisfy his burning, obsessive curiosity: does she or does she not have a mole on her neck? One of Connolly's informants had told him that, as a result of a shooting incident long after the trial, Diana had been marked by a bullet which had grazed her back. He once suggested, as a joke, that I go and find out if it was true. But he badly wanted to know.

The Erroll story contained all the right ingredients for Connolly and he approached it with the curiosity of a novelist, or a novelist *manqué*. To some extent he romanticised the Kenya characters in his imagination: the painstaking investigation seemed like a substitute for the serious novel he felt he ought to be writing, and about which he had always hoarded guilty feelings of unfulfilment.

Our article was well received and judged a success, as much I suspect for its evocation of time and place as its exposition of the story in a wholly new light. We had gathered a great deal of fresh material, on which my own researches were subsequently based, and Connolly was to add much more before his death. We had, in a sense, broken off the quest because of the need to publish, and the mystery was still there to baffle us, enriched, but perhaps deepened too. Connolly received many telephone

calls over Christmas, and letters afterwards, congratulating
him on his masterly effort, and a cable from the writer,
Quentin Crewe, also an Erroll murder aficionado, who had
written up his own discoveries in his column in the *Daily
Mirror*. His cable read, "Superb elegant amazing revealing far more than I have ever dared to hope many congratulations."

Letters arrived, containing peculiar memories and an-
ecdotes, like this one:

December 21 '69

Dear Mr. Connolly,

Your account of the Erroll murder in today's *Sunday Times*
Magazine was compulsive reading for me. This is the reason.

In 1945 my husband and I and two small daughters had a
holiday at Westward Ho in North Devon in a guest house, name
forgotten I'm afraid. Among the guests was a permanent resident,
a rather faded but elegant woman, beautifully dressed—Mrs.
Caldwell, the mother of Diana and Lady Willingdon.

We talked a little; she was quite friendly and obviously lonely.
One day she invited me to her bed-sitting room. It was full of
photographs in silver frames, carrying the atmosphere (as she
did herself) of Mayfair 1920s.

She spoke of Diana, saying she'd married a dreadful man,
presumably Delves Broughton. I recall the emphasis on "dreadful" very clearly. The case was miles away from people like my
husband or I, two professional people in a workday provincial
city, so I wasn't much interested then.

However, two incidents have remained in my memory very
vividly. Mrs. Caldwell went everywhere with a whippet dog. I
love dogs and used to admire him, especially his docile temperament. "Well you see, they're working class dogs, and used
to being kept under," said Mrs. Caldwell. It expressed perfectly
the caste system she took for granted, though she loved the dog.

Another time she left an expensive fur coat in the holiday-
makers' lounge. One of the guests, a London man with plebeian
manners, and a loud voice, picked it up in scorn saying, "Well,
the war's over and so's this sort of thing I hope."

I'd welcomed the Labour victory of '45, but this fellow put me, momentarily at any rate, on Mrs. Caldwell's side. My husband and I both agreed we hated his gesture.

Twenty years later whippet dogs appear with glamour models in *Vogue* and *Harper's* and anyone having a good fur coat in a guest house would be admired rather than scorned.

This gives a chance to say how much I enjoy all you write on Sundays. I've never forgotten your book *Enemies of Promise*, either.

Yours sincerely,
Evelyn Ratcliff

But others were not so impressed. On Christmas Day, Sir Iain Moncreiffe of that Ilk sat down and composed the following letter to the Editor of the *Sunday Times*. I no longer remember his reaction to it, but it was the kind of letter that would have touched Connolly on an exposed nerve.

Sir,

Before regaling us with servants' hall gossip, Mr. Cyril Connolly draws "indignant attention" to the War going on at the time of the death of Lord Erroll, whose only daughter was my first wife. It's as a talented writer rather than a military man that we think of Mr. Connolly, which is perhaps why he forgot to mention that Lord Erroll had recently returned from the Eritrean campaign, where as a Captain he had been awarded a mention in despatches.

It was also vinegar on a wound to read that the East African pioneers "took so much out of the world and put so little back." Lord Erroll did not own "seats" at Slains Castle and Rosenglass. He put his few pennies into Kenya, where he was a leading elected member of the Legislative Council. And my own father lost more than nineteen-twentieths of his outlay, when he put two thirds of his fortune and all his labour into clearing the virgin bush: no pun is intended to link him to those dozen or so forward looking families who were so much ahead of their time as to anticipate the permissive society so brightly hailed by our *avant garde* in this Day & Age.

Yours truly,
Iain Moncreiffe of that Ilk

It was, in fact, not the East African pioneers that Connolly had accused of taking so much out and giving little back, but those same "forward looking" families in Happy Valley that Sir Iain had linked to the landscape with his schoolboy pun. Twelve years later I arranged to meet Sir Iain—at White's—and we spent two enjoyable hours talking about the case.

We faced in addition a storm of complaints at the Press Council from members of the Erroll family. The layout of our piece contained a full page blow-up of Erroll's head lying on the mortuary slab, showing the fatal bullet wound and the scorchmarks of black powder. Lord Kilmarnock, Erroll's brother, complained that this especially, and the article in general, were in extremely bad taste; that it should not have been published without first having been shown to the Erroll family, and that the underlying suggestion of Erroll's homosexuality at Eton was "a most damaging piece of imaginative reporting calculated to cast an aspersion on Lord Erroll's character as a schoolboy." Connolly replied,

Surely the investigation of an unsolved mystery of thirty years ago, which received international attention, which has been the subject of one book, as well as innumerable articles in many countries, and made legal history, is in the public domain.

If all the members of the families involved were consulted, that of the accused as well as of the victim, which would now include some grown-up grandchildren, nothing would get published at all about this or innumerable other crimes or scandals, from Tranby Croft onwards . . . Surely the press is entitled to disregard the general wish of all families to keep their skeletons in their cupboards.

On the "bad taste" and the photograph of Erroll, Connolly wrote,

I do not consider the article in bad taste given what has already been written and the thirty year time lag. I do not see how one can adjudicate about bad taste: very many people whose opinion I respect enjoyed the article and wrote or said so. I was not responsible for obtaining or publishing the photo of Lord Erroll's head but I gathered that it was published on the grounds that it brought home that an unsolved murder was not just a parlour game and that it was in itself a thing of beauty. I do think it is a tragic and moving photograph and brings out the extraordinary beauty of Lord Erroll which was to dog him through his life and lead to his undoing.

The "imaginative" reporting on Erroll as a schoolboy was not imaginative, said Connolly, and supplied the descriptions of two Eton contemporaries, one of whom was Sir Sacheverell Sitwell. Curiously, Lord Kilmarnock had also objected to the adjective "fascist" which I had applied to Erroll in my own copy, despite a mention of Erroll's apostasy from that cause. Connolly ended his long defence,

People in Kenya are still discussing the crime as if it were yesterday. [The virus] . . . will continue to affect authors and journalists who come into contact with it. The bad taste is not theirs, but arises from Happy Valley itself, whose denizens never let consideration for their children prevent them from doing exactly as they pleased.

But that was not the end of it. Connolly had pointed the finger at Gwladys Delamere as the author of the anonymous letters placed in Broughton's box at the Muthaiga Club. Her daughter, Mrs. Rose Hodson, came to her mother's defence at the Press Council, and said of our article, "Far from being a serious enquiry into the mystery, it is principally a salacious rehash of an old scandal." Yet salacious rehash would surely have been more easily dismissible as yellow press tittle-tattle than our serious enquiry. Connolly's study of Gwladys as the possible author of the letters was the result of some deep armchair reflection and was, in my opinion, an inspired piece of literary deduction—speculation, of course, but based on real evidence which he produced at greater length in his defence.

The underlying complaint against us was that we had dared to "rake up the past"—an old stick with which journalists and biographers are often beaten in the hope that they will feel a sense of professional shame—and that in this case, although old families were involved, we weren't prevented from doing so by some unwritten law of propriety. The attitude is a familiar one, especially from a prominent family with a notorious episode in its history. At these moments, its members will often assume a right of veto where none exists, and where the story has for years been in the public domain.

The problem is that mystery and scandal in high places are always good copy—a truth surrounded with hypocrisy—and since they supply history with its best thrillers and its most revealing asides, they will always be kept alive. For my part I agree with the conclusion of Mark Amory, editor of the *Letters of Evelyn Waugh*:

Deciding what would cause unacceptable pain or embarrassment can only be a matter of personal judgement, but I have taken the harsh view that the feelings of the children must be largely ignored; they must learn to live with the behaviour of their parents.*

Connolly and I were, in the end, exonerated from all the charges against us, except that of bad taste in including the photograph of Erroll. Connolly was wounded by the criticism and said that he hadn't wanted the picture, but to me it added enormous power to the story and gave a stark reminder of the horror of the moment when Erroll was killed.

* Weidenfeld & Nicolson, 1980.

11
ACUMEN
AND
INTUITION

As the strong man exults in his physical ability,
delighting in such exercises as call his muscles into
action, so glories the analyst in that moral activity
which *disentangles*. He derives pleasure from even the
most trivial occupations bringing his talent into play. He
is fond of enigmas, of conundrums, hieroglyphics;
exhibiting in his solutions of each a degree of *acumen*
which appears to the ordinary apprehension
praeternatural. His results, brought about by the
very soul and essence of method, have, in truth, the
whole air of intuition.

EDGAR ALLAN POE
The Murders in the Rue Morgue

If there was a thin man inside Connolly begging to
be let out, there was a detective inside him too, who had
been locked away for some time.

In real life Connolly was perfectly, almost comically
cast in the role of a fictional detective of the cerebral
school, a Holmes or a Poirot or a C. Auguste Dupin.
"Although no philosophic hedonist could be more deeply
attached to his favourite armchair," wrote Quennell, describing Connolly, "ever and again his armchair becomes
miraculously jet-propelled. Sweeping over his contemporaries' heads, it leaves them gaping far behind."

Like Holmes with his cocaine, Connolly had his own distinguishing passions and weaknesses, but he also had the vast general knowledge with its unexpected areas of specialisation common to that school. And as a literary critic, he relied entirely on his powers of deduction and analysis. Thus Inspector Connolly, *bon vivant* and bibliophile, could linger in his hothouse, studying his precious carnivorous plants, while the station hacks rushed about mesmerised by physical clues, destroying, as often as not, the really important evidence. No matter. Connolly already possessed the solution.

So, while I searched for surviving witnesses, sent off telexes to faraway stringers, collected documents, raked through old newspapers and society magazines, and immersed myself in the story, Connolly resumed his detective work with an exhaustive study of *Debrett's Peerage* and the Eton school list of 1918. His aversion to the study of titles was over. He took on the manner of a St. Just in his methodical manner of collecting details on his contemporaries and on characters even remotely connected with the central cast. For example:

D.B's servants. Fifteen + Wilks. *Alfred* The Personal Boy. Takes tea to DB at 7 a.m. Does not go into study. Began work on 16th December. Goes to Nyeri with DB and (hired) driver on 27th. *Abdullah bin Ahmed* Head boy, employed 6 months (May) obtained from club. Gets petrol from the dhobi *3 or 4 days* before E's death. No previous bonfires made. *Mohamed bin Sudi*. Houseboy for 4 months (study etc). Saw DB place revolvers in study. Found 3 cartridges on floor. *Olei s/o Migoya*. Shamba boy, had worked for Dr. Geilinger who also used pit to burn rubbish. 3 shamba boys were gathering rubbish, collecting it for 3 days. *Omari bin Juma* DB's telephone boy. Same work as Mohamed. Who was Mohamed? Was he the missing Somali?

Then there was the following exhaustive record of the marriages and liaisons of some of the characters:

Les Affaires

DB	Lady (Jock) Buchanan Jardine
	Kath Carnarvon
	Phyllis Delamere
DB	= Vera
Vera	Lord Wharncliffe
	Ld. Moyne = Ida Rubinstein
	Hugh Sherwood (?)
DB	= Diana
Diana	= Vernon Motion, Broughton, Colville,
	Delamere
Gwlad. D.	= Hugh Delamere
	Erroll
	Alastair Gibb
	= Sir Charles Markham
	Denzl
	D of Gloucester
	P of W
Soames	Nina
	Gloria
	Alice
Alice de J	= Frédéric de Janzé
	= Raymond de Trafford
	Joss Erroll
	Dicky Pembroke—Diana—Paula
	Soames (unlikely)
	Lizzie
Paula Gelybrand	= Marquis de Casa Maury
	= Bill Allen
	= Boy Long
	Dickie Pembroke
Idina Erroll	= Gordon
	= Wallace
	= Erroll
	= Halderman
	= Soltau
Mary Delamere	= Cunningham Reid

Connolly alerted his friends. He resurrected the gossip
network of the 1930s, and with the generous expense ac-

counts of the period, many lunches were arranged. He began to call me, very early in the morning from East-bourne, for lengthy discussions on strategy. If my own mental print-outs of *Debrett's* faltered during these early calls, he could be sharp and impatient as his mind raced on. I remember him snapping one morning, "You must get your *card index* in order." Yet if I had fresh gossip for the files, or new evidence of any sort, his mood would instantly change.

The sheer volume and detail of Connolly's notes still surprise me each time I open the notebooks or examine the unpaid invoices, railway menus and errata slips on which he worked at the puzzles in his fluent, almost min-iature handwriting. At one point he attacked the complete cast of characters in his exasperation: The notes illustrate the anguish Connolly felt at the intractability of the puzzle:

What a Set!

Shit E
Crook DB
Drunk JC
Villain (sadist) J. Carberry
????? Soames
Murderer Alice de Trafford (Husband in prison)
Gig. Lizzie L.
Drunk Portman
Dotty Gwladys Del.
Only nice people Pembroke, Paula Long

Casualties

Alice de Trafford	suicide
"Boy" Long	drink
Molly, Countess of Erroll	drink and drugs
Guy Repton	drink
June Carberry	drink
Broughton	suicide
Erroll	murdered

The earliest entries include extracts from Connolly's diaries of 1967 and 1968, which already contained some valuable leads. On his trips to Nairobi he usually stayed with Jack Block, the urbane proprietor of Kenya's best hotels, and his wife, Doria, at their house at Muthaiga. The Blocks were among the few people in Kenya who knew who Connolly was. Pam Scott, with whom he also stayed at Rongai, introduced him throughout his stay as "John O'Connor." As a result Connolly sulked at her meals—he had also hurt his back—and Pam Scott became exasperated with his silence. "He was like a stuffed pillow propped up against a chair," she told me later. "He might as well not have been there." Sir Michael Blundell, leader of a white settlers' delegation at the Lancaster House Conference on independence in 1960, was under the impression that Connolly was the Editor of *The Times*.

With the Blocks Connolly met Lazarus Kaplan, known locally as "Kappie," Broughton's former solicitor, and a friend of Jack Block's called Prince Windishgraetz. The latter told Connolly that Dr. Joseph Gregory, the G.P. who had given evidence in Broughton's defence, had claimed that Broughton had confessed the murder to him while he was in jail, but that Broughton had decided to deny it vigorously as soon as he saw the court and realised that he might have a chance. Gregory had a remarkable memory for the idiosyncrasies of his patients; he was also known for his fanciful Irish imagination.

There was an obvious flaw to the Gregory story, at least as Prince Windishgraetz had reported it: why would Broughton go to the great expense of hiring Morris, if he was prepared to plead guilty? But Windishgraetz had touched on other local beliefs which Connolly had recorded. It was thought at the time that Broughton had been very short of money; whatever was left was in trust, and he couldn't touch it. According to Windishgraetz, before Broughton left England for Kenya, he had met a hard-up English officer and persuaded him for £1,000 to cut some family portraits from their frames and make off with them, for which Broughton claimed the insurance.

The ruse was successful, and Broughton then suggested that the officer "steal" some family pearls, for which he would also claim the insurance. The officer at first refused. Broughton told him that the pearls would be left in the glove compartment of his car outside a restaurant, and he could please himself. The officer changed his mind, and again Broughton collected the insurance. Windishgraetz described Broughton to Connolly as a man who thought himself above the law; he was bored and now thought he could commit the perfect murder. Jack Block added to this by saying that Lee Harragin, the son of the former Attorney-General who prosecuted the case, had told him that Broughton had gone up to his father after the case and said, "Bad luck, old boy, you knew I did it, and I knew I did it, but you couldn't prove it."

Block said that Broughton was acquitted because Scotland Yard, to whom the spent bullet found in the car had been sent, had said that it was not fired from one of Broughton's registered guns, but later had wired to say that they had made a mistake. By then it was too late. Broughton had been acquitted.

Block also told Connolly of a local rumour that pointed to Alice de Janzé as a suspect. A contemporary and neighbour of Alice, Mrs. Eileen Leslie-Melville, had agreed to look after Alice's house while she went away for a few days, some months after the murder. In her absence her houseboy came to Mrs. Leslie Melville and produced a revolver which, he said, he had found by a bridge, under a pile of stones on Alice's land. Mrs. Leslie Melville took the gun and said nothing. It lay around in her house for several years afterwards. Quentin Crewe had heard this story, too, from her son, Jock Leslie Melville, and had reported it in his column.

Connolly met Kaplan, Broughton's solicitor, on the day after these conversations. Kaplan immediately corrected two of the rumours: Broughton had indeed approached Harragin in the courtroom after the trial, but what he said to him had nothing to do with the case. Kaplan would not divulge what it was. He added that no bullet had been sent to Scotland Yard, but Churchill, the ballistics expert, was asked if a Colt could be ''broken.'' (Soames had said in evidence, and it was crucial for Broughton, ''I think it was a gun that broke, but I am not sure''— describing the weapon that Broughton had used in the shooting practice on his farm. It was believed that in all Colts the cylinder swung out from the frame sideways.) Although the Colt company had sent a wire to say that all Colts had five grooves and a left-hand rifling in the barrel, this particular question had never been put to them. Churchill had replied by cable that there *were* such Colts which broke for re-loading, but the telegram was not produced in court. There was no proof of authorship and it was rejected as inadmissible.

Connolly asked Kaplan if Broughton had done it. He replied, ''The answer is X minus 1; anybody but Broughton.'' He added that there had never been a shooting with less blood and that the murderer must have been an excellent shot. The killer, in his opinion, could have been a jilted girlfriend, or the husband of one, or a political assassin. The police, he said, had been extremely inefficient in gathering the evidence, particularly in their failure to examine the car for fingerprints.

A poll taken in Kenya among the white population, either now or soon after the trial, would put Broughton as a suspect low down on the list. The most popular choice would be a jealous woman—Alice de Janzé (''the fastest gun in the Gare du Nord''); June Carberry, on the presumption that she, too, had been Erroll's mistress; Gwladys Delamere; or Diana herself. After that the *cognoscenti* would cite Mrs. Wirewater (although she was in Cape Town at the time of the murder) or her husband, who may not have been in Cape Town, and who was aware of Erroll's current affair with his wife. The letters we received from Kenya residents, past and present, after the article appeared, are one source for this contention, and it was both men and women who suspected a woman of the murder. Otherwise the evidence is based on some 150 separate conversations with Kenya residents or exiles.

Broughton was usually discounted because all the evidence seemed to have been exposed at the trial, with nothing proved against him, and it was easier and more enjoyable to put up other suspects. Moreover, Broughton could be discounted on physical grounds. Yet the idea of a conspiracy has always been popular. Higher on the list than Broughton would be his hired accomplice, either a Somali, or another jealous husband, or a lover of Diana, committing the crime on Broughton's behalf.

Finally there was the question of a political assassin. This was first suggested by Morris in the trial in an attempt to show that there were others with a motive to kill Erroll. Erroll had turned against the fascist cause, and now apparently even had overall responsibility for interning Italian fascist sympathisers in the Colony; might he not have been the target for political revenge? Morris mentioned Count Rocco, a famous eccentric who lived in a huge Tuscan villa on Lake Naivasha, as a possible suspect. He had been placed under house arrest and shortly before the trial his house had been surrounded by police armed with shotguns, on a tip that Rocco was planning to escape by hot air balloon. (He was later interned in South Africa.) Poppy replied in court that Erroll was not responsible for internment, and there the matter rested.

Connolly then wrote to Diana (Lady) Mosley, wife of Sir Oswald Mosley, former leader of the British Union of Fascists, to ask if political assassination of renegades from the movement had ever been contemplated, or carried out. She replied from France,

The political motive for the murder seems far-fetched to an almost insane degree doesn't it. If I believed in political assassination, I can think of a world of candidates for my Charlotte Corday knife, & Lord E. is not one of them. But I don't.

An assassin who was not part of the Muthaiga Club inner circle would have had great difficulty in discovering Erroll's movements that night. To have followed him by car on his various trips, driving at his habitual eighty miles per hour, would surely have attracted attention. It was a line of speculation we never thought worthy of serious investigation.

Connolly left Nairobi in 1967 convinced, like Kaplan, that Broughton was innocent. And in his notebook two years later, on May 18th, 1969, when we were already well into our researches, he wrote, "His [Broughton's] birthday is the same as mine. We Virgos are not men of blood. I don't think he did it, and I don't think he thought so either." Much depended on a knowledge of Broughton's character, of which we knew little at the outset, and he continued to be one of our suspects. But if he had committed the murder, it was done with a skill that seemed beyond him; he would have been blessed with astonishing luck, too, and had somehow managed to leave not a clue behind.

What had happened to him, we wondered, in the months after his acquittal? Had he maintained the same weary composure, the confident air of innocence that had been the hallmark of his extraordinary performance in the witness box?

Of all the strands of information that Connolly had picked up in Nairobi, the most intriguing was the emergence of the "English officer" mentioned by Prince Windishgraetz, the man who had apparently helped Broughton to carry out insurance frauds on his own possessions. Diana's pearls had been stolen in Cannes in 1939, from the glove compartment of a car outside a restaurant, and in the same year Broughton's pictures were taken from Doddington. Broughton was in England at the time. But that Windishgraetz should know about either of these events was at first a mystery.

We discovered from a British newspaper report that

both Scotland Yard and an insurance company had made some enquiries in Nairobi, alerted, apparently, by the frequent mention of pearl necklaces in the trial. If they suspected any connection with the pearls that Diana had lost in Cannes, they drew a blank.

Two sets of pearls had been mentioned in the trial. The first was the necklace that Erroll had given Diana, and which Broughton noticed her wearing as she lay in bed with Mrs. Carberry on the morning of January 18th. After Erroll's death a lawyer acting for the Erroll estate insisted on their return. Diana gave up this precious gift from her lover very reluctantly. She felt the Erroll estate had no right to claim them, particularly since Erroll had inherited them from his last Countess, Molly, and passed them on to Diana.

The other set of pearls, according to Broughton, had been bought in equal shares, in London, by Diana and himself. They were mentioned in the trial because, for some reason, Broughton had often brought up the subject of who should buy out the pearls from whom at the moments of greatest tension between them, notably at 3:30 a.m. on the night when Diana had been out alone with Erroll. Broughton would always turn the discussion into an argument. This had puzzled Harragin, the prosecutor, and he had used these discussions about pearls merely to demonstrate that Broughton was lying about his true feelings. A discussion about jewellery seemed to Harragin to be a mild and trivial topic compared with the anguish of losing one's wife.

Yet there was nothing trivial about a string of pearls, least of all to Diana. Pearls were the very symbol of her elevation, the inalienable proof of success that transformed not only the neck but the woman herself from a Lenare beauty into a baroness or a countess. She was only the part owner of this string of pearls. Broughton testified in the trial that he had offered her the choice: buy him out or give them back. Was this an attempt feeble though it seemed, to persuade Diana to change her mind about Erroll? Was there some connection between these harsh and, for Diana, difficult discussions and the other Nairobi rumour—for which there was, admittedly, no evidence at this point—that Broughton had rescinded on the marriage pact and the promise of £5,000 a year in order to put pressure on Erroll to give Diana up, and that Erroll's response had been to panic, telling Diana that the affair was over and that for her own good she should return to her husband? In this scenario, Diana might with some justification have turned on Erroll—the first man she had ever loved—with a truly vicious fury.

Early on in our quest, rumour and hearsay confused our ability to separate the two strands of pearls. But as a subject, the pearls acquired a magic fascination for Connolly as a key to the mystery. Was it not conceivable that Broughton's English officer, if he was in Nairobi at the time, might have been an accomplice to the murder as well? We had our suspicions about who this might have been, although so far we had nothing to go on but rumour.

In the meantime Connolly studied the whereabouts of each of the main characters, by day and by hour where possible, from the moment the Broughtons' aeroplane touched down in Nairobi on November 12th, 1940. He made countless lists, charts and timetables, particularly of the fatal hours from the end of the dinner party on January 23rd to the early hours of the morning, when June Carberry reported Broughton's second visit to her door. June's times were suspect and seemed to be based on either guesswork or deception. Connolly also seized on the fact that there was at least one hour unaccounted for in the movements of Broughton and June. Nobody had seen them between 10:30, soon after the dinner, when Broughton said something to Dickie Pembroke about a game of bezique, and close to midnight when Jacko Heath invited them both to a supper party in the dining room. June claimed that between these times they were both sitting in the most public part of the Club, near the bar, drinking brandy. Captain "Long John" Llewellin, one of the witnesses who overheard Broughton's complaining remarks about Diana, placed this conversation at around midnight.

It was 12:30 by the time Gerald Portman finally persuaded them to join the supper party, and according to June they didn't leave the Club for another hour after that. Perhaps the missing hour was of no interest to the police, and yet after the dinner party, and Erroll's departure with Diana, Broughton and June Carberry would certainly have been the focus of gossip and speculation. Surely one of the many witnesses would have mentioned seeing the couple drinking together. For ourselves the discovery was of no immediate significance and we filed it away. But was it June and not Broughton who needed an alibi? Connolly noted, "June's alibi depends on Broughton's visits as much as his does, and according to him, he never made them." If she were not to be believed, if she herself had done the deed or been an accomplice to it or was covering up for someone else, the only reliable times that night would come from Llewellin, who confirmed that the couple left the Muthaiga Club at about 1:30; Waiweru, Erroll's houseboy, who said that Erroll and Diana left his house at Muthaiga around 2 a.m.; and the milk boys, who found the car at between 2:50 and 3 a.m.

June and Broughton were driven back from the Muthaiga Club by a chauffeur, either his own or June Carberry's. Broughton's driver was never called among the many African witnesses, and there were rumours that he had disappeared the following day. Only Wilks could supply the crucial evidence. She had been up and about, making hot water bottles and providing quinine for June, until at least 3 a.m. on the murder night. But was she still alive, and where would one begin to look for her? We presumed that she had returned to South Africa after the case, perhaps to her home town of Durban. I sent a telex to the *Sunday Times* stringer in Durban, Humphrey Tyler, who worked for the *Cape Argus*, asking him to make what enquiries he could. Three weeks later he replied that he had drawn a blank. He had managed to trace a building Wilks may once have lived in along the Durban sea-front, but it had been demolished for redevelopment. Tyler agreed to continue his search, concentrating on that particular neighbourhood.

Connolly would write out the times again and again, as if the very act of repetition would produce something new. Unable to sort out the puzzle in his conscious hours, his subconscious, stirred by great anxiety and frustration, took on the work at night, beaming up garbled but none the less detailed scenarios.

His wife, Deirdre, was woken one night by terrible cries from her husband and found him wrestling with an invisible assailant. Once calmed down Connolly, with admirable professionalism, reached for his notebook and made the following entry:

CC's nightmare—approaching a small hut—time about 10—7 minutes to three. Inside is a victim/killer known to him whom he is going to liquidate—but it must be done before 3 a.m.— when he gets to the hut the victim seizes him, brandishing a knife. There has been a mistake—either the clock is slow or the time set was a trap. CC is just about to be killed when he screams for help, flailing about the bed. The scream was loud and like a dog or a wolf howling (corroborated by D). Not heard by Elizabeth Bowen [the writer, a guest in the house] in her room. Time: about 3:30 a.m.

There were two recognisable ingredients in Connolly's nightmare. He had made some notes just beforehand about a kiosk, briefly mentioned in the trial, which stood near the road somewhere between the house at Karen and the murder spot. He thought at one point that it might have sheltered a murderer lying in wait for Erroll. Three-thirty a.m. was also a highly significant time (as were the ten minutes before 3 a.m.—the estimated period within which

Erroll's death occurred). It was the moment when June claimed that Broughton had paid his last call on her, and it was the moment, too, when she said she heard Diana's dog barking. Connolly became fixated on the barking of the dog and made a long entry in his notebook of the court evidence on the subject headed "Dog Talk." Harragin had begun this part of his examination of June Carberry with the question, "Is there a dachshund in the house?"

My own searches in the meantime had produced a complete set of the police pictures taken at the scene of the crime, including the photograph of Erroll's body lying in the mortuary. The source was a retired East African civil servant living on England's south coast, to whom I gave a promise of anonymity. In terms of clues the mortuary picture of Erroll's profile, showing the bullet wound, is of no more than clinical interest. But the photographs of the car, leaning into the murram pit, taken from many different angles, and those taken through its open front doors, showing Erroll's body hunched in the footwell, instantly recapture the macabre reality of the moment. The scene is exactly as the murderer left it, although the pictures were taken in daylight, four hours later, and evoke the cold stillness of the drizzling mornings in that altitude, with their sharp scent of rained-on earth and vegetation. Because of the position of Erroll's body, his hands clasped in front of his bowed head as if he is praying or cowering in terror, they reek of the violence of his last moments in that confined space and give an uneasy feeling of intrusion into the intimate few seconds between life and death. An arm appears at the edge of one photograph, holding open the door of the car for the photographer against the tilt of the car, revealing the body on the floor inside and heightening the sense of peering in on something forbidden and taboo. When the picture was taken, Erroll's body was still warm.

You could speculate at length on these photographs. A possible scenario, which also agrees with much of the prosecution's version, is that the killer rode with Erroll to the junction, where he asked to be dropped off so that he could walk home. He shot Erroll either as he was getting out of the car, or just afterwards, through the window or the open door. Erroll's feet were on the brake and clutch, the car was in gear and the engine running. As the bullet hit him his feet slowly eased off the pedals and the car began lumbering, its front wheels already turned to the right to negotiate the corner, towards the murram pit, carried forward by its thirty-horsepower engine. Erroll fell sideways on to the passenger seat with the movement, the wounded ear staining the seat cover, and the car came to rest in the murram pit. If he had had the strength, Broughton might have pushed the body into the footwell in an attempt to free the pedals.

At first sight it seems certain, both from the photographs and from the police experiments, that the body could not have fallen naturally; that the steering wheel would have blocked it, that it could only have been pushed there by force. If the murderer got out of the car before it began rolling towards the murram pit, he must certainly have followed it there. The car was found in gear and the ignition must therefore have been switched off *after* it came to rest. The lights, as we have seen, could only be switched off with pliers. Did the murderer panic at not being able to switch off the lights, and, wanting to drive the car farther off the road, make an abortive attempt to push Erroll's body away from the controls? The easiest way to do this would be to sit on the front seat and push the body forwards and downwards with one's feet. The rumpled carpet on the floor in the back of the car and the marks of shoe whitening on the back seat could have been made by the murderer climbing into that position. For support he would have grabbed the armstraps, which came away, and which were found lying on the floor in the back. Bewes was convinced they had been wrenched out although Butcher, the mechanic who examined the car, testified that the armstraps had been *unscrewed* since the previous day; Mrs. Carberry, who always used the straps, remembered them in position on the evening of the murder. One has to conclude that Butcher was wrong, that the wrench marks were simply not visible, the fittings loose. Why, after all, would anyone unscrew a pair of armstraps and throw them on to the floor?

And yet it *is* possible, as one of the police witnesses admitted under questioning from Morris, that the body fell into position naturally. In the simple experiment of sitting on the edge of a bed, falling sideways and then rolling limply on to the floor, you end up in the identical position in which Erroll's body was found. The jolts of the car as it rolled over the rough ground, and its sharp impact against the murram pit, could quite easily have caused the body to slip under the steering wheel, since the bulk of Erroll's body and hips were already slightly to the left of the wheel after he had fallen sideways. If the body did fall naturally into the footwell, the only obstacle to the theory that a woman had committed the crime was removed.

THIS LEFT US with two main groups of suspects to consider. First, those who fired revolvers at Nanyuki, using black powder bullets, and secondly those who knew Erroll would be returning to Karen a few minutes or so either side of three o'clock and could wave him to a stop and open the door. Group one included Broughton, Soames, Diana, or anyone they might have provided with a gun. Group two included almost everyone who knew Erroll and frequented the Club and his house. Lezard, Portman, Llewellin (and their girlfriends), Mrs. Barkas, Alice de Trafford, the Carberrys, Lady Delamere—all knew of Broughton's 3 o'clock deadline for his wife's return.

How efficiently were their alibis checked? And was it possible to go back along the road so many years later? In his certainty that Broughton had committed the murder, mesmerised perhaps by his own cleverness at discovering the bullets, and his eagerness to get a conviction, had Poppy looked elsewhere, in any depth, for a suspect? He had certainly produced a ragged prosecution case against his chosen man. The problem of the Colt, with its left-handed rifling, on which his case had foundered, had been completely overlooked. Yet Ernest Harwich who, in the trial, had given this crucial piece of evidence (and proved that a Colt could not have been the murder weapon), wrote to the Editor of the *Sunday Times* soon after our article, upset by the impression he thought he had given, that he had withheld this piece of information until he was asked about it in court. On the contrary, he wrote,

Up to the time of the preliminary examination before the magistrate I did not know, nor was I told, that there was any question of a Colt revolver being used. Had I been so told, I would have scotched the Colt concept once and for all . . . the signature on both sets was so obvious and so identical that there was never the slightest doubt about them. As it was, the C.I.D. were not left under any illusion by me that either the murder bullets or those found at Nanyuki could ever have been fired from a Colt. It seems to me now as it did at the time that it would have been far better for the prosecution's case to have conceded this point rather than try to force a link between Broughton's Colt, the Nanyuki gun and the murder weapon.

Later we lunched with Harwich, at the Mitre Hotel, Oxford. He was the image of the upright, detached ex-officer and policeman. He told us that he had been summoned from Uganda, where he had been Assistant Director of Security, to help with the case, and that when he arrived in Nairobi he was denied access to the Government laboratory by Maurice Fox, the testy chemist who squabbled in court with Morris, out of jealousy at Harwich's intrusion. Harwich also expressed the officials' conventional dislike for the Muthaiga crowd. He found them "totally selfish, self-centred exhibitionists" for whom the trial had been little more than a platform for their histrionics. He recalled that for most of them the problem of establishing alibis was that they had been too drunk to remember where they had been or with whom they had been sleeping on the night of the murder.

We also received a letter with a Hampshire postmark from Anstis Bewes, the businessman seconded to the Kenya police, who had been the only officer to take detailed notes at the scene of the crime and in the mortuary. Apart from the intrinsic fascination of being able, for example, to read his first-hand account of the overpowering smell of scent inside the Buick, Bewes's notes confirmed our growing suspicions about the inadequacy of the C.I.D. investigation.

One of his duties at the time of the murder had been to attend sessions of the Legislative Council to report to his superiors any debates relevant to the police and their work. Bewes wrote:

About the time of the murder, Mr. Wright, an unofficial Member (Aberdares I think) raised the question of the Police Force, emphasising the lack of *esprit de corps* and gross inefficiency at the top—reports of considerable moment were made, he alleged, and no action was taken. Discontent was rife throughout the Nairobi Force, and it was the unhappiest in the Country. Isherdass (later murdered) stated that complaints were not made by NCOs through the commissioner for fear of victimisation (he stated this to me after the debate and not in the Council). I have merely added this note in order to indicate that this particular murder investigation *may* not have been carried out with 100% efficiency in view of the lack of keenness on the part of many of the regular officers.

Bewes had made another interesting entry in his notebook at the time:

Mrs. Napier [a neighbour] knew Miss Wilks, and on the day after the murder, Miss Wilks came to say she couldn't stay in the house any longer with "Lady B. drilling it into her again and again what she must tell the police." If Miss Wilks said such and such a thing took place, Lady B. said "No, you have got it wrong. *This* is what happened," and so on. Miss Wilks said she was nearly demented with it all. She told Lady B. that if she went into the witness box she would tell the *truth*. Miss Wilks added that, on hearing of Lord Erroll's death, Mrs. Carberry did not wait to dress, but put on her dressing gown and drove post haste to Erroll's house, returning with a jewel box which she, Miss Wilks, helped Mrs. Carberry carry into the house. It was very heavy. Police went round and took a statement from Miss Wilks. Mrs. Napier was asked to make a statement but said she did not wish to. All this was reported by me to Chief Inspector Elliott.

Bewes's notes hint at a major problem that faced Poppy and his fellow officers. They were dealing with a homogeneous crowd who were accustomed to patronising officials and policemen, and who treated the law with a kind of amused contempt.

Any testimony they produced could always be corroborated by their servants, who could be bribed at a higher price than anything Poppy could find out of C.I.D. expenses. Lying to Poppy was nothing compared with the sexual deceptions, which also involved purchasing the servants' silence. The Somali servants, in particular, famous for their secrecy and indirectness, would be more than equal to an ambitious policeman in his early thirties, new out of Scotland Yard.

For evidence of the rapid reflexes of the Muthaiga group, threatened with the imminent arrival of detectives in their midst, one need look no further than the separate statements of Broughton and June Carberry, taken only fifteen minutes after Gerry Portman's call at 9 a.m. telling them of Erroll's death, when the police were already on their way to Karen. Despite Broughton's later claims that he was so drunk that he could hardly remember anything, he and June were both definite in their statements that the exact time of their return to the house the previous night was 2 a.m.

At first Broughton told the police that he had never left his room after going to bed. After June had told them of two visits to her room, he told the police, "I might have gone out into the corridor at 4 a.m. or so, to switch the lights off; I can't remember."

WAS POPPY STILL ALIVE, and could he vouch for these alibis he had collected? The cast of characters was severely depleted by 1969. The one great survivor was Diana, Lady Delamere. Of the rest, Gwladys Delamere, Lezard, Soames, Idina, Alice, were all dead. So was John Carberry. June was still alive in Johannesburg, although old and sick and dying of drink and drugs.

One of the finest reporters in South Africa, Benjamin Pogrund, who was famous for his courageous exposés of the evils of apartheid in the *Rand Daily Mail* and who was also the *Sunday Times* stringer in Johannesburg, was defeated by Mrs. Carberry. He rang her many times and made several appointments to see her, but she was never there when he arrived. He wrote, "She's a mighty difficult person. My discussions with her on the phone range from long meanderings about nothing to curt refusals to discuss the matter as being too far in the past. I gather she's an alcoholic."

Some of the minor characters were still around, like "Long John" Llewellin, who had been in the Muthaiga Club on the evening of the murder and who had seized joyfully on some inaccuracies in our article, informing us, for example, that Alice de Trafford's favourite pet, "Minnie," was not a cat, as Connolly had reported, but a dachshund dog. The last picture we had of Llewellin, who died sometime in the mid-1970s, was in a letter to Connolly from a friend who was visiting Kenya in 1973.

Dear Cyril,

I thought of you yesterday. I went shopping in Nanyuki and called on Long John Llewellin—aged 85, sitting on his verandah. Black patch over one eye—lots of patches on the tweed jacket —very dusty verandah with dried cacti in pots. Two dirty but attentive houseboys—a well stocked drink tray and two dachshunds who were given meticulously prepared dinners. The dogs' coats were the only things which shone. A very faded copy of THE number of the S. Times Magazine lay on a table, with Diana's face so faded that it had almost disappeared like the Cheshire cat's. "Had I seen anything of that writer fellow lately? Can't remember names." I said I hadn't seen you for ages . . .

Dickie Pembroke, who had retired to Kent, had been right under Connolly's nose for years. The writer Antonia Fraser remembers the sadness and frustration of Connolly, in their last conversation before he died, when they both realised that a frequent guest at a country house they often visited in Kent, a "gentle, sweet, terribly nice, very boring" man whom they had always tried to avoid, had been Dickie Pembroke himself.

Kaplan was alive, of course, and so was Dr. Gregory. But what of Hugh Dickinson, Diana's close companion whom she had called "Dicksy Ducksy," who had been a guest at Doddington before the war; who had come out to Kenya to be near her; who had been on that extraordinary hunting safari with Broughton and Diana after Erroll's death? He told the court that at the time of the murder he was in hospital in Mombasa, his foot poisoned by coral. He would surely be interesting to talk to, if only we could track him down.

In the middle of May 1969 Kaplan signalled that he was coming to London, and offered us his help. Connolly arranged a lunch for him at the Connaught Hotel on May 14th, and invited Francis Wyndham and myself. Kaplan had written to say that he had a copy of the typescript of the trial, which we badly needed, and a manuscript of his own, which he hoped Connolly would help him to get published. Wyndham wrote to Connolly on May 11th,

Dear Cyril,

I can't tell you how excited I am about the article on the Erroll murder. It's a wonderful subject and in your hands will be really superb . . .

The more I think of it the more I agree with your solicitor friend's remark that the key to the whole thing lies with June Carberry. She said Sir Jock visited her room twice that night to ask about her "touch of malaria," and that she had a long talk with Diana—thus giving them both badly needed alibis, but also giving herself one as well. Of the five people who knew what happened at Karen that night: i) Lord Erroll was dead, ii) Diana didn't give evidence, iii) neither did Wilks, iv) Sir Jock said he was drunk and could remember nothing, not even his "alibi" with Mrs. Carberry. So Mrs. C is the *only* source, and may have been telling lies or the truth or a mixture of both.

As you see, I'm beginning to be obsessed as well and am so much looking forward to seeing you and the solicitor and James Fox on Wednesday—Connaught Restaurant at one—for an unbridled discussion. Funnily enough, at lunch today I met a girl called Tessa Reay and suddenly realised that she must be Sir Jock's grand-daughter. I find it hard to believe these people were (and are) real—they seem *more* than real, like characters in fiction . . .

Kaplan arrived at the Connaught at the appointed hour—a neat, small, worried-looking man—and he picked his way through our many questions, exonerating Broughton, his former client, at every turn. Connolly's notes, edited here for clarity, record the conversation:

Kaplan was convinced that Broughton never left the house; that the theft of the revolvers was genuine, that the blood on the golf stocking was animal blood. In his six months in prison, he said, Broughton would without doubt have given something away to the warders or the South African soldiers he was constantly drinking with, if he had been guilty. He didn't think Broughton's motive sufficient. He described Broughton as an unjealous, equable person, although after the trial he had become more and more deranged by alcohol and "nerves." "You gentlemen approach it from a psychological angle," he said, "as a lawyer I studied the facts. The prosecution case was based on bullets, ours on his never leaving the house. You will never get anywhere if you think Broughton did it—that was already rejected by the jury." June Carberry's veracity was never impugned, and nobody questioned her story. But Gwladys, Lady Delamere's evidence was very biased, and Diana, urging Morris to cross-examine her had said, "That woman is lying. You must go for her." Kaplan recalled standing under a full length portrait of Erroll in his coronation robes at Oserian some years after the trial and asking Diana, "Do you still think about him?" She replied, "How dare you ask such a question." Asked what he thought Diana's reaction would be to our writing about the case, Kaplan answered "boredom."

We discovered little of great interest from Kaplan, and his memoirs turned out to be dull and uninformative, but he was a useful ally, and the transcript was of immense value to us.

Soon after he returned to Nairobi Kaplan, having originally asked for his help to be acknowledged in print, suddenly withdrew his support, sending letters to Connolly that suggested great anxiety, and communicating to us through intermediaries that he wanted all traces of his cooperation to be removed from the record and finally demanding—his last communications arriving through a firm of London solicitors—the return of the transcript. Connolly hurriedly copied almost half of its 600 pages into his notebooks in longhand. Something or someone had given Kaplan a bad fright. He died less than a year later.

BY JULY that year Connolly had tracked down Poppy, using that classic instrument of investigative journalism, often the last resort—the local telephone directory.

He was thrilled by the discovery and congratulated himself in his notebook. It was not entirely a coincidence. The towns of the south coast of England—Brighton, Hastings, St. Leonards, Eastbourne—were a catchment area for retired civil servants from the British Empire in the late 1950s and 1960s: fortresses of middle-class gentility where displaced Englishmen, returning from abroad after many years, used to the status and the relative comforts of a ruling class, would eke out their marginal reward from the old country. We got to know many of the hotels and tea rooms along that coast in our meetings with returned colonials.

There was one restaurant which never failed to lift us out of the depression brought on by these establishments: the Starlit, an old haunt of Connolly's, on the roof of the Metropole Hotel in Brighton. It was one of the finest buildings along the front, with its magnificent high-level view, from the restaurant's vast windows, of the unspoilt Regency terraces along the strand below, and the two Victorian piers reaching out to sea. The food in the Starlit was exceptionally good and we made it our place of rendezvous with our contacts whenever we could manage it. Unsuccessful cooking could torture Connolly to the point of suppressing all other interest except his own pain. At the Starlit, especially in fine weather, our lunches were usually a success.

Poppy was our greatest Metropole catch. Connolly recorded our first meeting: "July 5. Saturday. Excellent lunch over the sea where I used to lunch with Ian [Fleming] and Osbert [Sitwell]." I remember Poppy as an imposing, friendly man, who ordered sherry, shrimp cocktail and rump steak, a menu that never varied in our subsequent meetings, while Connolly poked into every corner and crevice of the menu looking for fresh delights. The eating never affected Connolly's attention, neither could it affect mine: he forbade the use of tape recorders or even notebooks at every one of our interviews, relying on total recall and the writing up of our notes together as soon after the event as we could manage it. Apart from his usefulness in filling in the basic narrative, Poppy had some points of crucial interest to make.

On the question of alibis he was adamant. There was no question, he said, that each one had been checked beyond a doubt. Dickinson was in hospital on the coast recovering from a foot so badly poisoned that it had almost had to be amputated; both Nancy Wirewater and her husband were in South Africa; John Carberry was at home at Seremai, Nyeri; Alice de Trafford was in Nairobi at the Muthaiga Club, in bed with Dickie Pembroke. (Poppy confirmed that Alice was the principal woman suspect.) "Lizzie" Lezard was in bed in a spare room at Erroll's house at Muthaiga, and had heard Diana and Erroll come back from the Claremont and leave again for Karen.

Portman was staying, of course, at the Club. It had been widely suspected in Nairobi, after the murder, that someone was trying to silence Portman. On the eve of the preliminary hearing in the magistrate's court, he was found naked, beaten unconscious, lying at the foot of a staircase in his own house. The truth of that, said Poppy, was that Portman had in fact been clubbed on the head by the irate husband of his African maid, whom he had tried to seduce. Gwladys—who Poppy agreed had a motive of jealousy— Llewellin and all the rest were accounted for, but Poppy had left his notebooks with the police department in Nairobi, and couldn't remember all the details.

He did not think that Broughton could have planned the murder with anyone else, and it would have been impossible, he said, to trust an African. He found the African servants "good chaps" in general and usually truthful, and the mutual dislike between Kikuyu and Somali would have ensured that anyone who disappeared or came into money would be informed on. Broughton's driver had not disappeared, said Poppy, he simply was not needed to give evidence.

Poppy believed that the love note which Broughton had thrown into the grave, apparently on Diana's behalf, was really a taunt of his own; he was saying, in effect, "See what you can do with it now." And one other detail stood out in his mind: he found it incredible that the jury could swallow Broughton's assertion that after a hectic morning driving about—to the police station, on to the mortuary, into Nairobi to rebook his ticket for Ceylon, all the while apparently shaking with nerves—he should come straight home and light a bonfire with a large quantity of petrol "because he loved it."

Poppy, of course, had his professional pride to defend in these conversations, and however open he was to suggestion, his certainty of Broughton's guilt and the various alibis seemed overconfident so many years later. Ignoring the obvious flaws in the prosecution case, based on the evidence he himself had marshalled against Broughton, and the requirement under English law to prove guilt beyond a reasonable doubt, Poppy insisted, for example, that a jury in England would have brought a conviction against Broughton—a highly dubious contention. He said it was very difficult in Nairobi to get an "impartial" jury; that one of the jurymen, called Head, was Broughton's barber, and gave him the "thumbs up" sign when the jury returned to court with the verdict.

I asked Poppy whether he had heard the story of Broughton going up to Harragin after the case and saying, "Bad luck old boy, I did it . . ." He had never heard of it.

"But Harragin was a strange fellow," said Poppy. "Very fond of curry. When he came to lunch with you he'd take off his coat to show he was expecting to sweat from the curry you were going to give him."

He thought it was possible that Harragin would have become Chief Justice of Kenya if he had managed to convict Broughton, and he must have taken the acquittal hard. He, Poppy, hadn't minded too much. In a case like that, he said, you get so tired of answering questions that you long for it to be over, and you don't really care who wins.

Poppy, a young and already successful police officer, had done a diligent job of organising the investigation—often hampered by the inexperience of his colleagues who carted away the body and the car, for example, before a proper examination had been made for fingerprints. His discovery of the Nanyuki bullets was an inspired piece of sleuthing. And the decision to prosecute on the evidence at hand rested, finally, not with Poppy but with the Attorney-General, Harragin.

12
THE MAYOR
OF
NAIROBI

OF ALL THE MEMBERS of the Muthaiga group exposed by the trial, Gwladys Delamere seems to have been the most disliked by the colonial official class for her high-handed manner. They were particularly incensed by the fact that she had clearly lied in court and had produced blatantly biased evidence against Broughton which, given her unpopularity, had had the effect of swaying the jury in his favour. Harwich described her to us as "a formidable old dragon who bossed them all about." Others, including, it seems, the whole English community in Zanzibar, even believed Gwladys to be the murderess. The debate must have livened up the atmosphere of that sweltering claustrophobic island. It is evocatively recalled by a reader of our article, Margot Irving, who wrote from Ankara in 1970:

I was particularly interested in your article because in 1941 I was living in Zanzibar. My husband, Francis Irving, O.B.E., was Comptroller of Customs and Economic Controller then. Our small European community in Zanzibar had either met the principals concerned or knew a lot about them from hearsay. We read avidly the almost verbatim reportage in the *East African Standard*.

It was the general opinion among us that Gwladys Delamere had engineered the murder. She knew Joss would be bringing

Diana back to Karen House around about 3 a.m. We opined that she hired an African, who crept into the back of Joss' car while he was inside the house, and who shot Joss at the junction. We never thought D.B. had done it—he was too infirm.

The motive? Sheer possessive jealousy. Gwladys adored Joss. She was his "intermittent mistress." But when Diana arrived on the scene Gwladys knew she'd met her Waterloo. Rather than let Diana have him, she arranged his murder. "Hell hath no fury . . ." Of all that hard set of Happy Valley, Gwladys was the hardest of the lot. But none of us thought she had had a secondary motive in causing D.B. to stand trial.

All this was, and is, mere conjecture. However, I thought you might be interested.

Gwladys was certainly keen on Erroll, there is no shortage of evidence for that; Kaplan, Paula Long and Lady Barwick, who will appear later in this chapter, all mentioned her strong affection for him at the time of the murder. But what of her new dislike for Broughton? She had been the first to entertain him when he arrived and yet, when her old friend was up on a murder charge, she was even prepared to use the witness box to vent her spite on him.

The first discrepancies in her evidence concern the advice she gave to Diana and Erroll on the night of January 12th at the Broughtons' house at Karen. At first, Gwladys said, she advised Erroll to leave Diana alone, but realised that this was useless. Did she then advise them to elope and "leave a note on the pin cushion"? She denied this, but June said in evidence that she was with Erroll when he telephoned Gwladys and that Erroll had said, "Gwlady, we have taken your advice, except for the note on the pin cushion." She also denied saying to Broughton that evening as they sat on the sofa watching the dancers, "Do you know Joss is wildly in love with Diana?" She *had* tried to talk to Broughton, she said, but he wouldn't listen—he was watching Joss and Diana dancing with an expression that registered "anger, misery, rage, brooding, intense agitation and restlessness." (Was this burst of eloquence more of a reflection of Gwladys's own feelings as she watched the youngsters locked together on the dance floor?) Broughton said that when Gwladys broke the news to him, he was deeply upset "and I rather neglected my duties as a host." Several times in court Gwladys contradicted herself, always backing out of admitting her twenty-year-old friendship with Broughton and finally whittling him down to an "acquaintance."

Morris opened his cross-examination of Gwladys:

Q: How long have you known Sir Delves?
A: On and off for twenty years.
Q: You knew him in England?
A: Yes.
Q: And you renewed your acquaintance here?
A: That is so.
Q: You knew him when you were married to your first husband?
A: I did.
Q: Were you and he great friends?
A: Never.

When asked in court about her evidence, Broughton said

Parts are correct and parts are very incorrect indeed. On our arrival in the country, Lady Delamere not only had lunch with my wife and myself but dined with us and treated me as a very old friend and told me I had never looked so happy. Now apparently she has taken a dislike to me. This I fail to understand as I knew her during her first marriage in England. I knew her quite well and saw quite a lot of her. When she was married to Lord Delamere I stayed up at Government House, Entebbe for a week and we played golf together and were most happy and amicable and the best of friends. Lord Delamere was almost my greatest friend out here and a near neighbour of mine in England. Nobody was more surprised than I was at her evidence . . . It was entirely fabricated.

We sought in vain for an explanation of Gwladys's attitude. At last we found one. From another witness in the trial we learned that an unkind remark that Gwladys had made about Broughton had been repeated to him and he had given her a dressing down in public. After that she was always getting at Broughton, in front of Diana or anyone else. ("A real bitch," said the witness. "She had it in for him.") It began to emerge that Gwladys was in a state of some emotional confusion. In 1928, the year she rolled the Prince of Wales on the floor of the Muthaiga Club, and even during the 1930s, she was generally seen as a kind, loyal friend, much admired for her "attractiveness," for her lovely pale skin and black hair. Now she had become bossy, touchy and "unbalanced"—the word that always occurred to the friends who remembered her at the time of the trial. ("*Very* unbalanced," insisted Paula Long.)

It was these reports that suggested Gwladys to Connolly as the authoress of the anonymous notes left for Broughton in his rack at the Muthaiga Club. He wrote, "I suspected the change of life and what used to be called 'getting a thing' about someone." (But Gwladys was only forty-three, rather young for the change of life.) Connolly had also suspected a woman as the author "from the use of such expressions as 'there's no fool like an old fool' and 'the eternal triangle.' " Certainly the staccato style, brusque and emotional, is common to both Gwladys's evidence and to the anonymous notes. In the end Connolly used the transcript to prove his point. He wrote,

I'm quite sure she wrote the anonymous letters. Listen [to her testimony]:

Q: You said to her, "Do you know that Joss is very much in love with you?"
A: Yes.
Q: And she said yes?
A: Yes.
Q: And you said "What are you going to do about it?"
A: Yes.
Q: Then you went upstairs to the bedroom and you said to her "Does he want to marry you?"

A: Yes.

Q: And she said yes?

A: I expect so.

Q: And you said that you were fond of Erroll and he deserved some happiness?

A: I don't remember saying he deserved some happiness.

Q: Do you remember saying you were very fond of him?

A: Definitely, yes.

Q: And you deny that you said he deserved some happiness?

A: I said I should like to see him happy.

Q: And you told her that he had been unhappy with his first wife?

A: Yes.

Q: And that his second wife was too old for him?

A: Yes.

Q: And Lady Broughton said, ''I am fond of Jock'' meaning her husband?

A: Yes.

Q: And you said ''He is an old man and he has had his life''?

A: I deny that.

Q: Do you regard him as an old man?

A: Yes.

Q: You know that she is very much younger than he is?

A: Yes.

Q: You said to her, ''Take your happiness where you can find it. There is a war on''?

A: I may have said that but with Your Lordship's permission I would add that I asked that they should both go and speak to Sir Delves about the whole situation.

Then, at the very end of her evidence came the question from a member of the jury which we have already heard, but which is perhaps worth repeating in this context. It seems to illustrate the jury's reaction to Gwladys.

Q: When you described the accused's disposition as morose do you mean habitually so?

A: Yes, I have always thought so.

Q: Would the word ''reserved'' suit equally well?

A: No.

Q: It may be that he was only morose towards you?

A: If so, he must have been morose for twenty years.

The first anonymous note read, "You seemed like a cat on hot bricks at the club last night. What about the eternal triangle? What are you going to do about it?" The third, "There's no fool like an old fool. What are you going to do about it?" The second note, "Do you know that your wife and Lord E. have been staying alone at the Carberrys' house at Nyeri together?", was written by someone in close touch with one of those three people. "My strong reaction to the letters was that they were written by a jealous woman," Broughton said in court.

In his defence at the Press Council hearing, Connolly wrote: "The expression, 'What are you going to do about it?' seems typical of a woman accustomed to getting her way, as was the Mayor of Nairobi. It is, of course, a common expression, but not when used so aggressively." "Hot bricks" suggests Gwladys, too. Indeed she overdid them in her description in the preliminary enquiry of her lunch with Broughton at the Club after the funeral when she said, "He talked about the events of the day. He mentioned his wife with unhappiness, with rage, with every possible reaction within a quarter of an hour." Most significant, perhaps, were the disparaging references to Broughton's age ("He's an old man and has had his life . . .", "There's no fool like an old fool"). Gwladys herself had been married to a much older man, Hugh, Lord Delamere, who died three years after their wedding. She had been a widow for ten years by 1941. Did she long for a younger man—and see all her disappointments and failures mirrored in the ageing Broughton?

The English critic and crime writer Julian Symons wrote that one of the worst mistakes made by Poppy was not to have traced the typewriter on which the notes were written. Mrs. Rose Hodson, Gwladys's daughter, in her complaint to the Press Council, wrote that it was absurd to suggest that Gwladys, who was unable to type, would laboriously tap out such notes with one finger. And yet if she had really developed such a feeling of spite against

Broughton, it was the perfect way to get at him. And if she was so keen on Erroll it was also a method to make Broughton "sit up" and put a stop to the affair.

Harwich said that it was generally believed that Gwladys lied in court because she was desperate to prevent her affair with Erroll from being mentioned. He also said that there had been a row between Erroll and Diana on the night of the murder initiated by Gwladys, who had ordered Erroll to give Diana up; a case of jealousy masquerading as sound advice.

Morris knew of Gwladys's feelings towards Erroll and said to her in court, "I am going to put it to you that you were vastly interested in Lord Erroll's happiness or what you conceived to be his happiness?"

"Not vastly," replied Gwladys.

And yet she was keen enough on Erroll to be one of the first arrivals at the mortuary and to ask Bewes for the indentity disc around his neck. The Mayor of Nairobi— no doubt to her embarrassment—was told that she was not allowed to remove his effects without permission from a higher authority than Bewes.

We had a further hint, after the appearance of our article, suggesting Gwladys as the authoress of the notes. Valerie Ward, later Barwick, but then married to a settler, Roddy Ward, had been a close friend of Gwladys's two daughters and of Gwladys herself. She told Connolly that late in 1940 she had been a member of the Aga Khan Club for influential Indians, and often used to dress in a sari. She began to receive, in her Muthaiga pigeonhole, type-written letters with messages that said, in effect, "How can a nice, well brought up English girl go about mim-icking the Indians?" She did not find them really offensive, but they hurt, she said, because they were unsigned. She consulted a "great friend," Walter Shapley, a Nairobi solicitor, who discussed the matter with Lord Francis Scott. Shapley sent for Mrs. Ward and told her he was sure that the letters came from Gwladys Delamere.

"He said that she was in such a peculiar state that it was best to ignore them." She never spoke to Gwladys again, and "did not regret her death."

Supporting Connolly at the Press Council in 1970, she wrote in her affadavit:

I know that Lady Delamere was greatly attracted to Lord Erroll and enjoyed the attention which he paid to her, but when Lady Broughton arrived in Kenya, Lord Erroll diverted his attention to her.

It is not unnatural for an older woman to feel jealous of a younger and very attractive woman stealing the attention of her admirer, Lord Erroll. I gather that Sir Delves Broughton received some typewritten letters informing and then reproaching him over the affairs between his wife and Lord Erroll. In my view it is more than likely that the author of those anonymous letters could have been Gwladys, Lady Delamere.

Gwladys was apparently at home at Soysambu on the night of the murder. She died, of a stroke, in 1943—the result of high blood pressure.

13

BULLETS
IN THE
GARDEN

AT OUR LUNCH at the Brighton Metropole, Poppy told us that Jack Soames had been suffering from acute anxiety during the trial—he was "in a terrible state" as he waited for a full ten days to be called as a prosecution witness. His nervousness might have arisen simply from the fear of letting slip evidence that could incriminate his old schoolfriend. So much depended on Soames's memory of whether Broughton was shooting with a Colt at Nanyuki that day.

If Broughton did commit the murder, Soames's evidence provides a peculiarly neat back-up for Broughton's own story, suggesting a complicity, a conspiracy or even mutual blackmail between the two men. It was to Soames, his one trusted Eton friend, that Broughton went for sympathy about Diana's affair with Erroll; and it was to Soames, too, that he wrote his "bread and butter" letter with its oddly detailed description of the revolver thefts and its announcement that he would "cut his losses" and go to Ceylon. (It was written the day after the theft occurred, and apparently delivered to Nanyuki two days later.) Then there was their urgent drink together at the Avenue Hotel on January 28th, when Soames already knew that the police intended to search for bullets on his farm in five days' time. This was just after Broughton and Carberry, who had come to stay in the house at Karen, had been discussing ballistics and comparison microscopes.

Finally it was Soames's evidence that had clinched the ballistics argument for Morris. Kaplan described Morris's hand pressing on Broughton's shoulder as he asked Soames, "And if Sir Delves tells His Lordship and the Jury that this gun was not a gun that broke [non-Colt] but one in which the cylinder fell out [Colt] you would not dispute that?" and releasing his grip as Soames replied, "I would believe him."

If Soames had committed the murder himself or lent Broughton the gun and the ammunition, the ballistics evidence would in no way be contradicted. Of the three live rounds found in the grass by the police, one contained black powder, one contained ordinary powder and the third was left unopened for the court to decide what to do with it. There was, of course, no provable link between these live rounds and either the murder bullets or the spent "Nanyuki" bullets found in the grass. Of the eleven empty .32 cartridge cases found lying about, four had Smith & Wesson markings and four Remington markings—and all eleven bore the mark of an identical firing pin and were thus fired by the same weapon. Therefore either Broughton was lying when he said that he took an unbroken box of fifty rounds to Nanyuki for the target practice, or Soames provided some extra .32 ammunition, possibly the black powder bullets. (The idea, raised in the trial, of previous target practice on the same site can be discounted. Although it did occur on the Soames estate, this particular range was chosen at random, had never been used before, and was only twenty-five feet in length.) Thus the black powder evidence, at least, was equally damaging to both men. Possibly it was Soames's .32 that they used for the target practice—and for the murder. It was only Broughton and Soames who swore that Broughton had brought his own revolvers to Nanyuki for target practice—a perfectly normal suggestion, apparently, to make to a guest on his way for the weekend. There was, of course, a war on.

Was it during Broughton's second visit to Nanyuki to
see Soames, a week before the murder, that they hatched
the murder plan together and concocted the story of the
stolen revolvers? This would assume firstly a knowledge
of ballistics and secondly that Broughton intended to use
his own gun, the idea of the theft being to draw attention
to the misleading firearms certificate. Why, after all, should
Broughton write so quickly and in such detail about the
theft? Did he write the letter at all? Soames said, "I eventually burned it." But did he burn it before the murder or
afterwards? Had he kept it, it would have been valuable
evidence for Broughton. Was it after the meeting at the
Avenue Hotel that Soames and Broughton agreed to the
story that he had brought his own Colt to the shooting
practice on that first weekend?

HARRAGIN: Did you notice what kind of gun it was to look at?
SOAMES: I understood it was a Colt, but I could not say.

At some stage Connolly wrote in his notebook:

How they did it
Soames
Took some of DB's cartridges at practice or at second
visit. Discussed how to eliminate E. then—had motive
connected with Alice or some other woman—could have
produced native killer (almost only suspect with long experience of them)
Possibilities:

1. Did it himself
2. Provided killer
3. Framed DB

considered honest by Kaplan—"almost the only one"

Soames (Nanyuki) bullets were fired by Soames from
a .32 S&W. He only used the .38 to fire one bullet when
police came later.

He *had* a .38 but used a .32 at practice, and used same to shoot E.

The black powder was his.

Connolly had missed a crucial point, however. Soames claimed that he had practised with a .38, and the police did find five spent .38 cartridges in the grass during their search at Nanyuki, apparently left over from the revolver practice.

Soames's evidence concentrates on the revolver theft, the "cutting of losses" by Broughton, his drunkenness, and the planned trip to Ceylon. And yet he was a prosecution witness. Harragin never pressed him. If Morris had been prosecuting, Soames would never have got off so lightly. The exchanges are worth looking at again.

Q: Can you remember what he said in that letter?
A: Yes, he thanked me for having asked him to stay with me and he also said he had had two revolvers stolen, some notes and a cigarette case. He also said that he had fixed up the matter we discussed.
Q: What did you gather from this?
A: I gathered that he had taken my advice . . . He was going to Ceylon I think.

The "drunkenness" evidence, the description of Broughton "passing out" at Soames's house supports Broughton's story of drunkenness and fatigue on the murder night. It was frequently emphasised by Broughton that this new habit of drinking spirits led to *sleep* (Broughton: "Since I arrived in this country I have taken to drinking whisky and gin as a night cap," etc.), and that when the affair started between Diana and Joss, he began drinking to excess. At other moments Broughton let slip that he had been sleeping badly, and that weekend Soames started him on Medinal ("oblivion's boarding card," as Connolly described it) to make sure he would sleep (even though he had already passed out). Soames almost went too far, once again, in his testimony:

Q: On the night he arrived at your house on that last visit, what was his condition?

A: He arrived perfectly all right. We had a whisky and soda at six o'clock; turned on the wireless at 6:45; had two more small whiskies and sodas and he passed out completely.

Q: What did you say to him?

A: I was very worried as I did not see how he could get into that condition after three small whiskies and sodas. I said I could not understand how a man could pass out after three whiskies and sodas.

[Soames seems to have omitted the word "small" as he repeated the sentence, for fear of straining the point. A barrister with whom I once discussed the case said, "In a murder trial a witness will *qualify* a statement if he thinks it is going to condemn the accused."]

Q: Did he make any reply?

A: Yes, he said that since the trouble with Lady Broughton and Lord Erroll he had taken to whisky and gin and that always sent him to sleep because he had never drunk spirits before.

Even Broughton in his own testimony found it necessary to tone down Soames's descriptions of his excessive drinking.

Then, when Harragin had asked him, "Do you remember which hand the accused fired with?" Soames had replied, "the right hand"—in other words, the crippled hand. (Broughton agreed with this in his own testimony.)

"And how did Sir Delves shoot?"

"Very badly," said Soames. "He looked like a beginner."

Yet Broughton in evidence said that he had been taught in the army to shoot a revolver with either hand, but that he found it easier to shoot with his left hand. His vanity also forced him to disclose the fact that he had shot twenty elephants with a rifle since the accident to his right hand and the onset of arthritis.

What kind of man was Soames, and why might he have helped Broughton to kill Erroll? Frédéric de Janzé thought him worthy of one of his inimitable anonymous portraits in *Vertical Land*. He called this one "Just a Bold Bad Man," and pencilled "Jack Soames" in the margin. It is one of his better attempts:

As he sits over his port, his slanting green eyes light when he sees one shiver to his tales of goring buffalo or tossing rhino.

As he walks in the garden moonlight his sensuous mouth tightens when the girl at his side gasps at his tales of debauch and treason.

His body, an athlete's, surges around a weird and lurid mind; diseased things attract him in the abstract; rape and murder would be his profession.

When 'flu breaks out he believes in being scarce. He loves a noise; his spick and span hair licked to perfection; he hunts by profession.

But all must think that: "Nevil, Nevil, is such a little devil with the girls."*

In 1979 I traced Dushka Repton, the beautiful Russian exile who had been a neighbour of Soames in the late 1920s and the 1930s, to a flat in London near the House of Commons, in a block that was alive with armed policemen—on the roof, in the entrance hall, in the corridors. When the small, emerald-like figure came to the door and peered at me, it was clear that she had almost lost her sight. She told me that the security was for the Secretary of State for Northern Ireland, who lived in a nearby flat. She had taken pity on the policemen and, despite her near blindness, took them down a cake each day, bought on her slow and difficult weekly expeditions to the Army and Navy Stores. She lived alone in the flat, which was dark, with a large sitting room. She felt her way into the kitchen, asked me to pour her a drink of

* Frédéric de Janzé, *Vertical Land* (Duckworth, 1928).

brandy and water, and said, "It is almost painful for me to talk about Kenya. I was so happy there."

When we discussed Soames, she said that she had read the description in *Vertical Land*, and that it was more or less correct. She said that he was extremely handsome, a wonderful dancer, with broad shoulders. "But," said Mrs. Repton, "he was a compulsive, pathological liar. He told me in great detail how he had been tortured by the Bolsheviks in the Caucasus. I was completely taken in and then, by an odd chance, I discovered that he had never been to the Caucasus.

"He loved to boast of fanciful things," she went on, "and of his exploits with women, but a lot of it was talk. He would tell a story about a prostitute who liked to go about crushing little birds in her boots, for example. He had a vivid imagination of horror. He and Carberry were great friends, and well-suited to each other. They loved to sit around talking and planning murder. Carberry even boasted that he had committed two murders, and I wouldn't be surprised. Poor Gloria, his wife, died a complete alcoholic."

But she and her friend Nina Drury, formerly married to Soames, had discussed together whether Soames would have committed murder. "Nina said he would be much too frightened to perform an act of physical cruelty, even though he was at heart a sadist and a voyeur of a very low degree."

Like many other men, Soames once took a fancy to Alice de Janzé, at the time of her affair with Erroll in the late 1920s. Soames, according to Mrs. Repton, made a pass at her and she turned away. In irritation he said to her, "You smell of death!"—a cruel reference to Alice's lingering consumption. But would that be enough to turn him against Erroll, out of jealousy and hurt male pride?

In Kenya in 1979, searching for clues and characters, I went to Soames's old house at Bergeret near Nanyuki, thinking that some of his former servants might still live in the area. The house is still there, with its large stone fireplace, occupied now by a white settler who was shortly selling up. The garden was still kept up on an impressive scale, with its enormous lake, surrounded by the nearest African equivalent to an English country park of the eighteenth century. In Soames's time, I was told, elephant and giraffe would appear from the low scrub at the foothills of the Aberdares almost every evening, and rest in the grass just across the river which flowed past the house, as the guests took their sundowners on the veranda. But the forest has since been cut back here for settlement, and the animals have moved elsewhere.

I did find Soames's former Somali servant, the anonymous witness who has already described the routine of Soames's house parties, living beside Lake Naivasha, working for a young polo-playing businessman. He was an old man, dressed in a red fez and sneakers, with a dry sense of humour and a somewhat snobbish longing for the standards of the colonial days. He gave a vivid description, translated here from the Swahili, of Soames's irascibility and unpleasantness:

Soames was very bad tempered and unreasonable. If he was driving along the murram and a car in front threw up dust as he approached, he would overtake the driver, make him stop and swear at him, telling him he shouldn't throw dust in his face.

Often, he would lose his temper with the car itself if it skidded in the mud, or slowed on a hill. He would shout, "Go on, get on you bloody old car," and slap its side like a horse.

One day we were at Limuru, going down the escarpment on our way to Nairobi. Everybody's car was stuck in the mud and Bwana Soames said, "Oh fuck this, I'm not going to get stuck in the mud. I'm going to GO, GO, GO, GO, and if I don't get through, I'm going to burn the car." Then he kicked and hammered it, and almost turned it over trying to get it out of the mud. All the other people were stuck. The mud was very bad. I [and another servant] made a track and we got through. We were all wet through and cold, and the colour of Soames's wife's hat was running down her face.

She said, "What about our friends? We've got to help them." Soames said, "Bugger them." We got as far as Muthaiga, very dirty and wet. We went to No. 1 cottage. The servants were given money by Mrs. Soames and told to go away and come back tomorrow, but on the way out we met Soames who said, "Where are you going?" We said, "Memsahib gave us the money to go away." Soames said, "Certainly not. Not until we've showered and dressed."

On a trip to the Kenya coast the same year, I picked up confirmation of a story that Poppy had mentioned in passing, which might explain Soames's anxiety at the trial. Soames had left the country soon after the case for an extended holiday, said Poppy, "in case more bullets were dug up in his garden." There was a suggestion that Soames was involved in illegal arms dealing at the time of the murder. One hot Saturday I drove down the flat coast road, south of Mombasa, past the palm forests and tourist hotels to look for Dan Trench, the son of Maxwell Trench, who had been Carberry's partner in the distillery at Nyeri. Dan had been in his twenties when the murder took place. I was told he was a senior beachcomber, down on his luck, and a drinker. He lived near the hotel that his family once owned, which now belonged to the Government. He was said to be a bar historian of some accomplishment, whose pedigree as a member of the inner circle of old surviving settler families gave him a certain distinction along the coast. He had become, in other words, a "character."

I found him about midday in the compound of the Trade Winds Hotel, in a Crusoe-like shack shaded by jacarandas, near a hire shop called Mike's Bikes. He was sitting at a wooden table on the "veranda"—which was no more than the exposed front half of the wooden box in which he lived, and roughly the size of a small ship's cabin. He was not so old, and there was no trace of senility about him, but he was emaciated, skeletal almost, and marked with severe skin cancer. As I began to talk to him he picked at a plate of fish with a fork, with a deadly lack of interest. I recited the names of the people in whom I was interested. "How the hell do you know all those names?" he asked.

On the veranda railing was a sign saying "Office," and on the table itself another that said, "Private." "They come and think they can sit around," said Trench. "I don't get half what I'm owed." I had been warned not to drink with Trench. It wasn't that he couldn't hold his liquor, but he had a serious ulcer which he had neglected—mostly through lack of proper nourishment— and a drinking bout, it was said, might kill him. The conversation began slowly and reluctantly on his part. He was forcing himself to eat the fish. Then he called for a beer, and then another. We proceeded to the hotel bar on the beach, and drank for four hours by the sea. He refused not to drink. He was amazed that I should know so much about the old Happy Valley crowd, even though I told him that I had been working on nothing else for some months. "I must say, you buggers who come out here really know your stuff," he said, and then having conceded the point, he addressed himself in intimate detail, varying fancy with accuracy, insult with praise, to characters who had died, in some cases, thirty years before. He talked a lot about Carberry, his father's partner, especially his cruelty to animals, which, he said, was legendary, and which had begun according to Trench when he was four years old. "His mother said to him, 'Today is Christmas Day and I want you to be especially kind to animals, particularly the cat.' John came back later and said, 'I've given the cat all the canaries to eat.' "

"He had one horse called Morning Glory and another called Mafuta," said Trench, "and he used to race them against each other. He'd put gramophone needles in the bits to see if they would go faster. He'd time the horses, swap the bits, and run them again and again."

Dan Trench remembers the tortures inflicted by Carberry on Dan's sister, Nancy: a toy was sent to her when she was quite small with the message on it, from Carberry "Not to be opened until my arrival." When he arrived the box was put in the middle of the room, he opened it, and produced a large child's doll. Then he took out a knife and slit its stomach open. The child wailed and screamed in terror as hundreds of gold sovereigns poured on to the floor. The rule was that all foreign exchange must be declared and Carberry had devised many ingenious ways to circumvent it. When he was finally jailed for eighteen months he called it "the happiest period of my life."

Drinking into the evening, Dan Trench and I often wandered off the point. "Hemingway came down here as a sick man, before he died. He couldn't leave this bar. He was scared as hell. He'd hired a marlin boat for three weeks, and he never once went out."

Around five o'clock we got on to Alice de Trafford. "God, there's only one bloody woman left I know who could come in here and every head would turn," said Trench.

Then we left the bar and walked down the sand for a mile, climbed over some jagged rocks, up a steep hill through cactus and trees and there was the ruin of Alice's coast house, roofless and overgrown, but with traces of her wallpaper and her paint. Dan Trench remembered building her the water tank in the garden: there was never enough water. If Alice had too many guests arriving, she would build on new rooms two or three days in advance. Not a single room in the house was square.

At some point that day Trench told me about Soames the arms dealer. At the time of the trial, he said, Soames knew that the police were investigating a tip-off that he had been receiving stolen military property. A million rounds of .22 ammunition had been stolen from the Gilgil depot, for example. Trucks, too, had been stolen and stripped down for spare parts, for which farmers would pay high prices. Handsome profits could be made reselling the equipment to countries like the Congo. Nothing was proved.

Soames also had a partner at the time, Jack Band, a priest turned dairyman who lived with him at Burgeret, whom Trench knew to be smuggling military equipment and arms to Abyssinia at the time. This fact was officially discovered after the war and when I later checked the story with Poppy, he agreed on its accuracy.

I could imagine Soames falling in with a murder plan, rehearsing the various possibilities with Broughton on that gloomy drunken weekend, and finally saying to his friend, "Of course, there is one other solution. You could just get rid of him." After that Soames would have been an accessory to the deed. I could not imagine him doing the deed himself—and his alibi would be too difficult to establish, with all the servants knowing his movements. But if he knew of Broughton's plan, why did he point out so readily to the police the exact spot where the firing practice had taken place? If Soames didn't tell them, perhaps the servants would. If there was one houseboy for the whiskies and sodas, one for the generator and so on, there was almost certainly one for revolver practice. There was no activity, it seems, apart from Soames's violin playing, that wasn't servant-assisted. Or did Soames know that the discovery of the bullets would be the very detail that would exonerate Broughton? To be sure about Soames, however, one would have to be sure about Broughton's guilt.

14
MISS WILKS AND THE MISSING HOUR

V E R Y   C L O S E to the final copy deadline for our article, almost too late to be of any use, a long telex arrived from Humphrey Tyler in Durban reporting an interview with Dorothy Wilks. He had found her, living with her widowed sister on the sixth floor of another block of flats along the Durban sea-front, and he had talked to her for an hour.

It was a fascinating document. First it seemed almost miraculous that Wilks could be exhumed from the past to describe the night of the Erroll murder so many years later. At the same time, the material caused us some frustration. Although Tyler had done an excellent job, there were gaps and details that needed checking again with Wilks, questions arising from what she said that would occur only to aficionados as steeped in the evidence as ourselves. There was not time to go back to Wilks, and when I resumed the search ten years later, she had disappeared once again from the Durban sea-front. Nevertheless, she had clarified some important points. What follows is an edited version of Tyler's own account of their meeting (Wilks referred to her former employers throughout as "Sir Delves" and "Lady Diana"):

The night of the murder at the Broughton house, Miss Wilks was alone. She wasn't frightened. She was often there alone.

She used to turn all the lights on, and play the piano loudly downstairs. The servants' rooms were right away from the house, and the dogs were locked in kennels, away from the leopards which used to prowl around the grounds.

About 1 a.m. Miss Wilks was surprised by a knock. It turned out to be June Carberry's driver. He said that Mrs. Carberry was returning to the Broughton house after the party. He brought a suitcase of clothes and Miss Wilks led him upstairs to one of the guest rooms, where he laid out Mrs. Carberry's clothes, and left.

At about 2 a.m. Sir Delves returned, with Mrs. Carberry. They both went upstairs, followed by Miss Wilks. At the top of the stairs there is a long corridor. Sir Delves and Mrs. Carberry stopped. Mrs. Carberry thanked Sir Delves for a "lovely party." Sir Delves said, "Goodnight, June darling." Then he went one way down the corridor to his room, and Mrs. Carberry went the other. "And that was the last that anybody saw of Sir Delves that night," said Miss Wilks. She herself went to Mrs. Carberry's room. Mrs. Carberry complained of a fever. Miss Wilks fetched her some quinine tablets and some whisky, then sat and talked to Mrs. Carberry for a while.

Some time later, perhaps an hour, another car arrived and there was a knock on the door. Miss Wilks went down to open it. "Lady Diana nearly fell into the room; she must have been leaning on the door when I opened it. She had a face like thunder. Lord Erroll was with her. It was obvious there had been a fight. There was none of the usual lovey-dovey stuff between them."

Miss Wilks pointed out a tray of bottles, and suggested Lord Erroll have a whisky. "Why, Wilkie," said Lord Erroll, "don't you know I never touch whisky?" Diana complained she was hungry. A tin of biscuits that was usually kept for her was up in Sir Delves's room. "He hadn't been sleeping well," said Miss Wilks, "so I fixed him a Thermos with something warm to drink, and I took up the biscuits. Lady Diana was away, so I had left them in Sir Delves's room. When Lady Diana said she was hungry, I said I would fetch them down. But she said not to worry. But I wish I had gone. I might have changed the whole trial if I had. I would have been able to tell the court definitely whether Sir Delves was in his room at that time—or not."

Miss Wilks mentioned to Diana that June was upstairs and that she had a slight fever. Diana went upstairs to see her. Miss Wilks picked up a jewel box that Diana had brought back with her and dropped on to a table, and took it upstairs to Diana's room. Diana spent a "few minutes" with June, then went downstairs again. Miss Wilks went to June's room and sat talking to her. She did not hear Erroll's car driving away.

After some time—"perhaps about half an hour"—Diana came upstairs again, and went to June Carberry's room. Miss Wilks herself retired. She could hear June and Diana talking excitedly. She wondered "when on earth they would stop." In the end they did stop. She presumes that Diana went to her room, to sleep. She herself then turned in. It was very late. She heard nobody else stirring.

After the murder was discovered, the police questioned her "but they didn't get much out of me. I told them I wasn't a clairvoyant." She said that she was questioned for hours. At the end of it all, she was very tired. The investigating officer took her aside. He said gently, "Wilkie, off the record, who do you really think murdered Lord Erroll?" "I didn't think. I just blurted out. I was surprised as anybody. I said, 'Diana.'"

"Oh, you should have seen her," said Miss Wilks of Diana. "She had those special kind of lips. Sensual lips. And those eyes! And her skin! The sun never touched it. I saw her in the bath once, stretched out with £90,000 worth of pearls round her neck. I asked if I should take them off, but she just laughed and said, 'Leave them be, Wilkie.' Oh, she had a figure on her. And couldn't she ride! She was just like one with the horse. Not like Sir Delves. He had a gammy arm, you know, and he always used to fall off."

Miss Wilks still swears she doesn't know for certain who committed the murder, although towards the end of the interview she looked up wistfully and said, "It does look like Sir Delves did it. It can't hurt him to say that now, can it?" She continued, "He was a fine man, Sir Delves. He wasn't like the rest of them. Aristocrats? Lords and ladies? Don't talk to me about aristocrats. I hate their guts. Of course, Sir Delves was an aristocrat as well. But he was different."

Did she lie to the police to save Sir Delves? She was quite shocked by the question, and so was her sister. "Oh no," said Miss Wilks. "We weren't brought up like that, you know, I would never tell a lie. Of course, under some circumstances I might omit something. But I would never tell a lie." Then, quite startlingly, Miss Wilks said vehemently, "But June Carberry did. She lied for him. She even perjured herself in court, and I don't blame her . . .

"After the murder, before he was arrested, Sir Delves tried to get me to kill him," said Miss Wilks. "I haven't told anybody else that, not even my sister. He called up to me, and asked if I had a minute, and I said, 'Yes, Sir Delves,' and he came upstairs, and he had this syringe all ready. He was holding it with the needle pointing up, and he asked me to stick it in his arm. But the needle was broken, and I couldn't do it. Just as well. Just imagine if I had! He didn't tell me then that it was poison, but he did tell me later, poor man. It was all so sad, really. I don't think anything would have happened if he hadn't married her. He should have just kept her, like he did before."

One day after his arrest, Miss Wilks visited Broughton in jail. "He looked happier than I had ever seen him before. He even told me, 'Wilkie, I'm much happier here than I ever was in Karen.' "

Wilks was not the only person to whom Broughton communicated feelings of relief, almost of well-being during those weeks of prison routine. And in court he said, "I think I received more genuine kindness and thought both from the prison officials and prisoners than I ever have outside prison." Wilks's story of Broughton asking for help with his broken syringe also has the ring of truth. Morphine was very much on Broughton's mind ever since Soames had provided the Medinal, a week before the murder. He had even arranged for it to be smuggled into the jail in case the verdict went against him.

Had I been able to interview Wilks myself, I would have asked her whether Broughton appeared to be drunk as he climbed the stairs; whether he needed June to support him; and to confirm or deny that she was "drilled" by members of the Karen household on what she should tell the police. In the end, since there is no question of Wilks lying to protect her former employers so many years later, at least it may be accepted that Erroll and Diana did appear at the door, and that Erroll was not killed on his way to the house at Karen.

Wilks makes some interesting points: Broughton apparently was not sleeping well, despite the whisky nightcaps; and she disagrees with June's times. Her information backs up the possibility of June inventing all the times that night, in the knowledge, perhaps, that Wilks would never be able to refute her story. Wilks ultimately gives June an alibi, Broughton no alibi, and Diana a loose alibi, by introducing the "half hour" she spent downstairs.

Would Wilks not have heard Broughton shuffling along the corridor for his two visits to June's room—was that what she meant when she said June perjured herself? Or heard the barking of the dog? She appears to have been one of the last in the household to go to sleep, kept awake by Diana and June "talking excitedly." Were they talking excitedly because they both knew that Broughton had left the house to talk to Erroll? Did the deadline for the article get in the way of the one opportunity we had to prove or disprove Broughton's story by questioning Wilks more closely?

The following extracts from Connolly's notebooks—written after the Wilks text arrived—are added here, not as an elucidation of the mystery, but as an example of the kind of fevered puzzling in which he indulged each time new evidence was introduced:

JC heard no sound of creaks, doors, keys. The stairs creaked loud enough to be heard over the whole house.

DB could not have climbed down from the roof. "He slided down the bannisters"—Cressida (Connolly, aged 7).

DB could only have gone down the stairs when Wilks was getting hot whisky from the kitchen or quinine or hot water bottle— in case she heard him.

Wilks would not be likely to get bottle from JC's bathroom as water would not be hot enough at 3 a.m.

There was a loo downstairs where he could hide if seen.

Could he have used a rope ladder?

Coming back—not so easy—but Wilks asleep, Diana retires— only JC awake. Dog hears him? JC invents 2nd call, DB 1st estimates it at 4 a.m.

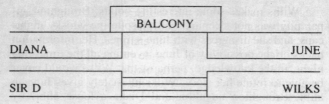

The upper storey of the house at Karen.

Wilks gives D a time when she could have done it too. Is that because she suspected her or vice versa? Wilks covers JC who otherwise might have driven DB in her car.

JC said she heard D and E talking and laughing—but they were not laughing but quarrelling—therefore she:

1. Didn't hear them.
2. They pretended they were laughing, not quarrelling.
3. They really were laughing. Wilks was wrong.

DB simply heard voices. Probably JC wished to hide the quarrel, it was still one of the better nights.

"There was a door open when D and E came back" (presumably from D's statement). He also had his veranda key—so he could have got out noiselessly by this door, perhaps returned by it.

Why did Wilks (or the others) not mention D bringing the dog back? Wilks especially.

JC's evidence covers up for DB, Wilks and Diana
Wilks's evidence covers up for JC
DB's evidence implicates no one else
Diana only made a statement

A door was left open. Anyone could have got in or out of it.
What do we know of Wilks anyway?
She says Mrs. C's chauffeur/butler left—for where? in what? did he come round the next morning?

One of the most interesting items in the Wilks interview was her description of the arrival of Diana and Erroll—the expression on her face "like thunder." It supported a popular rumour—a story believed by Diana's own friends to this day—that she and Erroll had had a terminal row on the night of the murder, after the dinner party. The theory, which varies little from version to version, is based on the idea that Broughton, while pretending to "cut his losses" and behave with scrupulous honour, had in fact reneged on the marriage pact and the promise to pay Diana £5,000 a year.

Broughton almost admitted as much in court, but he turned it round: Diana's integrity, he said, would have prevented her from claiming the money, and thus the financial part of the pact was effectively waived. Erroll told Diana at the last moment that without finance, the marriage plans were off and Broughton had therefore forced Erroll into officially taking over Diana, knowing that it would be impossible for him to do so. As a result Erroll had lost his nerve and backed away. Broughton was almost broke by this time. In any event he would certainly have been unwilling to finance Diana's affair with Erroll for three years, or until they could get a divorce. Diana herself was about to lose everything: miles away from home; a baronet, an earl; not one, but two sets of pearls, and above all, her romantic happiness.

Reading some of Broughton's testimony in this light gives it a new flavour. Here he is explaining his "dispassionate business discussion" with Erroll, within earshot of June and Diana and in view of Erroll's houseboy and garden boy, who described Broughton beating the table with his fist:

I think on that occasion I enquired about his financial position and Lord Erroll was rather evasive. I could not get out of him what his resources were. [It was surely common knowledge in Nairobi that Erroll was penniless.] I think he said he had not got very much. *I wanted to get out of him* [my italics] exactly what he was worth and I gathered it was not very much. I think he said on that occasion he was afraid Diana would not have all the things she had been used to, or a lot of the things she had been used to.

	Alibi	Motive	Opportunity	Temperament	Physic.*	Nan. bullet	Karen bullet
Gwladys Delamere	?	jilted	?	?	no	no	?
DB	no Pros yes Def	injured pride	yes Pros no Def	yes Pros no Def	yes Pros no Def	yes yes	yes no
Diana	no Wilks yes Mrs. C.	jilted at last moment?	yes acc. to Wilks	yes	yes except lifting body	yes	if she took some
June	yes Wilks otherwise no	jilted	no acc to DB	no	no	no	if she took some
Alice	bed with Pembroke	jilted	yes Poppy	yes shot R de T	no	no	no
Dickinson	yes Poppy	money or love of D	?	?	yes	no	?
Soames	yes Poppy	?	?	yes	yes	yes	?
Carberry	?	injured pride	?	yes	yes	no	??

*Physical ability.   Connolly's chart of the suspects.

In 1979 a close friend of Diana's told me that she had once said to her, quite courageously, "I always thought you shot Joss." "And she took it quite seriously," said the friend, "and very well, and said, insisted, that she hadn't. And I gave her my reasons, which were: he had made it clear to her that in no way could he marry her because, for one thing, she couldn't be divorced for three years and he had absolutely no money—the reverse: he was very badly in debt. And he more or less said the best thing you can do is go back to Broughton and call it a day. And in her rage she shot him. I said I thought this was quite a feasible thing. And she swore she didn't."

Broughton seemed always to be hinting after the murder that something had gone wrong between Joss and Diana. One could perhaps read too much into the following courtroom exchange, taken from Broughton's testimony, but it might also be read in the light of a letter Broughton wrote after his acquittal to a friend in England, in which he said, "Diana has been completely disillusioned about Erroll by revelations which have come out since all this trouble started."

In court he was asked by Morris:

You had some hope of everything coming all right in about three months' time when you returned from Ceylon?
A: Girls do change their minds.
Q: And had you ever heard of Erroll changing his mind?
A: Unless I am very much pressed I would rather not answer.
Q: I merely suggest to you that you had a double chance of everything being all right in three months?
A: Yes.
Q: You also knew Lord Erroll's reputation with regard to that sort of thing, that he was fickle in such matters?
A: If I am pressed to answer, yes.

If there had been an argument between Joss and Diana, why should it have occurred suddenly after the dinner, at which everything seemed to be so amicably settled?
There was no explanation for this and no hard evi-

dence to support the "row" theory, until Connolly stumbled on a witness whose story provided not only a plausible reason for the argument, but also seemed to explain the "missing hour" in the timetable of the movements of Broughton and June Carberry that night.

Lady Barwick, formerly Valerie Ward, who supported Connolly at the Press Council on the question of Gwladys Delamere and the anonymous letters, told Connolly that on the night of the murder June Carberry had invited her to dinner at the Muthaiga Club to celebrate Broughton's surrender. She and her South African friend, Laurie Wilmot, were dining elsewhere, so June asked them to come on to the Claremont Road House afterwards and join the party. Lady Barwick and her escort had drinks at the Club, at around 7:45. Connolly's note of his conversation with Lady Barwick tells the rest of the story:

She saw, and spoke to the following: Derek Fisher from Nanyuki, somebody Gaskell, who had an ulcer and drank milk, and Denzil Myers. June and Alice de Trafford were there; Long John Llewellin and his wife, Gypsy someone, Jacko Heath, still alive (1969) and married to Sally Billiard Leake!

After their own dinner she and LW go to Claremont in his camouflaged army car. They were first and were sat down at a long table. Had two dances. Then Diana and Erroll arrived, looking rather unhappy and sat at the end of the table—and later June Carberry and Broughton appeared! Their appearance caused consternation to Joss and D and they were obviously not meant to come. DB looked very white, started protesting immediately. They ignored everyone else. Immediately a terrific row started with DB shouting at Erroll and June booming away, trying to soothe them. It go so bad that she and LW got up and left and went to another club, Blue Room or 400 (up steps). She rather thinks there was someone else at their table. The row was fundamentally a scene of jealousy. Broughton and June then went back to Muthaiga—or where?

Next morning she was rung up because her Buick was the only one in Kenya besides Gibbs and the No. was almost the same (T 7341). [The Registration number of Erroll's Buick was T 7331.]

Poppy, who usually resisted the suggestion of gaps in his investigations, believed that Valerie Ward's story may have been correct; was impressed by the missing hour in the timetable, and he confirmed that the police did enquire about other Buicks, in case of confusion over the sightings of Erroll's car before the murder.

Broughton certainly planned to go to the Claremont Road House that night. He told Mrs. Barkas, Lizzie Lezard and Llewellin how much he was looking forward to it. Lezard understood that Jock would be taking June there as a dancing partner. June never specifically denied going to the Claremont. She simply said, in her evidence, "Joss and Diana went off to the Claremont. Jock asked me if I would like to dance and I said I did not want to, as I was not feeling particularly well." She supported that by the requests for quinine later on.

Diana and Erroll dancing together at the Claremont Road House had set off Broughton's rage on another evening, if the prosecution's information is correct, when he was heard to say to Diana before she left, "Shall I throw the champagne in your face, or break the bottle over his head, or would you rather I threw the bottle at your head?" On this final evening, had their departure again triggered off his anger, so carefully suppressed at dinner under the studied passivity and almost perverse generosity of the toast and the good wishes?

Why did no one else witness Broughton's scene at the Claremont Road House? Nobody was asked about it, and according to Poppy, Wilks was the only one among the witnesses who volunteered information. Lady Barwick's version of the last dealings between Broughton and Erroll before the murder, as reported here by Connolly, is close to the popular version:

Valerie Barwick. Part of her theory (obviously based on real knowledge): When it came to the crunch, DB said that he was not going to give her up without a test—he would say that he was not going to give her any money, after all, that if E's sentiments were genuine, he would say, "never mind, we'll manage somehow." If he didn't then they would fix him between themselves or some such expression. All this was tried on the last evening and E said something to the effect that he had only made love to her for her money and that without the money there could be no marriage—this could have happened at the club, the night club, the house afterwards, or on the way back to Karen (Wilks's description of Diana's anger). Perhaps the scene at the Claremont was the showdown and the moment when DB made up his mind to kill Erroll (though she thinks he had planned the murder for ages).

Reconstructing the scene from this new evidence, Connolly wrote:

The dinner was rather short—8:30 to 10:30 and ended in a *vin triste*, perhaps a quarrel after the Toast . . . D and E perhaps slipped away suddenly. E is surprised to see DB and JC at Claremont and there is consternation—Diana too. The row flares up and DB *threatens* Erroll. (VW and partner leave.) DB and JC return to Club and he starts off again "It's all very well June" etc. It is this *threat* he is so frightened of coming out, that he rushes up to Nyeri after the verdict of murder and asks her what she has told the police. She reassures him—only that he was in bad mood at Club. If he made this threat, D would *know* of murder as soon as death of E is established. Hence, can't abide DB.

The fact that no one gave away the visit of J and DB to the Claremont or the row there suggests that they *all* decided not to mention it. Purpose of DB's actions: to draw the enemy fire. He asks about prison conditions, fate of man who kills his wife's lover in flag. delicto—draws attention to bonfire.

If DB had hired a killer he would need an alibi and would therefore ensure Wilks being in and out of his room too—he might also make his presence known to D and E—but he behaved quite differently.

15

LETTERS FROM THE WANJOHI

Loneliness fixed Alice. Everyone was frightened of her.
BERYL MARKHAM

Alice de Trafford's marriage to Raymond had ended long before their divorce in 1938, and she was often alone in her house at Wanjohi, with her Ridgeback dogs and her pet eland. She had fallen in love, after Erroll's death, with Dickie Pembroke, her alibi for the murder night. Pembroke could never return Alice's affection with the same intensity, and she began to cling to him with suicidal devotion.

As she took up with Pembroke, so her affair with Lezard came raggedly to an end. It was a period of confusion for Alice. Patricia Bowles remembers that shortly before Diana's arrival in Kenya, while Erroll was conducting his affair with Mrs. Wirewater, Alice had talked about the possibility of getting Erroll back as her lover.

On the morning after the murder, Alice had begged Lezard urgently to take her to the mortuary to bid farewell to Erroll's body. They took along Gwladys, and Bewes recorded their arrival in his notebook. What he didn't record, but what Lezard saw, was that before Alice put the branch of a small tree on Erroll's body, she kissed him on the lips, pulled the sheet back, smeared it with her vaginal juices and said, "Now you're mine for ever."

After that Lezard suspected Alice—the murder fitted in with her morbid preoccupations. And there is a suggestion that she may have confessed to him. In later years Lezard was untypically evasive on the subject. Yet the writer Alastair Forbes, Lezard's flatmate in London after the war, is convinced that Lezard would have told him if this was the case, "Or if he had either done it himself," wrote Forbes, "or taken money to do it, or had it done without doing it, his most likely course in the circumstances."

Alice brought supplies, especially books, to Broughton in jail each day. She became fascinated by the trial, and filled with anxiety that Broughton might be convicted, a feeling she communicated almost daily to Patricia Bowles.

Pembroke had been expected to keep out of the public eye since his banishment but the trial, where he was a witness, and his subsequent relationship with the notorious Alice had exposed him once again. Pembroke applied for a transfer and in July 1941 he was posted to Cairo. This finally broke Alice's spirit.

The letters that Alice began writing to him, even before they parted that month, describe her own pathetic decline, and represent as well the last rites for Happy Valley. Pembroke's feeling towards her can be measured to some extent by the care with which he kept her letters until his death in England in the late 1960s.

The first letter was written in Wanjohi on July 23rd, 1941.

My darling Dickie,

It does seem absurd—even grotesque—to be sitting opposite you and writing you a letter. However with the length of time it seems to take, I'd rather send you—or give you—some silly nonsense to read from me on your arrival, than to envisage weeks more of lack of contact when you reach Egypt.

We've just had our "toasties" with much talk about the virtues of real or pseudo caviar.

For a moment I'm going to say sad things—& when the

G & T with dash has worked a little—cheer up again. I can't imagine the immediate future at all. Joss gone, then Dina,* now you—who mean the most of all. Even Paula [Long] is gone in a way. Our way of life lies apart and her big, bold paramour has changed her nature a little.

Lizzie is going.† Even you reproached me lately for being a little hard on him. I've never meant it really, for I count on him a great deal and am really fond of him. Anyway all of you are gone or going and my self-pity wells up when I realise that I can follow no one. You will surely smile with me when I say, "Thank God one can still recognise self-pity as such and not give it any greater dignity than just that." And now—what I said flippantly to Lizzie in my note, I mean with all my heart. Thank God I seemed unreasonable and was firm. We've had—for me at least—a lovely week. I hope I *can* bear the end, which is tomorrow, decently. I don't think I could have borne only the two days without being difficult and making your departure hard.

The next letter is undated, written from the Norfolk Hotel, soon after Pembroke left.

My Beloved Dickie,

. . . There are not a great many things to say, but there are a few. Firstly—that you have made me inconceivably happy for exactly five months and four days. There is not one single thought or word to break the continuity of that happiness in my memory.

Secondly the fact of you going away in these uncertain times, even for only a short time, as we hope, is pure and absolute pain . . . P.S. Funny how small and irrelevant thoughts intrude. One is that I forgot to tell you that if you have occasion to use that morphia, squeeze one good drop out of the needle before injecting in order to expel any air which hurts and blisters. Also do not take U93 for more than four consecutive days (3 a day *after* meals)—3 days is better. It will probably make you feel a bit mouldy, but should you feel really ill stop it at once. Some

---

* Alice is possibly referring to the fact that Lady Idina had been taken away from Happy Valley by her fourth husband.
† Lezard, too, was on the point of being posted to Cairo.

people don't tolerate it at all. Take it for a heavy cold and also if you have any sort of infection which won't readily clear up such as veldt sore.

At the end of August, Alice was discovered to have cancer of the womb and was waiting to go into hospital for a hysterectomy. She had also suffered another, bitter loss.

I really had to laugh—gloomy as I felt on arrival. The greetings I got from the Matron and the Nurses (almost all of which I've known for years) was for all the world as if they were welcoming me to a party. The night sister startled me a good deal by saying ''There's plenty of your maté tea here if you want it. You left a whole packet here last time and it's hardly been touched.'' I had intended sending out for some this morning!

Flo came down [to Nairobi] with me. We had a hideous trip—two punctures and of course no spare the second time. We arrived here at 7 but I wasn't hungry and didn't want the dinner, whereupon the Matron said ''*I* know what you like—you used to drink gallons of chicken broth last time,'' and everybody laughed heartily and I had a cup of chicken broth!

As to the operation itself—that is cheerfully referred to as ''the op'' and with much thumping of pillows and shaking of towels one is told how well one is going to feel. This part is all parallel with people telling you—''you *must* see this film or that play—you'll love it.''

And now I have one thing to tell you which I cannot bear to write about beyond the bare facts. ''Minnie'' [Alice's dog] is dead—I killed her entirely painlessly, she knew nothing—because that car hysteria was no longer limited to cars. Her distress was so great that I put her out. I feel as if I'd committed a murder. She trusted me so, all the time I was breaking my heart feeding her Nembutal in some of your pâté . . . I look forward to all these moves with an indifference amounting to distaste. I can't imagine what Wanjohi will be like without ''Minnie'' for company and the train journey to Diani. You once said to me impatiently ''Life must go on.'' Well, it need not. Look at Joss, look at Minnie. Life need *not* go on. In Joss's case *someone* decided that, in Minnie's case *I* did, and the length of our own lives lies entirely within our own hands (unless someone else gets at us first!)

September 17. I am OK surgically speaking and since yesterday quite healed up, but I feel simply frightful, weak and ill. I suppose this will get right but it seems very long. The Matron who is *charming* gave me a talking to before I left and said that I must expect to get periods of depression for some time and not to let them get me down. You know the books "What every young girl (wife) (mother) should know"? I felt this lecture could be incorporated in the series under the title, "What every old hag in the forties should know." What these periods of depression will be like, *plus* the ones I get anyway, I can't imagine . . . What I can see of the garden from my bed looks well and full of colour. The Eland was standing in the pyrethrum by the road as we came in yesterday and has become quite enormous. Quite terrifyingly big.

It is desolate beyond words without Minnie. She is the last person and I mean "person" except for Paula, left . . . I went out to Joss's grave, day before yesterday and I was glad to see that someone has put new pots of growing flowers there. Since the middle of May there have been only odd bunches of dead flowers there, and nothing kept up . . .

September 20. Bill Allen* is coming to lunch today. I've had long talks with him. He first said that he thought Jock incapable of "things" because he said he was one of the greatest cowards (in ordinary life) he'd ever met. He'd known him for years. He liked him, however. When I stressed the fact that the murder was about as cowardly as one could imagine he agreed entirely and thought it consistent. She [Diana] is a great friend of his ex-wife's (an awful woman, I know her) so I asked his opinion of her. He said he'd met her several times and took her to lunch etc. He said "I see nothing whatever in her," and that he'd been "abysmally bored" at lunch. Now that surprises me, for though I don't pick her as you know, I'm surprised at *anyone*—even Bill, finding her lacking in all interest. However he sticks to this.

* Once married to Paula Long; became head of British Secret Service in Ankara.

Alice made one try at suicide shortly before her final successful attempt, on September 23rd. When Patricia Bowles, her neighbour and friend, went to her rescue, she discovered that Alice had already marked each piece of her furniture for distribution to her friends. Patricia Bowles said:

Our house was at Kipipiri with the mountain behind it. Nancy Wirewater, Joss Erroll's old flame, was living at Clouds while Dina was away. And there was a joint birthday party of Alice, and someone else. All the guests were arriving. Flo Crofton was with Alice and sent a note over saying Alice wouldn't be coming because this time she'd done it successfully. The party was starting. I went to Gilgil to get a South African medical unit and he and I both got to work on the stomach pump. I felt awful bringing her back. She wanted to go. I spent the night with her trying to keep her off the Nembutal, which she had obviously hidden. She had her gun in the bed and passed out before she could use it. The second time she used it. I didn't go that time. I was terrified of having to do it again. It was absurd. We were always apologising to each other. Me for bringing her back to life and she for causing me inconvenience, and all the time almost asking me not to do anything.

Alice wrote two letters after the first attempt. To Dickie Pembroke:

My darling, I don't suppose for a moment you can understand why I am doing this. We think so differently.

Anyway please, please, believe that from my viewpoint at least I'm doing right.

I'm writing this in my garden on a glorious morning—drinking in sun and colour and peace, by the middle pool.

I love you very much as you know—too much to meet you as a different being later on.

The reason it was so intolerable for me saying goodbye at Kampala, was that I knew then it was final.

All my love Alice.

Give my love to Lizzie. I simply can't write again, and there is nothing more to say. A.

To Patricia Bowles, she wrote,

Me voilà encore! You wrote me a perfectly charming letter. It was sweet of you and gratefully received in the spirit of the moment.

But you see what I did not make clear—life is no longer worth living when you no longer care whether you are wanted or not.

I won't say more, but I think you'll understand, partly anyway.

If you will not talk of this at all, no one will need know that it is not post-operative depression. It is kinder towards Dickie and my children and better for you and Flo and William [the doctor who operated on her].

Love Alice
Love to Derek too.

When she finally succeeded, Alice tidied her bedroom and filled it with flowers, dressed up and put on her best bed linen. She left several notes. One was to the police —its contents were never released. The rest were to her children, to Dickie and one to Patricia Bowles: "By the time you get this," it read, "I'll have done it again. This time, I hope successfully." She also asked that a cocktail party be held at the grave.

16

THE GREATEST
POUNCER
OF ALL TIME

BROUGHTON DID HAVE one loyal friend
in England who had followed the case with close attention.
This was "Porchy" Carnarvon (the Earl of Carnarvon).
When he heard that Broughton had been acquitted, Carnarvon sent him a cable which was framed and hung on
the wall of White's at the insistence of Jimmy de Roths-
child. It read, "Hearty congratulations on winning a neck
cleverly." How Broughton must have treasured it as a sign
that he was still accepted in the fold of his fellow officers
and peers! Lord Carnarvon has written about his old racing
friend in his memoirs, *No Regrets*. The two men had met
in the army in 1914, and it is clear from the book that
Carnarvon considered he knew Broughton better than anybody. In May 1980 I wrote to him, asking for an interview.

There was a period in the early 1970s when Lord
Carnarvon was a star of the television talk shows in Britain,
playing the role of the unashamed feudalist and plutocrat.
He was the size of a jockey, but looked more like a bookmaker who had been out in a lot of bad weather, and
sometimes he spoke like one. He winked a lot and told
dirty jokes, and talked about women's legs and ankles.
When he laughed it all came out in one loud syllable:
"Hah!"

Forty years after Carnarvon had sent his cable to

Broughton, I drove down to his home, Highclere Castle, in Berkshire, with Tessa Reay, grand-daughter of Vera and Jock Delves Broughton. It was a warm morning late in May, with patches of coolness in the air and a bloom across the landscaped park. Golden pheasants stepped through the unfenced grass along the gravel drive. It seemed that nothing here had changed for centuries; certainly not since Broughton had come as a guest for the racing weekends in the 1920s.

I rang the bell at the front door, but there was no answer, so we made our way into the great Victorian Gothic hall, lit from a skylight, with its soaring pillars and leather wall coverings. In search of Lord Carnarvon we wandered into a large room glimmering with perfect Empire furniture, the chairs and sofas otherwise upholstered in the dark green leather favoured by the St. James's Street clubs.

Great clocks ticked together, yet next to the armchair beside the fireplace was a cheap green alarm clock with a black face and luminous hands—the only hint of present-day occupancy. Possibly this was the room where Lord Carnarvon took his naps. We called out into a passage beyond the brown baize door, but our voices echoed back. We separated and searched the ground floor. In the cloakroom was a sauna bath and a record of the Earl's daily steam temperatures. There were the usual racing caricatures and cartoons and a rhyme on the theme of declining sexual power.

> His sporting days are over
> His little light is out
> What used to be his sex appeal
> Is now his water-spout.

Then Lord Carnarvon appeared and briefly mistook me for Cyril Connolly. Half an hour later a butler also appeared and apologised for the doorbell being broken.

Carnarvon was neatly dressed in twill trousers, a greenish tweed jacket, and immaculately polished brown golfing shoes with studded soles. His speech delivery was part Willie Whitelaw (emphasis and bluster) and part Earl Mountbatten (rolling stentorian).

"Vera's grand-daughter," he said. "I can't get over it. Now. You'll have anything you want. You just have to ask." He faced the drinks tray. "Are you married and blissfully happy with lots of children?"

"No, I'm divorced," said Lady Reay.

"All right, darling."

"Darling Vera," he continued. "Now. Ask me anything you like. Most glamorous woman of her day. Quite, quite lovely. She was always being mistaken for Gladys Cooper, which I think gave her an enormous kick as she was very fond of people admiring her. I don't know any woman in the world who doesn't like being admired."

"Did you ever have an affair with her?"

"No. No. Certainly not. Never laid a hand on her. I find it damned hard to credit, but darling Vera, I don't think she willingly went to bed with anybody.

"Her interests were shooting with a rifle (probably used a shotgun too, but certainly a rifle). And there you are. And if you said to Vera, I'd like you to come with me to the source of the Mekong Delta, one thing and another. Where's that? Timbuktu or something. Will there be crocodiles? Yes, darling, guaranteed. Will we have to sleep under mosquito nets? And I'd say Oh, I haven't asked. Oh, yes I'm sure we will. Is it civilised? No. Not civilised at all. I'd love to go. I'm just giving you a picture."

Tessa Reay said that her grandmother had travelled to places which were then very remote: Burma and the Philippines, and had eaten human flesh. "Oh, I've no doubt," said Lord Carnarvon.

"I wouldn't have thought she was in love with Lord Moyne," he said. "My guess is that Vera said to herself, 'Here's Walter. I must be as nice as possible.' I cannot and do not believe that Vera was the sort of person who fell in love. I've never seen the slightest sign of her being unfaithful or anything else. I think she was one of those ladies who didn't ever want to hurt anybody's feelings; don't think she would ever consciously do so. I think she said to herself, 'I like the fleshpots, who doesn't? Well, there it is. Walter's mad about me and I'm not going to quarrel with him or anyone else.' But I find it very hard to believe that she surrendered herself willingly to anybody. Darling Vera. I don't think sex interested her.

"Jock in my opinion was a *weak* man," Lord Carnarvon continued. "He was *not* in any way a *brave* man." He leaned forward to emphasise the point, clearly resisting the word "coward." "I probably knew him better than anybody," he continued. "He faked a sunstroke in 1914 as he feared going to France. He was basically a dishonest person and rather vain.

"And when Vera wanted to go off with Lord Moyne, he would say, 'I hope you have fun. God bless you. See you when you get back.' That's not to say his feelings weren't hurt. He was too weak to say no—a *mari complaisant*.

"Vera probably said to herself, 'I'm no longer amused by Jock,' who wasn't a very amusing man—didn't tell funny stories or anything else. Hardly ever spoke. He was a very ordinary chap, neatly dressed, trim moustache. Perfectly nice. (The best-dressed men of the time were me, number one, Broughton, Jock Buchanan Jardine, Hugo Londesborough and Burghie Westmorland.) Jock was perhaps a little vain and I think damn stupid, if you ask me.

"Hate being horrible about anybody and never am, but I think he was. Not much grey matter.

"Do you want to know what Jock was most interested in? Going to the loo every day in the morning. There. You've got it straight from the horse's mouth."

I suggested that Broughton had run out of money by the time he went to Kenya, or that at least he was hard up. "He *was*," said Carnarvon. "Up at Doddington he'd lived high, wide and handsome. He'd betted and lost. And what's more, what he did was very dishonest. He'd rather make £10 crookedly than £100 straight. He, unbeknownst to Vera and the children, sold property and pictures which did not belong to him, which he'd no right to sell. Yoh, yes. Yes. Only weak men succumb to temptations to do dishonest things. That is a fact. I mean a man, poor devil, he's starving, he snatches a bun out of a stall. I can understand that. But Jock was never starving. I can imagine he would be very shy coming back to England, because he knew perfectly well that he'd done something which, if found out, he was liable to go to prison for. I'm certain he appreciated that."

Why, asked Tessa Reay, had her grandfather taken such risks to maintain such extravagance? "Because once you do something, my dear, you get accustomed to it," he said. "It's very difficult to give it up. Only strong men are able to do that. He was not a strong man and I'm certain that he was determined that what he'd got used to he was going to do for the rest of his days."

Our trio moved into lunch, across the great space of the dining room. Lord Carnarvon faced one of Van Dyck's monumental portraits of Charles I mounted on a horse. "Erroll? Knew him," said Lord Carnarvon. "Stoat." Stoat? "One of the greatest stoats of his generation—one of the great pouncers of all time.

"He was a *coureur par excellence*." *Coureur*? "Runner after. He certainly was. *Had* been very attractive. *Got* rather bloated in Kenya."

We lunched on ravioli, Highclere lamb with new potatoes, and strawberries. "Gorellas," said Lord Carnarvon. "G-O-R-E-L-L-A-S. Dutch. They come from Holland. They're better than Cambridge. Not so juicy, but they're good fruiters.

"Erroll was double-crossing Diana with Alice de Trafford," he continued. "That affair wasn't over at all. I don't think Jock Broughton had the guts to kill anybody. He could no more have shot Erroll with that hand than he could have shot an elephant. Damn bad shot. Incapable of lifting any weight. He couldn't have held an army revolver.''

But why did he take up with a woman so much younger than himself—one who was not particularly well accepted by his friends? Was he in love with Diana . . . ?

''He was a weak man, therefore I would have said he liked pretty women.

''He was not a great performer. He'd take a girl a box of chocolates to her bedroom and claim the rest; whether or not Diana was pretty at the time, never appealed to me, but that's neither here nor there. HA!

''There's no possible way of knowing,'' Lord Carnarvon went on, ''because what's one man's meat is another man's poison. I mean, to me, *hands* are very important things, *nails* are very important things. After all, hands caress the man. Therefore to be touched by anybody who bites their nails—ooghaargh—puts me off. Oh no, darling, don't look at your nails. They're not bitten. Ridiculous.

''It's one of the first things I look at. I am a person who pays great attention to hands. Lot of people don't. I've known *endless* men who pop it in, go to bed with a woman or anything else, who've got hideous hands. Think nothing of it. And so on. *Everybody* is different.

''I myself pay great attention to hands, and I pay a great deal of attention to legs too. If people have got hideous legs, fat legs, I mean to say—poor devils—they can't help it. They didn't make themselves like that. There again, I, Carnarvon, have always been *put off*.''

''What happens,'' asked Tessa Reay, ''to a woman when she loses her looks?''

''ZERO,'' replied Lord Carnarvon.

We were now clearly straying away from our subject. But is this how Broughton and his contemporaries talked?

"I have in my time known perfectly beautiful women, not a brain in their head, dumb as anything and I've said, 'I'm going to give you a barrelling *and* I'm going to enjoy it.'

"My first wife was quite, *quite* beautiful. Then Tilly [Losch, the actress—Lord Carnarvon's second wife] was very beautiful. She had a very rare thing. She had green eyes with yellow, amber pupils. Now you only see that once in a lifetime. And she had naturally dark, I think it's called 'Titian,' hair. Can't say she had the greatest legs —she's dead now—then she had been a dancer. Imperial Ballet in Vienna. Develops the calf and thigh muscles. Take lots, tuck in. Take lots of cream. Anything you want. Arrive sober and leave drunk. That's what I always say to my guests."

After lunch he showed us into an enormous drawing room lined with leather-bound books, densely furnished with more magnificent objects. I asked about the origins of a piece of furniture. Was it French? Italian? "Can't tell you how I got hold of it," he said. "All here when I arrived." He pointed out a chair and table on which he claimed Napoleon had signed his abdication at Elba. "See those scratches on the arm? Said to have been made by his finger-nails. In frustration. Soft wood at the time." The room in which we stood had been badly damaged by fire some years earlier. The plaster rosettes on the ceiling—"macaroons" as Lord Carnarvon called them— needed replacing. He was abroad when the builder cabled him with the estimate: £150 per macaroon. "I cabled back," snapped Lord Carnarvon, "NO MACAROONS."

Lord Carnarvon then sold a copy of *No Regrets* to Tessa Reay for £5.95, inscribed it and disappeared. He was gone a long time and I heard Tessa Reay calling out in some distant passage, "Lord Carnarvon? Lord Carnarvon? Where *are* you?" He returned to see us off on our journey back to London.

17
PALACES
AND
APPEARANCES

THE MOST REWARDING PART of our investigation into the mysterious temperament of Delves Broughton began with the moment of his acquittal. He had reacted slowly to the verdict. The judge was already thanking the jury, exonerating them from further duty, when Broughton was seen to blush, to light up with pleasure and excitement, and then, on his way out of the courtroom, to say to Harragin, according to one version of that ill-heard remark, "I'm afraid I've slipped through your fingers." In anticipation of the verdict, Diana and Kaplan had arranged a party for Broughton in Kaplan's house. A guest remembers its end of term flavour and the roars of nostalgic laughter when June Carberry raised her brandy glass and said, "It doesn't look too good for the old boy today."

Broughton described the acclamation and attention he received, and his own euphoria, in a circular that he mailed off to his friends in England a few days later, attaching a fulsome letter of congratulation from Morris. (On his return to Johannesburg, Morris was asked who he thought the murderer might be and had replied, "Good Heavens, I forgot to ask.") Broughton made a hundred copies of each document. His purpose was clearly to diminish the air of scandal surrounding the case; to brush the whole episode aside as an annoying interruption in his life; to project it now as an amusing story for his friends:

I only wish I could tell you the inner history, but it would be censored, so it is of no use.

It was a ridiculous case and I was a victim of unfortunate circumstances . . . I was in Gaol from March 6 until July 1st, and was never worried or depressed and kept absolutely fit all the time. Being on remand I could have my food and drink sent in and as much to smoke or read as I liked, but no drink [sic], which did not affect me in the least. I had lots of visitors and always walked for two hours each day and I have never felt better than when in Gaol.

I got a fellow prisoner to clean out my cell etc. and had no discomfort except the small, whitewashed cell 10' × 8'. I had a very comfortable bed and never had one sleepless night.

I read a lot and played games a lot.

Much of the Trial was frightfully boring, especially the evidence and cross-examination on ballistics.

I went into the box one Thursday and came out the following Thursday, actually five days in the box, three and a half of which I was subject to cross-examination by the Attorney General.

They never made me contradict myself or shook me in the least; I thought most of the questions futile, they were all easy to parry, but [it] makes one use one's brain and you have to be alert.

In this country they do not lock up the Jury till they retire to consider their verdict and that was the only time I felt any strain whatsoever, to my eternal shame. I own that I did then, and could not sit down for long on end, and kept walking up and down for three hours and twenty-five minutes.

When the verdict was announced at 9:15 p.m., in a crowded Court there was a sigh of relief from all the audience, the Court being packed; some clapping.

It took me ten minutes to come to and realise I was a free man; but I had a big group of people to shake hands with, headed by most of the Police.

I had practically the whole country solidly behind me from the start. I drove with some friends to a house where Diana was waiting for me. I would not let her come into Court the last day. She, poor dear, has had a much worse time than I have.

We then proceeded to make whoopee and had a very late night.

I never felt better or happier in my life than I did the next day. Neither my health nor my nerves were affected and I have, except for the wait for the Jury's verdict, never felt any strain.

The wicked part is that it has cost me £5,000 which I have not got and of course, as the Crown can do no wrong, I can recover nothing.

I got the best Counsel in Africa—Morris of Johannesburg.

I took the definite view that when your life is in danger, you cannot afford to worry about expense, also there was the obligation to clear my name for the sake of my family.

All the prison officials were kindness itself. There is more charity in prison than in most places outside.

So ends what would have been, except for the war, an historic trial, but, I believe that Jocelyn Erroll (the 22nd Earl) Hereditary High Constable of Scotland, who walked immediately behind the King and Queen and in front of all the other Peers, including Dukes on official occasions in Scotland, was the first Earl to be murdered since Bosworth,* the boyfriend of Mary, Queen of Scots, in the reign of Queen Elizabeth.

His family has been bound up with that of Scotland and has several times intermarried with Royalty and goes far back into the mists of Scottish history.

Is Broughton bragging? There is no mention of the tragedy of Erroll's death, or a hint of sadness at the loss of a "great friend," or even a reference to the unexplained circumstances of the shooting.

In his covering letter to Lady d'Avigdor-Goldsmid, Broughton wrote,

Diana has been loyalty itself to me since my misfortune overtook me, and what happened about her was largely my fault and bad

---

* Historically, Broughton is way off the mark. He may be referring to the Earl of Bothwell, who became Mary's third husband. Bothwell masterminded the gunpowder plot against her second husband, Lord Darnley in 1567, although Darnley was strangled by another hand. Bothwell died insane in a Danish dungeon some years later.

temper . . . [He added here the line about Diana's "disillusion-ment" with Erroll and the "revelations" that had since come out about him.] So I decided the only thing to do is to resume our life as if nothing has happened, and am quite happy. We are on our way to Ceylon where I have a job of work to do . . .

He ended the letter on a note of anxiety—with a standard question that occurs in each of his letters of that period that I have seen:

Do write to me darling and tell me truthfully how people have reacted to my case at home and whether you think I shall be able to come back after the war and resume my normal life or not. The worst feature of this b . . . y case has been having all my private affairs broadcast to the world . . .

After Diana's supreme effort during the trial, her rallying to her husband's cause, the prospect of Broughton reviving his plans to visit Ceylon, subjecting them both to a long sea voyage, must have been unbearable. By now their relationship was paralysed by guilt and suspicion, and Diana was not only frightened of him, she despised him as well. She had no choice but to go with him. Yet Broughton must have been aware, in view of all that had happened, that for Diana such a trip amounted to a form of torture.

Towards the end of August, at a moment when the war in Europe and North Africa looked particularly bad for the allies, Broughton wrote from India to a friend in England:

The Nawab of Bhopal was the best polo player in the World the last time I was in India in 1927 and is a Mohamedan. We stayed at Bhopal and then down to his country Palace 45 miles out where he had a very cheery party (all Indians). It has two lovely swimming pools and he has masses of ponies. Tennis courts etc., and they all danced out of doors on a laid down floor after dinner about 16 of them. I sat next to the "Begum" (his wife) on one side at dinner and a really lovely [word omitted] on the other, about 20. They all speak English perfectly. We came on here by train. This is a lovely "Palace" and we have 6 huge rooms and 4 servants to look after us. We have lunch and dinner with His Highness, who takes us out motoring and to see his other 3 palaces and on the lake in a motor launch. This lake is about 30 miles away, and we saw 2 tiger and . . . 3 leopards coming down to drink. This place might be a million miles away from any War. There are no Europeans and life goes on in exactly the way it did a thousand years ago, except for H.H.'s motors and the motor launch and every modern comfort in his Palaces. I should have said amongst the people. The town is most picturesque with cows (which are sacred animals) all over the streets. Peacocks everywhere, and monkeys everywhere. His Highness has the finest collection of Pearls in the World [Broughton's capitals], and studs of other priceless jewels. He showed them all to us last night. The collection is valued at 8 millions.

By the end of September Broughton and Diana were back in Kenya and Broughton had begun to write frequently to Mrs. Woodhouse. In November 1941 he wrote:

Darling Marie,

I haven't heard a word from you since your cable of congratulations. Did you get a long letter I wrote you with notes on my Trial. I went to Ceylon and India after my case was over to do a job of work and came back here end of September last. I had a lovely time in both countries and was entertained lavishly. It appealed to my delicate sense of humour in Ceylon as being just out of jail that the person who entertained me most was the Lord Chief Justice of Ceylon who most respectfully called me "Sir" all the time. I went out and back by the "Bank" Line. Very comfortable boats with very good food, cabins and stewards. Do you remember the effect that baby lobster we had at Southampton on the boat at the beginning of our trip to Madeira had on you. I have taken to farming on a large scale out here, and have put in a thousand acres of wheat, and sell £200 worth of milk a month and have guaranteed the Government to produce a thousand pigs this year and a ton of vegetables a week. I therefore work all and every day. The difficulties of farming nowadays are awful. One can get no spare parts and there is practically nothing in the shops. Luckily this is a perfect climate and labour is cheap. I pay my labourers 8/- a month so you can have about 20.

I have a very nice small house 10 miles from Nairobi with a really divine garden. Labour is so cheap that I can have 20 gardeners for the cost of one in England. I have 20 acres of grounds with tennis court (hard), swimming pool, 3 ponies, 6 dogs, 2 monkies [sic], 2 mongeese [sic] and peacocks. It has a divine view of the Ngong hills.

I am frightfully homesick. Do write to me tell me what people think of my case at home. I do long to hear from you and all about your dear self.

Give my love to Jim.

My fondest love to you darling.

Jock

Broughton's worry about re-establishing his position was now becoming an obsession. He had already told his jailer that he would commit suicide if his friends at home rejected him. Two weeks after the murder, some time before his arrest, he had seen the first signs of his ostracisation. He told the court, "Mr. Wheelock [his agent], Mr. Hopcraft [his partner], and Mr. and Mrs. Carberry came to see me, but none of the friends I thought would come to see me came near me." Soames, as we have seen, had left the country. The Carberrys had also left for Johannesburg soon after the trial. Dickinson had been sent to Abyssinia, Pembroke and Lezard to Cairo. There was no question of speaking to Gwladys after what she had said in court.

And as Carnarvon was cabling his congratulations from White's, so, across the street at Brooks's Club, debts were being settled. The Brooks's betting book records the following entry on May 25th, 1941:

His Grace the Duke of St. Albans bets Sir Mark Grant Sturgis £5 that Sir Delves Broughton will be hanged for the murder of the Earl of Erroll.

Yet Broughton felt the acquittal had changed all that. On his return from Ceylon, he hoped to be both a popular hero and a celebrity. Instead both he and Diana were ignored and shunned, "cut by everyone," as Kaplan remembered it. Diana was seen as the scarlet woman who had shamed the community. She was now verbally scorned in public, and not only by the officials. The whole gang of public school ex-officers, with one or two exceptions, had now turned against her. Broughton, surrounded with suspicion, was dropped like a hot potato. Bill Allen, on leave from Addis Ababa in June 1941, wrote, "I gathered that consorting with the Broughtons was looked on with an unfavourable eye by Lord Francis Scott, who was then Military Secretary."

The excommunication was swift and businesslike. The committee of the Muthaiga Club was the first to do its duty and ban them both from its precincts. This extract from a proposed history of the Club, written by a former member who has asked for anonymity, comes from the minutes of the meeting that decided on cancelling the Broughtons' membership:

Before the committee met in 1941 and before the Annual General Meeting, Lord Erroll was murdered. He was living at the Club at the time and was found shot in a motor car, on his way back from Karen where he had been dining [sic]. In his younger days his career was chequered and he was often in trouble with the Club Committee: latterly he had done an outstanding job of work as Secretary of the Kenya Manpower Committee. The circumstances of Lord Erroll's death, the titled and well known people involved, plus the fact that he was a member of the Muthaiga Country Club committee, brought it a great deal of unwelcome, lurid and inaccurate publicity. This went on for some months and reached a crescendo during the subsequent trial of Sir Delves Broughton for murder.

A picture was painted of a Kenya society which, even in a desperate war, could not stop from behaving in a frivolous and lax manner. The Club committee was, not unnaturally, extremely perturbed by events which it was powerless to influence.

However, when a party was given at the Club following the acquittal of Sir Delves Broughton, the Committee, after a Special Meeting, did act strongly about what they considered behaviour which brought the club into disrepute.

Whatever his good intentions, the author cannot cloud history with such discretion. The fact is that the Broughtons were told that they were no longer welcome at the Muthaiga Country Club. The main objection, as the author told me separately, was that "the acquittal of a person for the murder of a member of the Club Committee was being celebrated at the Club."

Thus life changed dramatically for them both. Broughton was now faced with the very things he dreaded most —loneliness and obscurity—and in his letters the signs of depression began to show. Significantly, perhaps, he began to talk about Erroll. He wrote to Marie Woodhouse, "I always had the sympathy of the general public as he was a professional breaker-up of homes with lots of enemies, and the popular saying in Kenya was, 'whoever had done it deserved a medal' "—a theme he was to repeat later on. And he began to regret his parting with Vera, echoing the conversation with Gwladys on the day of the funeral. To another English friend he wrote, "I have never had any luck after Vera and I parted after 27 years of married life. It has brought neither of us any luck." (Broughton is referring to Moyne's persistent unwillingness to marry her.)

The job of work that Broughton describes was in reality not very demanding—a light routine of office work in Nairobi, while his agent, Wheelock, and his partner, Hopcraft, managed the Lake Naivasha estate and the coffee plantation at Spring Valley. Indeed, Broughton's office routine came to a halt towards the end of 1941. As he began to talk about Erroll, so he made the one move that showed that neither he nor Diana could ever put his memory away. Broughton, incredibly, moved into Erroll's house. He rented the Djinn Palace on Lake Naivasha, which had been empty since Erroll's death. He even tried to buy it from the trustees' agents, but he couldn't find the money. Erroll's portrait in his Coronation robes was still at the top of the stairs. And there is, to this day, a picture in the hall of Molly Ramsay-Hill reclining on a *canapé*.

Broughton's farming land on Lake Naivasha was hardly a convincing reason for such a reckless move. The house, whose garden slopes steeply to the water, and its surroundings are hauntingly beautiful. But Lake Naivasha, then and now, is also a strange and lonely spot which gives off a sense of isolation and of danger as well. A cold breeze blows off the Aberdares, and there is always fresh news of drowning, though the water itself, which gets deeper year by year, looks harmless and placid. It was as if Broughton had gone there on purpose to confront his own desperate loneliness. He was to become intensely unhappy in the house, while his marriage to Diana entered the final stage of its painfully slow death.

One day Broughton went to visit Paula Long, who was recovering in hospital from a serious car accident. He confided to her his main worry, that he would have to resign from his clubs (the Turf, the Guards', etc.) on his return. She found this odd, but "typical of the vain and sociable." He said that he thought a service had been performed when Erroll was shot (a repeat of his new theme), that Erroll had "had it coming to him." She noticed the way he expressed it and decided that he was trying to justify *himself*—and, in effect, confessing to the murder. This finally convinced her that Broughton had done it— a suspicion she had already formed during the trial. She had often walked with him and found him "a perfectly good walker." But for her the crucial piece of evidence concerns the golf stocking found, charred and bloodstained, in the bonfire. Broughton had said he had never worn golf stockings. Mrs. Long not only remembers him wearing them "the whole time," but even had a photograph to prove it.

Broughton, she said, was a pathetic figure whose

pride had revolted at his humiliations at the hands of Diana and Joss Erroll and at the miserable uncertainty of never knowing what was being planned against him. He was besotted by Diana, she said, even after the trial, and wildly jealous. She described Erroll and Diana dancing, ''glued together as if they were making it. It was a *coup de foudre*, and Broughton looked on miserably.''

So, she surmised, Broughton got into the car, wanting to continue discussing the divorce (on one other occasion —the day before the murder—he had also chosen the close quarters of Erroll's car for an identical discussion). He rode beside Erroll, who may then have said ''something cutting,'' got out of the car and shot him, either with the car door open, or through the window. He would have had no problem, in her opinion, running or walking back home. In fact, because June almost certainly invented Broughton's alibi, he could have taken as long as he liked to get back to the house.

These recollections from Paula Long carry considerable weight in the final analysis. Much of what she told Connolly, and me some years later, revealed an uncanny intuition and perception about the events and personalities of the period—qualities for which she is well-known by her acquaintances.

THE BROUGHTONS knew almost nobody on the lake and even in that small and interdependent community they were treated as pariahs by everybody, except for one extraordinary man called Gilbert Colvile.

Colvile—only son of Major-General Sir Henry Colvile of Lullington Hall, Derby, and ''patron of one living''—had been at Eton with Broughton and Lord Francis Scott. He had become one of the most Africanised of Masai-lovers, and he was among the biggest cattle ranchers in the country. A small, awkward, chinless man, he was also a miser and a hermit, who lived in comparative squalor with his many dogs, and whose house had the sour, wood-smoke smell of the Masai *boma*. He dressed with con-spicuous shabbiness and knew as much about cattle as the Masai themselves. Before long he had turned into Diana's official protector, not so much against the hostile com-munity as against Broughton himself, who had become miserable and aggressive and whose drinking had begun to dominate his moods.

From now on Diana began to show an outstanding talent for managing a smooth transition between one hus-band and another, often with a dancing partner in the wings. A poignant description of this strange, suspended period of the Broughtons' lives came in a letter to Con-nolly from Hertfordshire, from Albert Andrew, written on Christmas Day 1969:

Dear Mr. Connolly,

I was enthralled by your account of the Erroll murder, and the first thing that I must do when I go to a bookshop is to try to order the other book on the subject—if it is still in print. As you are so obviously keen on the story, and background, I felt I must write to tell you the little I know. I only wish I could be more definite about dates. About March 1942 I was staying with the McCraes who had a bungalow by the shores of Lake Nai-vasha. We had heard that the (by then) notorious Delves Brough-tons had taken a house in the district, and Mrs. McCrae, Margaret her daughter and our neighbours, Captain and Mrs. Ralston all vowed that nothing would induce them to acknowledge them. (Lady D.B. was always referred to as "that woman.")

Then one day (I think early in April) I was alone in the house with Mrs. McCrae when one of the house boys came to tell us that there was a white woman at the door who wished to see the lady of the house. Mrs. McCrae went to see, and then brought in what proved to be Diana Delves Broughton. She was in great distress, as her husband had fallen from his horse. So I went with a couple of natives to the place she had described, and found Sir D.B. half lying in the bush, obviously in pain. We had to go back to the house for a makeshift stretcher to try to get him to the house; but in the meantime Mrs. McCrae had rung up presumably the Red Cross in Naivasha, and they came to take over as we were trying to cope.

After that Diana came to thank Mrs. McCrae for her help, and they were gradually brought into the lakeside circle. They must have found it very different from the circle they had known, for although there was plenty of bridge and tennis and dancing, there was none of the Happy Valley type of life. Diana, however, seemed eager to be friendly—I can well see how she settled down in Kenya. She wasn't really snobbish. Her husband didn't come so much. You say the break came in May 1942; yet I feel sure that they were together at a dance at the Country Club in June 1942. I distinctly remember dancing with Diana, and taking her back to her party which included Colvile and Broughton. Could there have been a short reconciliation about this time? Diana was always polite to him when we were around, and it was only when I was in Nairobi in the July or August that I heard of the rift. We were all sorry, but as she was young enough to be his daughter, we were not surprised.

Only one other person mentioned did I know, and that was Idina (I believe she was Idina Soltau when I knew her). Nobody could have been kinder or more thoughtful, and she was most certainly not snobbish. She was willing to be nice to anyone, and the last thing she thought about was class. She was exceptionally nice to her servants.

Frankly I found far more snobbery in Government, Army and Missionary Circles than I did among the so called good-timers. The last named would accept anyone but bores. If one played a moderately good game of bridge, and took one's drinks without becoming objectionable, one was persona grata with them. They probably were drones—but very amusing ones.

However, thank you once again for reviving memories of a most interesting part of my life.

Yours sincerely,

Albert W. Andrew

As Broughton's isolation increased, he began to see Mrs. Woodhouse as his only loyal friend. In early May he wrote to her and told her he wanted to come home.

My Darling Marie,

So loved getting your letter and I am so sorry to hear your news about Jim which came as a complete surprise to me. What a rotten thing marriage is. Nowadays it always seems to end in disaster. I shall come home as quickly as I can, but doubt whether it will be possible before the end of the war. I am very unhappy out here, thousands of miles from all my friends.

Do write often. I miss you unbelievably.

Broughton now made a mysterious trip to Mombasa. There is no indication of where he stayed, or what he did, except that, having barely recovered from his riding accident, he fell down a railway embankment and seriously hurt his back.

This episode is mentioned in a letter I received from Mrs. Molly Hall, known in her Kenya days as "Woody" Hall, who was now living in Mallorca. The letter, which was undated, arrived in February 1970.

Dear Mr. Fox,

Lady Nihill [wife of Sir Barclay Nihill, Chief Justice of Kenya from 1947–50, whom I had met] has asked me to tell you what I can remember about Sir Delves Broughton's last days. First of all let me make it quite clear that he did not confess to the murder, what did happen was this . . .

Jane Wynne Eaton [known as "Silver Jane," a famous East African aviatrix], who was living with me in Mombasa, asked him point blank if he did it—he remembered he had an engagement and left. No answer one way or the other.

On the other hand he would go over the whole business, his time in prison and the fact that there was *no* motive. He also talked a lot about his wife, Vera. Apparently she was in love with somebody else and hoped he would marry her if she were free—hence their divorce—Jock was heartbroken and felt he must get away, but not alone. There were *two* women who might make a trip with him, his first choice could not get away, but Diana "jumped" at the idea. The marriage was forced on them, as you already know.* After the trial, when he came out of prison, he spent two weeks in Mombasa. He would arrive in the morning at my house and more or less sit about all day. I have no idea where he slept. He vaguely talked about a tent and I suggested he might like to put it on a piece of land I had beside the house, where he could have a bath and my boys would look after him, but he said he was all right where he was.

Mombasa was jam packed with troops, etc. A tent: very mysterious. Where could he have put it? An African came to see him one day—not an ordinary African "boy"—very tall and hefty, possibly Somali. He walked on to the verandah, where we were having coffee. I gathered he wanted money.

Jock said, "He wants money for his food." I said, "Finish your coffee and tell him to wait for you in the boys' quarters." But I was talking into thin air. They were gone. Jock returned later, and the subject was not mentioned. Jock came with me to the Club one evening, to change library books. He liked to go to the Club, but would not go alone, although the Secretary had told him he was most welcome to use it. We had two whiskies, and I drove him back to my house. It was raining and I offered to drive him to his "tent"—but he would not hear of it, or come into my house, he wanted to walk! At this point I must tell you my house overlooked the harbour—a broad road, grass verge, quite wide, and a cutting for a little goods train. That is where he fell, right onto the lane below. He appeared next day in plaster from his neck to his waist, in great pain. I saw him off at the boat some weeks later. [Broughton had returned to Nairobi in the meantime.] No luggage, just a bed roll and his shaving kit. He travelled as a deck passenger, still in plaster.

I know Diana well. I've stayed with her at the Gin [sic] Palace when she was married to Gilbert Colvile. I was trying to cope with Micky Dew [née Grosvenor]. No nursing home would have her. A very difficult woman, with a whip in her hand or on her bed, which she used on her boys.

I often thought one day she would be murdered! I was rather frantic being in that house, but one couldn't leave her ill as she

* A common misapprehension in Kenya is that they were not allowed into the country except as man and wife—a notion that was quashed at the trial.

was. Diana and Gilbert came over to see us one day and with no hesitation at all, took us both off to the "Gin Palace." I only mention this because I don't like what you wrote about Gilbert Colvile. He was generous, shy perhaps, and charming. Diana went everywhere with him, into deepest darkest Africa, where he visited his vast acres and counted his cattle etc. Diana is kind and warm-hearted.

It does not seem to have occurred to anybody that Joss Erroll might have been murdered by a woman—a woman who used a gun in the Gare du Nord and wounded the man she married later. A woman who bound her head up in yards of chiffon, got into bed covered with flowers and shot herself after Joss Erroll's death. She had a motive, if you call unrequited love a motive.

I wish it were possible to talk to you. So difficult to write. A clue here and there, which might be useful. For instance, that mysterious African in Mombasa. Jock had obviously known him for years. The lost revolver. What could be easier than to give him the revolver and report the loss to the police? The boy could so easily have got into the back of the car that night while Joss was in the house. I hope I have been of some help.

Yours sincerely,

M. M. Hall,

The fall down the embankment, the mysterious Somali—Broughton was beginning to resemble Orestes, stumbling about Africa, pursued by furies. He managed to return to Nairobi, still in plaster, to make one last attempt to get Diana back. He asked Dickinson to meet him at Grogan's office, and begged him to intercede with her. When Dickinson refused, pointing out that Diana would never return to him, Broughton, by now "deranged with alcohol and nerves" according to Kaplan, began to shout and issue threats against them both.

In July Mrs. Woodhouse wrote to him with the news that her husband was dead. Broughton cabled back "Returning immediately." He wrote to her on August 9th, from Nairobi,

Darling Marie,

I am trying to get home as soon as I possibly can. Fly to Johannesburg, train to Cape Town, and then home by boat. All very mad and may take six months. I will contact you when, and if, I get back, immediately. Longing to see you again.

> All my fondest love,
>
> Jock
>
> I return alone.

In the end Broughton left for Mombasa in September of that year.

18
PEARLS
AND
OYSTERS

D I A N A ' S   F R I E N D Hugh Dickinson had now begun to move to the centre of the story. It was Poppy who
had told us—at first in the vaguest terms—that Broughton
was making threats against him, and it began to be apparent
that Dickinson was invariably present, in a minor role, at
the most telling moments in the drama, except, of course,
on the night Erroll was murdered. He was somehow in-
dispensable to the Broughtons.

The trusted friend from Doddington days with the
"outsider" tendencies, Dickinson's life revolved increasingly around Diana as the years went by. When he met
her at Mombasa, she handed him her marriage certificate
for safe keeping, as well as the contract—the marriage
"pact" that she had drawn up with Broughton—a gesture
on Diana's part that was never explained. The trio formed
up again for the safari in the Southern Masai Reserve a
few days after Erroll was shot. And, at the end, before
Broughton left for England, he needed Dickinson as a
broker between himself and his wife.

I knew Dickinson was still alive, but he seemed to
have lost contact with all of the old Kenya network, and
it took me months to track him down. Letters to his former
regiment and to the army records office at first drew a
blank. When I persisted I was given the wartime address

of his bank. Towards the end of October 1969, near the
deadline for our article, Dickinson telephoned me, to my
amazement, at the *Sunday Times* offices. He had received
my letter within a week, and was willing to see me. He
was now the managing director of an office cleaning firm
in London. His telephone number was listed, he said,
under his wife's maiden name. I set a date for lunch at
the Savoy Grill on November 5th, and sent a cable to
Connolly.

On our way to that rendezvous, I told Connolly that
there would be a photographer waiting in an alley outside
the entrance to the Savoy Grill, ready to take a picture of
Dickinson as he came out after lunch, and that at a certain
moment during the meal I would be called to the telephone
—the prearranged signal from the photographer that he
was in place. Connolly was seized with fear at the thought
of being caught out using such surreptitious journalistic
methods.

The menu, however, helped to calm his nerves. Indeed, for once it severely diverted his attention—his notebook records the opening round:

DICKINSON Nov. 5 (anniversary of DB's marriage).
Savoy Grill (oysters, partridges, claret!). Dickinson thin, grey,
pink faced, good features, quiet, reserved, nervous. [Dickinson's
hair was, in fact, blond, according to my own notes, with a slight
ginger tinge.] Hates publicity. Had a bad time after the trial.
Comes from old Northumberland family. Brother or brother in
law High Sheriff. Sherry. Talk of Savoy in old days. Kenya in
old days. Offers to tell whole story for £20,000.

The offer was turned down. Dickinson, however, did
not get up and leave, and the following is the essence of
our conversation, extracted from our notebooks.

He had met Diana at a cocktail party, and through
her, Delves Broughton. He was a frequent visitor at Doddington ("very comfortable, fairly lavish"). He kept him-

self always very fit, and could play twelve sets of tennis even now, and walk any distance. His relationship with Diana was extremely warm and close, but platonic. It was true that he had followed her out to Kenya. He and Diana regarded themselves as half brother and sister. He got into trouble with the army because he had obtained compassionate leave on these grounds to look for a house for her, but really he just wanted to be near her. When the truth came out in court, he was exiled to Abyssinia.

Diana was a "wonderful woman," a great animator of the scene. Her boyfriends before 1940 were Mark Pilkington, Rory More O'Ferrall and Broughton. They had had many happy times together, although he hadn't seen her now for eighteen years. Yes, it was possible that she did love jewellery and clothes more than men. She was certainly not promiscuous.

Erroll was the greatest "athlete" in Kenya, where there were many "athletes," and was undoubtedly the love of Diana's life. He was much disliked and his reputation contributed a great deal to Broughton's acquittal. There is no doubt, he repeated, that Diana loved Erroll madly, and he her, "in his way." He kept himself immaculate and was always better groomed than anyone else.

Delves Broughton was *devious* above all—even capable of writing anonymous letters—very intelligent, *not* sour by any means, good company, friendly and sympathetic, but *two*-faced. He could be charming to someone and say "dreadful old cow," etc. the moment after. He would pat you on the back and say "absolutely marvellous, old boy," when his real feelings were "bloody awful." He was crazy about Diana physically, but they hated each other like poison later—i.e., at the time of the Erroll affair. It was natural for such love to turn to hate. He did not recall anything, or any conversation on the safari to suggest that Broughton had done it—it was, in any case, an unmentionable subject.

He last saw Broughton in Ewart Grogan's office in

Nairobi. Broughton had fallen down a railway embankment in Mombasa, and his back was in plaster. He thought he'd gone round the bend, and said to Broughton, "Why don't you go into a home or something?" Broughton said, "I can't live without Diana. You know her best and you're the only one who has any real influence over her. Won't you see her and try to persuade her?" Dickinson told him that nothing would induce Diana to go back to him and he wouldn't bother to try. Broughton was furious, began shouting. Dickinson said he could do nothing. He should cut his losses and go back to England. "He said a lot of mad things at the interview."

Dickinson admitted that he had smuggled the syringe and the morphine into Nairobi jail in a chocolate box because Broughton had told him that if the case went against him he wanted to commit suicide. When it was suggested that Broughton had tried to frame him in an attempt to get Diana back, he replied that Broughton had a grudge against him because of his close friendship with Diana. He would say no more than that.

He thought Broughton was morally capable of committing the murder, but not physically so, and he couldn't think of anyone else. He (Dickinson) was physically capable, but was away at Nyali in hospital. A cactus spine had pierced his foot (coral according to Poppy), and he had nearly had to have it amputated. He described the theories of African killers as unlikely, though "any African would disappear and never be seen again for a few shillings." Erroll would have stopped his car for any European who flagged him down to ask for a lift, but for no African.

Dickinson did seem nervous when the murder was mentioned; but when the robberies were talked about he became distinctly uneasy. He was in the South of France with Diana, Mark Pilkington, Rory More O'Ferrall and a few others two months before the war started. Their car was outside the restaurant in which they were lunching and the jewels had been left in the glove pocket by Dickinson. "Damn silly place . . ." etc. They were all interviewed by the insurance company, but only Freddie McIlvray, who was a South of France playboy, saw the police. Dickinson knew nothing about the picture theft from Doddington.

The telephone call came from the photographer, and the lunch broke up. But Dickinson, instead of walking out of the side entrance of the Grill and into the photographer's viewfinder, went back through the hotel to the front entrance, and got into a taxi. The only photographs taken that day were of two shamefaced reporters, Connolly and myself, flushed with claret, emerging from the Savoy Grill.

That Christmas of 1969, Dickinson went to stay with his brother Roy, near Newcastle. A description of the family gathering came to us by chance soon afterwards. It seemed that as a result of the article Hugh Dickinson had become the hero of the hour, and the talk in the house throughout Christmas was of nothing but the Erroll murder. According to our source, Dickinson told them that he knew who had done it, but had sworn total secrecy. He had not done it himself, he said, neither had Broughton, although Broughton, he said, had engineered it. He himself had been offered £25,000 for the story (sic) but there were certain things that couldn't be done for money. To me the story echoed those Kenya rumours and the claims to unique knowledge that could never be substantiated.

But there was one other snippet from the Christmas weekend which I had thought nothing of, until I looked at the transcript again while writing this book. Dickinson had been asked by one of the guests whether his alibi—his stay in the hospital on the coast—was genuine, and he had replied by giving a large wink. In the witness box he made a slip that went unnoticed. He told Harragin that he went into hospital on January 18th or 19th, "for about a month." But to Morris, who was questioning him about his meeting with Diana and Erroll at Malindi a week or so before the murder, and who asked, "After that meeting when did you next see Lady Broughton and Sir Delves?" Dickinson replied, "I think the last day in January." Was it a simple mistake? If Dickinson had taken trouble to establish a false alibi, he would not have exposed the flaw so glibly, and in court. Or would he? A slip, after all, is a slip.

19

A GOOD RACING MAN

BROUGHTON WAS AWARE that he was taking a serious risk in returning to England. His son, Sir Evelyn, revealed to me in 1980 that his father's affairs at home were in a chronically bad state. Broughton had hinted at this in his circular letter after the trial ("The wicked part is that it has cost me £5,000 which I have not got . . ."). He took pains in his letter to justify spending the money on his defence in what seemed like an appeal to the trustees in England.

It had filtered through to Evelyn, then aged twenty-four, through chance conversations and the mumbled commiserations of his father's friends on the racecourse and in the City, that things had gone disastrously wrong with the estate. The vast wealth that Delves Broughton had inherited had dwindled to almost nothing in fifteen years.

Evelyn's father had cheated the trust by selling around 32,500 acres of Chesire farmland at perhaps £50 an acre. He had pocketed the money—some £1.5 million—instead of channelling it through the estate.

"My father had a mania that he was hard up," said Evelyn, "even when there was no justification for it."

Broughton had also made consistent, almost compulsive mistakes with his investments—gambling, from the distance of Doddington, on the foreign exchange markets, on the commodity market, and investing in "tin pot gold mines," according to Evelyn. Betting took its toll as well (Broughton bet heavily on illegal cock-fighting) and Doddington, which had to be full every weekend, was still run on a roaring scale. Only trivial economies were attempted. The Hill Street house was closed down for a few weeks at a time; the staff was moderately cut down at Doddington.

Evelyn discovered that the trustees of the estate, some of them employees of Broughton himself, had put up no resistance to his father's activities. So, at the age of twenty-four Evelyn asked his solicitors to challenge them, and confronted his own father. "I told him I'd heard that there was nothing left of my eventual inheritance," he said, "and asked where the money had gone. My father lost his temper. He came round the desk and chased me from his study with a riding crop."

Evelyn then hired his own solicitors, hoping to save what was left. "I tied him up to the extent of the estate in the first year of the war because he'd been a naughty boy. And whatever money there was in the kitty was practically bugger all. It was something like £50,000. All the money from the sale of the land was gone.

"I'd never thought of it before," said Sir Evelyn, "but now I see why he left for Kenya and closed down Doddington."

When Broughton arrived in Liverpool in November 1942, there was no member of his family, nor even Mrs. Woodhouse to meet him. That was perhaps not surprising in view of the difficulties of wartime travel and the secrecy surrounding shipping timetables. Instead, Broughton was greeted by two detectives from Scotland Yard, who were well informed of his movements. Cheated of his murder conviction, Poppy had sent information ahead that once more put Broughton under criminal suspicion, this time for fraud. But there was, for the moment, no hard case against him, and he was allowed to reach Doddington.

Nevertheless, the interview had a crushing effect on Broughton's delicate mental stability, held in balance until now only by the hope of a dignified return. That disappointment explains much of his behaviour in the following three weeks. He returned to Doddington almost in secrecy. The *Chester Chronicle* reported later that "very few people were aware of his return," and that he had stayed at the house of the butler, Mr. Martin, on a far side of the park, "where he had been seen out walking." Doddington, meanwhile, had been turned into a wartime school.

On November 24th, Broughton telephoned Eustace Bowles, a solicitor from Market Drayton, whom he had known for thirty years. He told him that he had been thrown from a horse (no mention of the fall on the railway embankment); that his back was in plaster; that it was very uncomfortable and that he was shortly to go into hospital to have it removed. Broughton asked, "Can I come over and see you sometime?" Bowles suggested December 6th, a Sunday.

By now it must have been clear to Broughton that his family knew of the extent to which he had defrauded the estate. He told Mrs. Woodhouse that he would contact them "in good time." He did visit Vera, who was living with her mother near Wrexham, to try to persuade her to come back to him, but she refused.

At some point soon after his arrival, Broughton had a chance meeting with an old friend, Alan Horne, a local horse breeder who had known him since the late 1920s, and in the middle of a long conversation, Broughton confessed to the murder. It was the first of two confessions he was to make in this period.

Tipped off by Quentin Crewe, we discovered that Horne was now living in retirement in Worthing, Sussex, and we met him there, in the Beach Hotel, in May and June of 1969. Slight, wiry, humorous and direct, he was immediately likeable. He was neatly dressed in tweeds, scrubbed and shining—a man obviously more at home in the stable-yard than in retirement in a genteel town on the south coast.

Horne had brooded for so long on his conversation with Broughton, had felt the burden of it so acutely, that he had written a play about the incident in a laborious longhand, in a red exercise book like a small ledger with a hard cover. Where his conversation with Broughton had been sketchy on facts Horne had used his own imagination. Connolly described the play as "too far fetched and hopelessly wooden, but exciting."

As a breeding consultant, Horne had often visited Doddington in the 1930s, but had given up horses in 1941. By 1942 he was a censor in the Security Branch in Liverpool.

On the day he met Broughton, Horne was travelling to see a friend in Malpas. He described what happened:

I broke my journey at a small village on the outskirts of Nantwich, Walgerton, I think, and had lunch there. I saw Sir Delves when I came out of the pub. He sat in a car belonging to a friend of his, and his friend got out to visit another friend, leaving Sir Delves in the car.

As I walked by he put his hand out of the car. He told me his friend would be back in half an hour. We started chatting, chiefly about racing matters, and eventually I touched on the trial. I said I was sorry to hear he'd been involved in all this trouble and strain and I saw it had ended all right. As I say, I was an old friend and we chatted for about an hour. He said, "I didn't do it, you know." I said, "I didn't think you did, Sir Delves." He began about the affair himself. He went from strength to strength. He needed no prompting from me. He was a distressed man. He was on perpetual edge, nervous, agitated. He used to be a happy-go-lucky fellow in the early days. He was smart, erect, handsome, military bearing, you know. But I think in his latter years, he drank quite a lot.

I remember he said, "If I tell you a few things, Horne, will you promise not to spill the beans?"

Broughton told Horne that he had planned the murder with a friend. He wouldn't mention names and referred to the accomplice as "Derek," who for reasons of his own, wanted Erroll out of the way. Broughton had allowed himself to be goaded into a plan whereby he would pay for an African, hired by "Derek" for £1,000, to assassinate Erroll. He also agreed to the revolver thefts. Broughton, who had been drinking too much, then regretted the plan, tried to call it off, but was told by "Derek" that the African was now uncontactable. According to Broughton, Erroll was in fact shot one day ahead of schedule.

The African had hidden in the back of the car in the driveway at Karen, shot Erroll at the junction and disappeared. Broughton then said that when the trial was over and he was brooding about it in Ceylon, he formed the idea that "Derek" had double-crossed him, and had gone ahead with the murder in spite of Broughton's efforts to stop it. Horne quotes Broughton as saying, "When I returned to Kenya I challenged 'Derek.' He flushed angrily and denied it, and there was something sheepish about his manner and reply which I didn't like." (It must be remembered that Horne had re-created the conversation from memory.)

We asked Horne why he thought Broughton had decided to tell him the story. He replied, "We were interested in racing and those connections create some bond which is hard to define—probably because some of them know a lot about each other, something which you don't find in other walks of life. If you're a good racing man, you're a good loser—I can't explain it."

Broughton spent his days taking his favourite walk around the lake at Doddington, talking to anyone on the estate whom he met by chance. He saw Mrs. Woodhouse every day. At his insistence they would read over the transcript together again and again while he flattered himself on his courtroom performance.

Mrs. Woodhouse had moved to Hastings in the mid-1960s and we met her there, in the Queen's Hotel, on a windy day in late July. We each took notes on her appearance.

Connolly: Aunt was a well known Cheshire horse woman. One son, now a doctor in Hammersmith. Dark, late middle-aged, cosy, sense of humour, nice brown eyes, rubbery smell. Keen on good old days. Tory party. Double whiskies. Suspicious at first (photo in papers) but unbent gradually. Loved crime stories. Hates Labour. Her sharpness!

Fox: Obviously strapping hunting gal in early days. Gin set. Typical of odd half of Broughton's entourage. Glasses. Tailored tweeds with sapphire horsey brooch. To a double whisky at tea time, craftily suggested by C. C., she replied, "A damn good idea."

Mrs. Woodhouse didn't come to the point immediately. She described the early days at Doddington, her dislike of Diana; how when he returned Broughton called Diana "a real bitch." Vera's wanting to marry Lord Moyne, she said, had been the cause of all his troubles. It was a further shock when his daughter Rosamund, whom he adored—and vice versa—got married. It was then up to Broughton to get a young and beautiful woman. Vera herself had been very beautiful, with green eyes and a wonderful figure. Rosamund would have come out to Kenya for the trial, but he told her she shouldn't.

She didn't think that Rosamund avoided him when he returned. He simply hadn't let his children know, and she didn't think that he had even seen Vera.

Broughton, she said, was very much in love with Diana. He was a most honourable and splendid man, and he couldn't stand this kind of dishonesty. It had crossed her mind that he might have been impotent, however. She noticed the great interest he took in monkey glands after a neighbour had used them with good results, but she thought that it may simply have been vanity, his declining looks, that concerned him. He was a very bad rider, but he was fit, and it was nonsense about his inability to walk over distances, even at speed.

He had taken to drink in Kenya with bad results. Until

then he had been wary of it because of his brother Brian, who was "a drunken sot." He used to come up to the house and Broughton would say, "That's why I never touch a drop."

"They were married on April Fool's Day," said Mrs. Woodhouse (in fact it was Guy Fawkes' Day). "And he wrote to me, 'I hope I'm not the April Fool.' But of course he was, poor dear.

"I saw him almost every day after he came back," she said. "He would come to collect me, driven by his chauffeur. Then we would go back to Doddington for tea or a walk. We had an affinity. Put it like that. We were both lonely.

"He was terribly worried about the tenant farmers' and the locals' opinion of him after the trial. They had placed bets in the pub on the verdict. He was living at the time at Badgers' Bank . . . He wanted quiet dinners. He couldn't stand the pace. I remember, he thought June Carberry a good and loyal friend, but thought Wilks as bad as her mistress, and completely on *her* side."

She and Broughton were discussing the transcript again, two days before he was due to go to Liverpool to have his plaster changed. "We talked a lot and went for walks together," said Mrs. Woodhouse. "He said to me, 'You know I did it, Marie.' I was dumbfounded. I said, 'You didn't, Jock.' He said, 'I've never run so fast in my life.' "

"You know, we laughed about it. He said he thought he was doing everyone a service, but you know, I think that was boasting a bit. He was trying to boost his morale."

Broughton told Mrs. Woodhouse that he had left the house after seeing Mrs. Carberry (official time: 2:10 a.m.) and had walked to the point of the ambush, and had then run back. He told her that the stealing of the pistols was genuine, and the murder was done with a third gun which he had later given to a friend to hide. "He didn't say any more, and I couldn't ask him about it in detail," said Mrs. Woodhouse.

She had the impression that Broughton was obsessed with the affair of Diana and Joss. He had written to her soon after it began. ''He told me that Joss Erroll had already been horsewhipped in Nairobi. I asked him why he hadn't done that, and he said he wasn't strong enough, and he wanted it to be final.

''We laughed about him stoking up the bonfire,'' she said. ''It was completely out of character.''

At the end of our meeting, as we stood on the pavement in the breeze, Mrs. Woodhouse said, ''Well, Cheerio, gentlemen.'' Connolly and I turned and struggled along the strand—he in a felt hat blowing about the brim—to a bar where we could write up our notes. Later Mrs. Woodhouse wrote to say how much she had enjoyed our article.

Two days after his last conversation with Marie Woodhouse, on December 2nd, 1942, Broughton went to the Adelphi Hotel, Liverpool:

He went to the Adelphi without me [Mrs. Woodhouse had told us]. We had booked two rooms and were going to a show to cheer him up. Jock was waiting to go into hospital to have his plaster changed to a lighter, more comfortable one. At the last moment I couldn't go with him because my son, Nick, was very ill and I couldn't leave him.

I rang Jock and told him, but he seemed to expect me to go anyway. He was a bit disappointed. He rang me back later and said, ''Are you all right, Marie—financially I mean?'' I should have known then. I said, ''Of course, Jock.'' I was always broke. He said he would see me next day. I said, yes, if my son was better. I tried to ring him the next morning, but the manager said Sir Delves Broughton was under treatment and wasn't to be disturbed. What a fool I was not to have realised what he was doing to himself. I knew he already had a tube of morphia in jail, in case the verdict went against him.

The *Cheshire Chronicle* reported what happened in the following three days:

. . . Miss Bridget Hayes, head housekeeper at the Adelphi Hotel, said that about 3:30 p.m. on Wednesday, December 2nd, she received a telephone message as to the arrival of Sir Delves.

THE CORONER: Did he seem a little fastidious?

MISS HAYES: Just a little. He asked to be kept perfectly quiet. He didn't want to be disturbed by anybody.

Q: Did you ask him if there was anything he would like or you could do for him and he emphasised that he didn't want to be disturbed?

A: Yes.

Witness added that Sir Delves told her his intended arrangements for the weekend. He said he intended going into the Northern Hospital on Sunday morning.

Q: Did he say how in the interim he was to be treated or not treated at all—rather unusual wasn't it?

A: Yes, he said he didn't want to be disturbed by anybody.

Q: That was from Wednesday to Sunday. That surprised you?

A: Yes. I asked "What about food?" He replied, "I don't want any food. I am looking after myself. I am preparing for an operation."

Q: Then you were not expecting to see him until after Sunday morning, neither at meals nor anything else?

A: That is so.

Q: A reference was made to the question of making his bed?

A: He said not to worry about it.

Forty-eight hours later, Miss Hayes found Broughton, much too late, bleeding from the nose and ears, and in a coma. She noticed a detail that would belong, more realistically, to a soap opera: a bottle label marked "Medinal" floating in the lavatory.

Dr. Ray Maudsley, Resident Medical Officer at the Northern Hospital, admitted Broughton at 6:30 p.m. on Friday December 4th. There was a puncture mark on the inside of the left elbow and several other puncture marks, but not into the vein. Broughton had taken fourteen injections of Medinal. He died at 2:25 a.m. on December 5th.

Mrs. Woodhouse was visited by the Cheshire police, and received an urgent message from Vera asking for a meeting. The question of suicide threatened the life insurance payments, and Mrs. Woodhouse understood that the family wanted to be sure. The coroner's verdict left no question, however, about the cause of death.

Broughton's casket was put in the family vault at Broughton parish church. He had sent Mrs. Woodhouse packets of coffee and tea from Kenya—something of a wartime luxury. After his death, they continued to arrive. She found this "rather morbid."

He had left two notes, both addressed to his solicitors. The most significant message was to do with the "strain" of the trial, and the fact that he could not face further charges. He ended the note with characteristic pomposity: *Moriturus te Saluto*. The second note said that, as a result of his back injury, he had blacked out many times on the journey home and since his arrival; that he had lost all sensation on his right side, and was becoming paralysed. He had therefore decided to take his life.

20
BLACKMAIL

> Gentlemen; have you ever heard anything so fantastic?
> Here is a man whose whole life is being ruined; having
> his wife stolen from him right under his nose; being
> made a complete fool of before the whole public of
> Kenya; and when his wife comes home he discusses
> who shall pay for a bit of jewellery. Do you
> believe a word of it?

For ourselves, Broughton's obsession with this one
particular piece of jewellery was certainly not to be dis-
missed so easily, if only because Broughton always brought
up the subject with Diana at the moments of greatest crisis
between them. A whiff of insurance frauds had always
surrounded Broughton in our minds ever since Connolly
had heard the rumour in Nairobi, back in 1967, that
Broughton had paid a hard-up officer to steal his pictures.

Pearls, in some form or other, had an insistent way
of coming back into the story again and again, and we felt
instinctively that the pearl trail would be a hot one to
follow, with its suggestions of accompanying blackmail.
Looking for clues, we found an original newsroom mem-
orandum in the cuttings library of the *Daily Express* in
Broughton's file—a rarity, since memos seldom find their
way into the "morgue." It was written by a newsroom

reporter on December 11th, 1942, soon after Broughton's death.

Memo Re: Sir Delves Broughton

The Manchester office tell us that they have heard this story from a local man for what it is worth.

It is to the effect that Sir Delves Broughton, who died in Liverpool the other day and whose inquest will be held on Monday, December 14th, was concerned with the Doddington Park robbery a few years ago. At the time of the robbery three pictures were missing, supposed to be valuable.

The pictures were never recovered and the insurance company were not quite happy about the whole thing, but paid up apparently to Sir Delves Broughton.

It is now suggested that since the murder case of the Earl of Erroll in Nairobi—Sir Delves Broughton was acquitted—someone in Nairobi has told the police that Sir Delves Broughton was very "sticky" to newspapers about the whole affair.

It is also suggested that when Sir Delves Broughton returned to Liverpool recently Scotland Yard were interested about the picture robbery and were on his track. It is not known whether Yard men interviewed him or not but his death is believed to be suicide. It is expected that some kind of white-washing verdict will be made at the inquest on Monday.

It was time for another lunch with Poppy at the Metropole Hotel, Brighton. Now he told us that the insurance company which had paid out to Broughton for the stolen pictures from Doddington and the pearls missing from Miss Caldwell's car had been alerted by the press reports of the Nairobi trial, particularly by the squabbles between Jock and Diana about pearls. But the insurance company's enquiries came to nothing: they found themselves pursuing, instead, the Erroll pearls. This, however, alerted Poppy. His informers in the Karen house reported continuous arguments on the subject. He had also seen a letter from Broughton to Diana, threatening to implicate her in a fraud unless she came back to him and returned with him to

England on the next boat. Diana was wondering what to do about Broughton's threats, so Poppy was expecting a visit. But it was not Diana who came to see him. It was Hugh Dickinson.

Dickinson told Poppy that he had "something to get off his chest." At the end of the interview, he signed the following statement

In the June before the War, Sir Delves Broughton came to me in London and said he wanted to talk over with me a proposition he had in mind. He said that the then Diana Caldwell must in no circumstances know of the proposition he was about to make to me. He suggested I should take the pearls which she was wearing and that he had bought for approx. £6,000, as an investment and which he had lent to her and which he had insured for approx. £12,000. The reason he gave for this was that he was hard up and she was also the same and that he thought I was a likely person to try and help as he knew I was extremely fond of her. I told him I'd think the matter over, as I could not possibly give an answer at once. He approached me later and again I stalled him. Later on he said that he knew we were all going in a party to the South of France and he thought that would be a golden opportunity. I said I would if a suitable opportunity occurred, but would make no promises.

In the South of France I was staying at Juan les Pins and she and X [Mark Pilkington] were staying at the Carlton in Cannes. The three of us together, with about half a dozen other people, had drinks in the Carlton before going to have dinner at a restaurant about 20 miles away. She and X were staying the night at another hotel, and so her luggage was put into the car while we were standing around waiting. When it had all been put in we motored in either two or three cars to dinner. In the middle of dinner, which was rather hilarious, I got up and walked out and removed her dressing case from X's car to mine and then returned to finish the meal. After dinner all dispersed and I drove down to a quiet place on the sea shore, opened the dressing case, put the pearls in my pocket and threw the rest into the sea. The next day I buried them and they stayed there until the day before I left to come to England, where I buried them again until I got in touch with DB. He told me to buy a deed box, put them in it and deliver the box to him at his solicitors, and, to avoid curiosity, to say when I handed them over, "Here's the box you said you would keep for me." I did this, but do not know the name of the solicitors. After a short lapse, he came to me and said that he had some pictures which he wanted removed from Doddington as they were extremely well-insured and he told me that if I refused to do this, he would ask his solicitors to ask Scotland Yard to investigate the box which I had left there, and I felt compelled to fall in with his wishes.

He told me to come to Doddington and he would show me what pictures he wanted removed, which I think were three in number, but I could not swear to this. It might have been four. He told me that I should need some collapsible step ladders which I could get at Gamages, a large bag to put the pictures in and a glass cutter to cut the glass from the lavatory window, and to hire a car from a London firm. He told me to go up and do it on a certain Sunday towards the end of October 1939 as he would be away that night, staying in an hotel in Liverpool. I went up on the appointed day and at about 11 o'clock at night started operations. I drove the car to about 100 yards from the house and parked it under a tree and tried to cut the glass in the window which he had indicated to me, but failed to do so.

I then walked round to the front of the house to have a look around and happened to notice that a window on the first floor was open about a couple of inches. It was a bright moonlight night, I climbed the drain pipe and got into the window and walked through the house, opened the front door and brought in the step ladder, bag etc. I cut the pictures out of the frames, and, two of them being too large to get into the bag, I cut them into smaller bits. I then returned to the car and drove away. When I had driven for about an hour, I stopped the car at a lonely spot and, as Broughton had suggested, tried to burn the pictures with the help of some petrol. I failed to do this. I then returned the pictures to the bag and motored on again for some time until I came to a small river which ran right up against the road. I fastened the pictures to the step ladder and, with the aid of it, sank them. I then drove back to London.

That was the end so far as I was concerned, with the exception that later on I had some conversation with him when he told me that the insurance company was being rather awkward about it, but that he thought it would be all right. I was never offered and would not have thought of accepting any consideration for what I had done, except that he gave me back the pearls with which he had been blackmailing me. I did not know what to do with them and did not want to put them into my bank as my financial position was bad and I thought they might be curious. So I asked Diana Caldwell if she would put in her bank for me a box with some private papers, telling her the reason I did not want them put in my bank. This she did, I think in her name, but I could not be positive.

I was told after I had removed the pictures that the firm which had done the valuation of them was bogus. Broughton told me that the reason he was having trouble with the insurance company about payment was that he had recently increased the insurance enormously and the insurance company was unable to find the firm which had carried out the valuation, as it had turned out to be bogus.

Dickinson told Poppy that he had "never had such a hot time going through Customs"; that among the jewellery thrown into the sea was a jade brooch, a gold and platinum bracelet watch, and three blue stone bracelets. Among the pictures he destroyed were two Romney portraits of members of the Broughton family.

Miss Caldwell had received a cheque from the insurance company for £12,730 10s. od. The pearls had ended up without her knowledge in her own deposit box. No wonder Broughton would continually bring up the subject of jewellery with Diana. But the idea was macabre in the extreme, and revealing of his true nature beneath the calm, patrician exterior. Diana in this scenario would live the rest of her life with a man she despised, under the everlasting threat of blackmail.

It is also clear what took place in Grogan's office between Broughton and Dickinson, when Broughton demanded that Dickinson persuade Diana to come back to him. In his confession to Horne, did he intend "Derek" to mean Dickinson, in revenge for Dickinson having resisted the blackmail and informed on him to Scotland Yard?

Dickinson told Poppy that if Broughton were going to blackmail him, he would bring Broughton down as well.

Thirteen years later, when I telephoned Dickinson, I was shocked to hear the frailness in his voice. The sporty confidence that I remembered from the meeting with Connolly had disappeared. He told me that his wife was in hospital, her thigh broken in a mugging attack, and that he had undergone open heart surgery. The last ten years had been painful and sad. He immediately agreed to see me and I suggested the Ritz.

His face was handsome, a little anaemic and he had acquired the charm and attentive politeness that often comes with old age. We tried to order drinks from a young Hispanic waiter with a sycophantic grin. Dickinson said, "I'll have a dry martini." This simple request was misunderstood—a frustrating wrangle began about methods and ingredients. Dickinson stared after the waiter and said, "What an extraordinary man." The Ritz had declined. Dickinson had recently found it impossible to fill the basin in the washroom: there were no plugs. "At the *Ritz*," he said. "The chap regretted it. He said they couldn't have plugs because people *took* them."

We began by correcting some biographical details, and quickly cleared up the confusion about his alibi. He had been transferred to Nairobi Hospital with his poisoned foot—that was how he had been able to see Broughton and Diana at the end of January. He also said that any inside knowledge of the murder itself, reported by Dickinson to his friends and relations, had been pure speculation.

I found Dickinson moving, sad, very dignified and I nearly abandoned the idea of showing him his confession, which he hadn't seen since the day he signed it forty years before, and which he must have thought was buried for ever. But he was also relaxed, resigned, and the past seemed to be something he enjoyed talking about. So I told him that I thought Broughton had tried to blackmail him; that I had brought with me his confession made to Poppy. He flushed just a little and there was silence between us. Then, with the same polite composure, he said, "He *was* trying to. He was being a bit awkward. That [the confession] was to try to cut the ground from under his feet."

I gave him the document, which he read slowly, his hands shaking at the edges of the pages. He dropped a page on to the floor. Halfway through he said, "It comes to life now. How did you get this?" He read on and said, "It would certainly add flavour to your book."

A second round of drinks was ordered. Dickinson continued reading slowly and with great concentration. He looked up and said, "Good Heavens, I'm going to be famous or, rather, notorious." When he had finished reading, he said, "I shall never forget that night as long as I live. It was absolutely fantastic." He then described the evening much as he had in the confession, adding, it may be said, some picturesque details.

"You have no idea how *tough* canvas is. You think it's paper thin, delicate. But I had to chop and chop and chop. So I cut these beastly things out—each of them about that size"—Dickinson pointed to the rococo mirror in the cocktail bar—"and I walked out of the front door like a gentleman, found a quiet field and tried to burn them. All the petrol burned away, but the canvas just wouldn't burn. I was so exhausted that I fell asleep driving to London and ran off the road. But Godfrey Davis didn't seem to mind."

I asked if he was forced to steal the pictures because Broughton had blackmailed him for his part in the pearl robbery. "Yes, Broughton was doing all the batting at the time," he said. "For me it was just rather an adventure and a challenge." But finally Dickinson refused to help Broughton: "After the trial he wanted Diana to come slinking back. That's why he tried to blackmail us both. I said, 'To hell with it, she'll do what she wants.' " (Diana later made it clear to me that she herself was not in a position to be blackmailed by Broughton.)

When Dickinson returned to England, on a troopship,

he was taken off ahead of all the other passengers, by Scotland Yard detectives. He was never charged: "As soon as they know you're making no financial gain out of it, they lose interest in you," he said. Instead, Dickinson co-operated with the insurance assessors. Broughton, to whom he had eventually returned the pearls, had intimated that he had hidden them in a tree trunk at Doddington. Dickinson and the assessor spent some days walking over the estate looking for them. They never found them, although Sir Evelyn Broughton remembers that the pearls were eventually found by an estate worker and returned to the insurance company.

Dickinson talked, finally, of Diana. He seemed apprehensive about her; he was perhaps still under her spell. Their relationship had always been platonic, he said, but they were very close and he would do anything for her. Diana's maid in Duke Street, before the war, had once called him a "fetch and carry man." Diana had taken great exception to this and Dickinson said, laughing, "It's not something I liked being called." But Diana, he said, wanted jewels and titles and "I didn't want to step out of my league." They had not spoken for twenty years. "I was devoted to her," he said, "still am in a funny way."

21
WHITE ROYALTY

D R E A M Y   D A Y S at the Muthaiga Club—the last
stage of the quest in 1979. The crackling of insects in the
room, ants from nowhere suddenly collecting on dead bugs
outside the metal window, the rain dripping down on the
banana leaves. The sensual thrill of returning to familiar
pleasures, the sour smell of woodsmoke, bright red earth,
metallic guitar rumbas wheezing from the taxi radio.

The pleasure of all bedrooms in good British colonial
clubs—and Muthaiga is a fine example—is their enormous
size and their spartan airiness. The doorways into these
spaces are on an equally grand scale. There is also spare
Indian-made custom furniture, circa 1930, an isolated
washbasin along one wall, a water decanter, a hard floor
of green or brown linoleum, and a luxurious bathroom,
where the thundering of hot water echoes against the cream
walls.

Bachelors are often billeted in the Military Wing—
the cheapest sleeping arrangements available—but I was
directed to more luxurious quarters, in a room that was
reached along a communal balcony. The Club rules in my
desk drawer were unchanged (members bringing their own
liquor will be charged; no snakes to be brought into the
Club; members upright after midnight in the public rooms
still to be charged, by the hour), and there was the vital

stationery: the bar chits coloured white, the others green and pink for every category of need. There were many servants to make the long journey, chit in hand, from the rooms to the bar and back. Was this the room in which Portman was staying and where Broughton changed into evening dress on the night of the toast; Portman, flushed with the martinis and the thundering hot water?

Tea is brought at 6:30 a.m., unless members leave special instructions, in the sturdy, pale blue tea sets of the *civilisation anglaise*. The tea is always extra strong and this is the moment for reverie and luxury, for the sensation of the early tropical light in the short rains, the sweet smell of vegetation, the coolness, the calls of the nightjars, the unbroken sound of sweeping in the yard outside and on the balcony. It allows a two-hour break before muster in the dining room for the great Swahili breakfast of paw-paw and "bacon na mayai," the *Daily Nation* and the *East African Standard*. Time to speculate on images of the Buick 6 at the junction of the Karen and Ngong roads.

In the members' study I reviewed the complaints book:

4:30 a.m. woken by native sweeping leaves. 5:15 a.m. woken by tramping of watchman putting out lights. 5:30 a.m. woken by trundling of some handcart behind bedrooms. For some 30 years this native (or his ancestors) has been sweeping leaves before daylight. Is this necessary?

Another: I like the military wing. It is peaceful. One is spared the shrill cries emanating from the rooms of married members engaged in beating their wives into submission.

At midday, the light shines off the trees as bright as crystal. In the Club secretary's office, a servant had come to complain to the Club manager—a former Kenya District Commissioner—that he had been insulted. When the servant was originally accused of taking cream from the dining room, the manager had said, "I suppose you've drunk it." The manager now said, "If you can't see it's a joke,

if you can't take a joke, I've really got no time for you."
The manager refused to apologise, and the Club servant
refused to leave until his sense of honour was restored,
which seemed an unlikely prospect.

At a dinner party in Nairobi to which I'm invited, the
table is set with a large arrangement of bougainvillaea
petals in a Waterford bowl, silver candlesticks on a polished Queen Anne table made by a local joiner. Persian
rugs; sherry with the soup; piri-piri juice; pigeon and par-
tridge; fried bananas and claret.

Topics: Different species of flame trees—Nandi and
Abyssinian. Only Nandi in Kenya when Elspeth Huxley
arrived. Criticism of greed and waste of new Kikuyu nou-
veau-riche farmers. Defence, up to a point, of the venality
of Kenyatta; of his obtaining a large acreage near Nakuru
for which he neither paid nor compensated the owners,
because he had thus stabilised a warring tribal area.

Everybody has their version of the Erroll murder.
There is reverence and admiration for Diana Delamere. A
woman says, "God she's clever, Diana." Speculation follows on her value; the total acreage she now owns, and
the settlement left by her husband, Tom Delamere. From
now on, this is all we talk about until 2 a.m.

"You should see her at the fishing competitions at
Malindi. All alone, jewels from head to foot, walking
down the pier to her marlin boat. She almost always comes
back with a fish—and marlin are hard to catch now off
the coast."

First man: "Well, she's got class. More than you
could have said for Wallis Simpson."

Second man: "Same type of woman. Exactly the
same."

Third man: "You have to take your hat off to her."

And you do. When she first took up deep-sea fishing,
she was severely seasick, for two or three seasons, an
ordeal that would quickly finish off any ordinary person's
enthusiasm for the sport. But Diana was determined to get

over it. She went out time after time with the rod in her hands, and a bowl on her lap, and finally got the better of it.

For a Nairobi hostess, the Erroll murder was a topic that always promised sparkle. Indeed, it was the only topic guaranteed, for the last twenty-five years, to keep the guests in thrall, a topic at which the locals could excel, and at which they could compete as historians. A knowledge of the affair, of the inner story, was a measure of how well you knew the country, and Diana's formidable and continuing presence added the spice of indiscretion. Neither was it remotely parochial gossip, to make you look provincial to the metropolitans on their way to the game reserves: it had acquired cultural edge, on a par with stories about Karen Blixen and Hemingway.

Diana publicly suffered from it, from time to time. Once in the mid-1960s at a lunch with the late Duke of Gloucester, who was visiting Kenya, and with several local politicians including Kenya's former Attorney-General, Charles Njonjo, the topic turned to the recent murder of a local nurse. A former colonial politician, looking in Diana's direction, said in a loud voice, "At least we don't have white murders any more." Njonjo was irritated. He had already managed to laugh off the Duke's remark to a prominent Kikuyu politician: "Do you buy your wives one at a time, or by the dozen?" Njonjo is reportedly fond of Diana and has offered her some protection by joining the board of her management company.

Her rise to wealth and, in a way, to fame, had been purposeful and dramatic. After the murder, bitterly down on her luck, and shunned by the rest of that smugly censorious colonial community, her future had looked decidedly uncertain. She did receive a letter of commiseration from Nancy Wirewater in Cape Town, and Mark Pilkington, her old boy friend, wrote to say that he was coming to be near her, but he was killed in North Africa soon after Diana read his letter. The worst of it, perhaps, was that for a while she had to stay near to her husband.

But then Gilbert Colvile entered her life; the man whom nobody could remember having even talked to a woman before, and who had certainly never had an affair.

There is a scurrilous legend current around Lake Naivasha that Diana asked Broughton's partner, John Hopcraft, with a view to her next conquest, "Who is the richest man in Kenya?" At that time the Delamere estates were only just beginning to recover from the ravages of the inter-war years, many acres had been sold to pay Lord Delamere's bad debts, and Colvile (who sat as the Chairman of LEGCO when Delamere was away) was certainly near the top of the list.

"He was the most boring man in the world," said his neighbour on Lake Naivasha, a trophy-hunting Austrian called Baron Knapitsch. "He could only talk about cattle and rain." "He didn't drink or smoke cigarettes," said my Somali acquaintance. "The only thing he was interested in was the Masai. He had so many dogs it was like the grass."

Colvile, educated at Eton and Sandhurst, formerly a lieutenant with the Grenadier Guards, and a member of the Guards' Club, was looked down on by the Somalis I spoke to—possibly because of his love for the Masai—and when Diana married him, all her servants left, knowing his reputation for parsimony. But there were more snobbish reasons. The Somali had various charges to lay against Colvile:

"Colvile's mother lived at Gilgil and ran a hotel."

"She wasn't like a Mazungu [white person]."

"She didn't have English customs [she was partly French] and used to carry milk [on her head]."

"She had little respect from us because she didn't play tennis, polo or bridge, and Colvile was the same."

"The cows used to come into his house." (An exaggeration.)

"He used to drive a car with a Masai Moran carrying a spear in the front seat." (Translator: "Note the distaste in his voice.")

Perhaps Colvile was a misanthropist. He was a lonely, taciturn, dour man, according to Sir Michael Blundell. "He would appear at the Meat Board, on which Tom Delamere also sat, in a large, wide, pork pie hat, crushed on top. No socks, of course, and a rumpled, lightweight tweed suit. When I tried to call him Gilbert, he said 'My name's Colvile.' "

An acquaintance of Diana's saw it like this: "During and after the trial no one would speak to her. She had to give up all the clubs, and couldn't stay in any hotel. Colvile was a great woman hater. He met Diana and thought, 'This woman is really tough.' He felt about her as if she was a man. He wrote to her and said he would do anything for her; that he belonged to every club in Africa as a founder member and with his money he could fight the lot."

As soon as Broughton was out of the way, Diana brought Colvile to the Djinn Palace, cleaned him up, and in January 1943, a month after Broughton's suicide, married him. Colvile was only five years younger than Broughton. "He bought her Erroll's house, the Djinn Palace," said an acquaintance, "and he gave Diana his family jewels. He *loathed* Delves Broughton." Diana told a friend, Dushka Repton, that she was down at the bottom; nobody would talk to her; Colvile picked her up and she would never forget the gesture.

True to his word, Colvile not only let up on his legendary meanness—Diana, for example, was allowed to spend money on a string of racehorses at Nairobi, and a large part of the estate was given over to her on her marriage—he also encouraged her social life elsewhere. Diana was often seen at parties as her social life blossomed again, with a steady dancing partner, Jack Hilton. Colvile didn't mind—a social life required a dancing partner. Diana and Colvile were, nevertheless, said to be deeply devoted to each other. She called him "my little monster." "No, darling," a friend remembers her saying, "I can't come tonight, I promised to take Pooey [her nickname for him] to the cinema." (Had he ever been to the cinema before?) But few people could understand the combination—how Diana could stand this man, and why Colvile had given up the habits of a lifetime and devoted himself to a young and fashionable woman from whom he expected nothing.

To Poppy, Colvile had been an odd fellow indeed, and he concluded that his strange existence before Diana's arrival was due to a homosexual obsession with his favourite tribe, especially with its young warriors. There was not much room for unconventional behaviour on the frontier, apart from an acceptable degree of drunkenness and promiscuity, but "going native," which was what Poppy suspected of Colvile, was of course unforgivable. For Poppy it could be explained only in terms of sexual aberration.

By the early 1950s, Diana's moment of purdah was over and she began to attend every social event. Soon enough a race meeting at Nairobi was not the real thing —not a truly *royal* event, you might say—if Diana wasn't there. There was a 400 Club in Nairobi too, and Diana was often seen there with Jack Hilton. Her comings and goings were written up relentlessly in the local gossip column, "Miranda's Merrier Moments." A woman remembers seeing her at the 400 Club during this period. "She wore a beautiful black dress and splendid emeralds. She had a beautiful figure. One couldn't do other than just gape."

But there had been a tragedy in their lives. Diana lost two children—the first lived for ten days, the second was stillborn. Diana and Colvile adopted a daughter, Sarah, known as "Snoo."

When Diana first met Tom Delamere, son of the pioneer, with his red hair and small stature, she didn't like him. Colvile and Delamere, however, were close friends, despite the fact that Tom's father, Hugh Delamere, had shown a marked preference for Colvile, whom he had treated with more kindness than his own son. Diana, Colvile and Delamere began to be seen out and about together, moving as a trio between the Djinn Palace and Soysambu, the Delamere ranch.

Diana, who had felt, she said, nothing for any man since Erroll's death, now fell in love with Tom. The unwritten pact was genuine this time and Colvile, although unhappy to lose Diana, never let it disturb his friendship with her or with Tom. He agreed in 1955 to an amicable divorce, even promising Diana that she would inherit all his remaining estates when he died. In that same year the Hon. Mary Delamere sued her husband for divorce, citing Diana, and Diana married Tom Delamere, whom she nicknamed "Bear" and "Buzzer."

At the wedding, Diana said to Kaplan, "Third time lucky." (She was overlooking Vernon Motion, her first husband, the support player for Carroll Gibbons's Savoy Orpheans.)

The Emergency came and went and independence under Kenyatta arrived. When Colvile died, he left everything to Diana. The most conservative estimate of the proceeds of Diana's sale of Colvile's property, to raise death duties, was £2.5 million.

I FIRST LAID EYES on Diana at Nairobi racecourse one day in 1966 when I was working on the *Daily Nation*. She was smallish, like English Royalty, and she dressed and seemed to behave like Royalty too. She wore the grandest chic that Hardy Amies could produce, yet in her puffy white melon of a hat and her fabulous jewellery she had a dazzle that in Royalty would have been considered excessive. It came as much from her striking face and ice-blue eyes as from her costume. I thought that perhaps she was overdoing it—that even at Ascot, let alone Nairobi, she would have stood out; that she was not, you might say, *discreetly* rich in her appearance.

I felt that if she were not so conspicuously adorned,

projecting as she does an air of great wealth, of power, always attracting attention as if she were permanently on parade, there would be none of the speculation that exists about her origins. It is firmly believed in Nairobi, for instance, and quite incorrectly, that Diana "came from nowhere." Chorus girl and mannequin are the most generous suggestions in the Muthaiga Club bar. "She has made herself very respectable," said a woman member, "because she *wasn't*, you know." And yet Diana is proudly thought of by most whites as the most fascinating woman in Kenya, the symbol of white survival and profitable co-operation with the black ruling class after independence.

On that afternoon she was presented with an enormous silver racing trophy, the Uhuru Cup (she and Delamere always had the finest horses), by Jomo Kenyatta. The two great survivors smiled conspiratorially together and I remember thinking that once again Diana had managed to charm a rich and powerful man.

The Somalis were amazed that she never took off her many pieces of jewellery before lowering herself into her swimming pool at Kilifi. She clearly felt "undressed" without them—yet for them the impression she gave was of somebody stepping into a whirlpool fatally weighted down with bright stones.

A friend of mine once saw her in the Muthaiga Club wearing a cape fastened with powerful magnets, and was fascinated to watch her pull these apart and then let them snap together. He noticed that she had borrowed several books from the library at the Club in a series called "Real Life Murders." At independence, the statue of Lord Delamere was removed from Delamere Avenue in Nairobi when it was renamed after Kenyatta, and brought to the garden at Soysambu. There the peacocks were provided with mirrors which encouraged them, in their vanity, to peck at their own image. Diana would say, "*Go* on."

Antonia Fraser wrote to Cyril Connolly,

I have always been obsessed by the case. Obviously everyone sees something different in it: in my case it was not so much Jock Broughton as Diana, the *femme fatale*, and how some women are accident prone, something I often brood about (Mary Queen of Scots fitted into this). Imagine my excitement on sitting in the Muthaiga Club in about 1958 and seeing a leopard of a woman stalk by in pale gold jersey (everyone else in tatty cotton) with hair and skin the same colour, and even a fur coat on her arm (the temperature was about 75) and hearing a murmur, "Diana Delamere." One of my theories about a *femme fatale* is that she often feels rather *cold*, compared to everyone . . .

"Cold" and "hard" were epithets often ascribed to Diana, and yet people close to her would praise her loyalty and warmth towards her friends. "She is very nice to ordinary dull people," I have heard it said.

She is always surrounded by ladies-in-waiting. She is frightened of being alone. It is not always easy, I was told, for the ladies-in-waiting to devote so much of their time to her, but in the case of Diana, "an order is an order."

"She was always faithful and kind to Tom, who was a difficult man, and ill for a long time," said a friend of Diana. "She was patient with him, and he was rather strict. He didn't want her running around."

"Soysambu was rather gloomy," said the friend. "They lived extremely well; not vulgarly, but they didn't play down their riches. Their servants were always immaculately dressed in green fezzes, boots and white breeches. One day I was sitting alone in the drawing room, and one of these wonderfully dressed servants came in. He can't have noticed me. He went to the drinks tray, picked up the whisky decanter, took a long gulp, put it back in its place and walked out of the room. I was very impressed by that.

"Diana bothered about her clothes. There was tremendous preparation for Ascot, and the moment it was over they were planning the next one, drawing up the costumes with Hardy Amies and so on. She has one great quality as a woman, Diana. She would make you feel that you were *the* chap she would dominate.''

Her friend's description of the servants' uniforms is not quite correct: at Soysambu they do wear green fezzes, but their uniforms are long khaki tunics with green cummerbunds and long khaki trousers. On the coast at Kilifi they are dressed in plain white, and the ''boat boys'' wear trousers or shorts of navy-blue drill and navy-blue tee-shirts with the name of Diana's boat—*White Bear*—on the chest. On special occasions the boat boys also wear white.

Another feature of Soysambu life—and one of special luxury—is the breakfast arrangements. In the evening, as the guests change for dinner, a printed menu card with a gilt surround lies on the table of the bedroom, with a rose beside it for a buttonhole. An enormous variety of tropical fruits and cooked dishes are listed, for the guests to tick their preference. Breakfast may only be taken in the bedroom. A friend of mine who once stayed there said, ''I gathered that Diana didn't like the idea of young men wandering about early in the morning. One was not encouraged to emerge with too much haste.''

CONNOLLY FINALLY MET HER, before we wrote our article. The unsuspecting hostess in question was clearly innocent of any disloyalty to her friend. Connolly recorded the encounter in his notebook:

1st meeting with—at dinner with Lady Hoare. 14 Selwood Terrace. July 23 (69).

Diana wore a simple summer dress, black and white flower pattern, close fitting, with 5 strand enormous pearl necklace and small diamond clip.

Medium height (not little), short blonde hair, big blue eyes, small aquiline nose. Mouth *not* turned down discontented. Voice rather metallic, but not at all dead, vibrant with hint of gaity and laughter. *Not* a little woman. Must have been dazzling.

Reminds me of 1. Duchess of Windsor as entertainer and builder-upper of rather stupid elderly husband.
2. Diana Cooper twenty years ago.
3. Figures of the charm school of the 20s and 30s i.e. Doris Castlerosse, Lady Queensberry (Mrs. Follett). But not, like her, devitalising.
The kind of woman one associates with Cannes, Scotland, Ascot, St. Moritz as they used to be but not with giving house parties or any particular purpose except pleasure—not at all Bohemian.

Also present the Walter Bells, he an ex-intell. officer (Kenya). Good dinner.

Topics
Her passion for Rome. Stays in the Hôtel de Ville. Top suite (air-conditioned). Likes queers but husband says he has "no time for 'ginger beers' " as they were called in the army. She stood up for the "nice ones" who tell her if her hair style is correct, notice her clothes, etc.

Opinions
Can't bear South Africa, nothing would induce her to live there. Loves Kenya, would rather stay there and never leave it than any other country. She has "lovely" farm at Lake Naivasha and house at Kilifi on Mombasa side. D. farms at Elmenteita, and she goes to the coast for her health in the winter. Likes Alan Bobbé's grill [a Nairobi restaurant]. Didn't drink *anything*.

Bought a Michonze painting for £600. Took a "little Gainsborough" to be cleaned—"a family thing" (DB?)—a portrait of a young girl (child) with blue collar, white dress.

Anti Wilson, pro Kenyatta. Lord D held forth on African politics with Bell all evening. Talk of Eton. She said to him, "I know you think it's a very bad sign to have no lobes to your ears, but here's someone else without them"—meaning me. She took off her pearl earrings and raised her hair to show her ears to me. He calls her "Buzzy."

Essentially a charmer and manager of men—one could understand being crazy about her thirty years ago if one was the right sort of man (for her). Faintly common or perhaps merely worldly. Diamonds and sapphires and pearls. They drove me to Victoria to catch my train, very friendly. The snake farm at Kilifi. I said the man looked like D. H. Lawrence on an off day. "A very off day."

She had been down to the City, was told to "hold on to her blue chips." Slump would go further. Thought of giving a farewell party at Aspinall's—did not like cocktail parties—then her friends could gamble if they wanted to. Thought Kennedy business a tragedy. Lord D was very against War. Thought everyone should be taken to see *Oh What A Lovely War!* to know what it was about. All rather Sandy Wilson. She had not been to Jack Block's house or seen his pictures. Mentioned Chester races. Flies Alitalia—has old boy friend in the company. Loved racing.

In 1979 I saw Diana Delamere on Nairobi racecourse once again, sitting in the Delamere box, a widow now, but looking a lot younger than when I saw her in 1966, and still dressed in Hardy Amies Royal. The husband of her current lady-in-waiting raised his trilby hat at every move she made—at her getting up, her walking down the staircase and crossing the enclosure towards the paddock, then at her return to the box to watch the race. The Delamere box is at the extreme north end of the members' stand, and she sat in the corner in a red hat, directly opposite the winning post.

She lunched in the members' restaurant with her entourage, including her stepson and heir to the Delamere estates, Hugh Cholmondeley, now Lord Delamere. When the loudspeaker was switched on, before the first race, a loud and prolonged scream—feedback—was piped into the dining room where we sat. I saw Diana mouthing with bridled irritation as the howl continued, "For *God's* sake."

Even though I expected a flat rejection, or worse, if ever I brought up the Erroll case in her presence, there was always a slender hope that one day in the right circumstances she might talk, however briefly, to a serious historian of the subject. That possibility had to be carefully protected. It would have been convenient but in some ways dishonest for me to write that Diana refused to talk to me if my request had been made in an unsuitable setting.

The racecourse was not the place for it. She was too exposed there. One doesn't after all lobby members of the Royal Family at Ascot. The telephone was no good, either. You could lose it all, for ever, in a few seconds. Our first contact had to be a face to face meeting. And it had to take place on the reporter's most ancient battleground: the front doorstep. But approaching her in her own stronghold at Soysambu looked impossible from the road. There was a distant gate in the middle of the African plain, a sentry box and a steel barrier across the road, and from these the track disappeared across the bush and over the horizon. For an unwelcome reporter to announce himself on a field telephone from a remote sentry box would plainly have been absurd. Another eighteen months were to pass before Diana and I finally met.

22

ABDULLAH
AND THE
AFGHAN PRINCESS

BEFORE TRAVELLING up-country I drove out of Nairobi to Karen on a still and hot afternoon, to look at the murder site again, in the hope that the terrain itself might reveal some clue to the events of that fatal morning. I knew the drive well from previous years: out of the Nairobi suburbs along a straight road that passed Nairobi racecourse and Jamhuri Park where I had once covered the annual Agricultural Show and, much impressed, watched Kenyatta declaiming and waving his fly whisk, leading the massed chants of *"Harambee"* ("Pull together") in the days of "nation building" after independence.

The Karen and Ngong roads, at whose junction the Buick was found, are now surfaced with tarmac; this and St. Andrew's Church, a wood and stone building which stands a few yards from the old murram pit, are the only visible changes in the immediate vicinity. When you look at the site, you are immediately struck by the sharpness of the turn the Buick made as it passed the junction and veered towards the murram pit. The first impression I had was that Erroll had swerved to the right to avoid an oncoming car on the wrong side. Yet it is also possible that after the right turn and the shots, Erroll slumped forward on to the wheel, and his foot left the clutch, causing the car to swing into the grass in a tight curve. There was always that lack of any clear-cut evidence at the scene of the crime.

The land between the junction and the Broughtons' old house is a large meadow used for cattle pasture, divided by the road that Erroll drove down and along which Broughton may have walked back. Struck by the distance between the house and the junction (2.4 miles is farther than it sounds), I was at first convinced that the murderer must have been waiting for Erroll at the junction, and that he must have been a hired assassin rather than a member of the Karen household. Of one fact there could be no doubt, at least—that if the murderer were Broughton or anyone else in the house, he or she took a lift with Erroll on the outward journey. What I saw put a great emphasis on Broughton's ability to cover that distance at the speed required to meet June Carberry's alibi. (Diana was overheard to say at the trial by Harragin's secretary, "He's not nearly such an old crock as he's making out.")

The Broughtons' house now lay behind heavily constructed steel gates and it looked locked and empty. Its present owner was Kenyatta's former son-in-law, Udi Gecaga, at one time a director of the English mining conglomerate, Lonhro. He told me that the driveway and the entrance to the house had since been switched from one side of the house to the other, otherwise nothing in the house had been altered.

I took off one afternoon from Wilson airport, heading north—in a small aeroplane you are airborne and climbing six or seven seconds after the brakes are released—and flew across the hilly, rich-looking plantations of the Kikuyu, then past Nyeri Hill, whose summit shot by just below the wing-tip. Its tree-covered cone is a milestone for low-flying aviators and marks almost exactly the border between the Kikuyu settlements and the great Masai cattle plains that reach from here nearly to Lake Rudolph. Flying low along this broad valley between Mount Kenya and the

Aberdare range, over the great expanse of the smooth greensward that sweeps in a long, gentle rise into the foothills of that mountain, must be one of the most exhilarating trips you could make in a small plane.

The pilot, David Allen, is a professional game warden; the other passenger was his wife, Petal, daughter of Sir Derek Erskine. We came down on the grass strip outside the garden of their house, which faces Mount Kenya and is a few miles from Soames's old farm, near Bergeret. That evening we fished for trout on a wooded river under tall and un-nameable African trees, and were casting again soon after sunrise the following morning.

Some years earlier, on a hurried reporting trip I had made to Nairobi, Sir Derek Erskine had told me a story about Broughton and a horse of Erskine's called Pantaloon—a story which had seemed significant and which I had always wanted to follow up. In the meantime Erskine had died. But the rest of his family, who had provided me with limitless hospitality on this trip, remembered it clearly. It transpired that Sir Derek had committed his memories to tape soon before he died, including those of Broughton and Pantaloon. That night his widow, Lady Erskine, offered to play me the recording.

Although Broughton had his own stable of horses, she told me, Pantaloon was a particularly fine-looking animal, always flattering to its rider, and on the morning before the murder Broughton, who had often told Erskine that he would like to buy the horse, asked to borrow it until the following Sunday. That day Broughton was alone in Nairobi, waiting for the result of the inquest. Diana and June Carberry had gone to Nyeri. Erskine described the Sunday afternoon when Broughton returned the horse, around 4 p.m. He was one of the few people who knew the real cause of Erroll's death.

Jock Broughton rode up to our stables looking extremely weary on a very tired and weary looking Pantaloon. I was very shocked to see this. Jock more or less tumbled off Pantaloon and staggered into our house. We asked him if he would like a cup of tea and he said, "No, I've been for a very long ride which started at half-past nine this morning. I've had nothing to eat and I would like some gin." My wife brought him a bottle of gin and a tumbler and he drank off a tumbler just as if it had been water.

Then he said to me, "Have you heard anything about Joss?"

I said, "Well, nothing except that he is dead."

"But what on earth happened?" said Jock. "Could it have been a heart attack?"

And I said, "Yes, most certainly, it could have been a heart attack."

"But," he said, "he was so well on Friday night, what could have brought on the heart attack?"

And I said, "That is quite easy to answer. It was caused by a bullet through the back of his neck."

I watched Jock very carefully as I used these words, and from that moment on there were no doubts in my mind as to who had murdered Joss Erroll.

What makes this conversation all the more significant is a remark Broughton made the previous day, before the murder had been announced, to Kenneth Coates, a junior police officer. He told him, "I am public suspect number one now."

Now, two years after that, a great friend of mine, Arthur Orchardson, who used to ride for me and was Kenya's leading rifle shot, was riding out by the murram pit when he came across what looked like a rusty weapon. He dismounted and picked it up and there was a pistol which he brought to me and showed it to me and immediately we decided that this had better be done away with and we buried it where it could never be found again.

At lunch with the Erskines two days later, I met a woman known as the Afghan Princess, a woman who seemed utterly English, who told me that she remembered Lord Erroll. She had been in this district all her life and her late husband had been A.D.C. to that same Duke of Gloucester who had irritated Njonjo, the Attorney-General. Together they had lived out the Emergency, staying put on their remote farm after most of the whites had abandoned the country for the town. "He shot one," said the Princess, referring respectively to her husband and a Mau Mau fighter, "at the bottom of the garden."

When the Princess invited me to stay the night I packed up and went with her, although I had no idea how much she knew. She lived in the same district, near an outpost for retired settlers known locally as "Blood Pressure Ridge." Her mother was from a ruling Afghan family and had married her father, an Englishman, in India. Thus the Princess was a true "Anglo-Indian," although to speak to her she might have spent all her life in the southern counties of England. Down the drive came a pack of ten or twelve of the fiercest and loudest dogs imaginable. The Princess was a breeder of Rhodesian Ridgebacks, so-called because the hackles along their spines are permanently raised.

It was immediately clear that the Princess knew almost nothing about Erroll: her only quote which I thought worth recording was "Erroll was good at everything." Nevertheless, she was extremely hospitable, although the Ridgebacks occupied all the seating space, and it seemed unwise to ask them to move. Only the Princess's chair was empty, and I sat in it. Her daughter-in-law, who lived with her, said, "That is *her* chair. Just thought I'd let you know. Don't suppose it matters for tea."

At six, the silent Somali head servant laid the table for dinner, with the place mats with the hunting scenes, the pickle bottles and the silver salt and pepper pots, and the water jug with the beaded linen cover.

The food was superb. Sherry, as usual, with the soup; filet mignon, carrots and perfect little roast potatoes. There was then a pause, and the pause turned into a wait. The expected savoury did not appear. Her kitchen had recently burned to the ground and a temporary one had been set up across the yard, in the darkness. The Afghan Princess became impatient and very cross. (To the switchboard operator at Nanyuki she had screamed, "Oh, wash your ears out, you *ber-luddy* man.") The Swahili word for "where" is *"wapi."* Now the Princess got up from the table, approached the threshold, and shouted into the darkness, *"Wapi Seconds?"*

Out of the African night came an exquisite béchamelled egg with anchovy, in a perfect pastry tart, cooked on a paraffin stove somewhere near the chicken run. All was well, yet I wondered how the Princess had survived, badmouthing these Africans so venomously all these years. In Nanyuki I discovered that she was considered merely eccentric; that she had performed many acts of kindness and that these weighed greatly in her favour.

The Afghan Princess released me the following day, and I left for Lake Naivasha, and the last traces of both Erroll and Broughton, the present estates of Diana Delamere. I rented a house once owned by Kiki Preston, the lady with the silver syringe, in a wild and isolated recess of the lake—a place to write and a base for investigative sorties, where, except for Stefan, the houseboy, I was alone.

Early each morning I would walk along the edge of Lake Naivasha beneath jacaranda and pepper trees and large and ancient thorns, putting up flights of water birds along the shore. When I felt the real heat of the sun I would turn back for the coolness of the fresh paw-paw and pineapple already laid out in the shade for my return. It seemed to me that the surface of the lake had changed, often dramatically, each time I looked back at the water. First it was a mirror lake traversed by gangs of enormously beaked pelicans whose progress left no single impression on the glassy water. A minute later a sudden wind had transformed it into a blustering Scottish loch with a surface current and whitecaps. The light can change with an equal suddenness. At times there is a clarity of detail at great distances when, for example, each branch of a thorn tree on the far bank is minutely sharp to the eye. Instantly it will become a dull strip of grey, and without a cloud in the sky to account for the change. This can produce mild hallucinations as the middle distance advances and recedes, and you can soon begin to feel oppressed by the strange gloom of this lake, with its isolated houses and its wide lawns that slip into the water as if the lake were slowly flooding. When loneliness was beginning to affect Broughton's mental stability, how desperate he must have felt in these surroundings.

Two miles around the bay from the garden of my own house, I could just see the top of the white crenellated tower of the Djinn Palace above a clump of trees. It had been restored by a German businessman, and the old Moroccan courtyard with its fountain and mosaics now looked like a well-furnished garden centre. The fountain had been filled in. The woodwork, however, and the mosaic bar had been left intact.

During the war years there was distinguished company on this wild part of the lake. The late Aga Khan lived in the Preston house and Prince Paul of Yugoslavia in the house next door, sharing the same lawn.

That house is now owned by Baron Knapitsch, the trophy hunter. The Baron has shot so many animals, large and small, commemorating each by the horns, that the gentlemen's cloakroom, taking up the overflow from his cavernous sitting rooms, bristles with the antlers of dik-dik and Grant's gazelle. The Baron has even arranged two enormous fallen branches in an arch in the garden, to remind him of a monumental pair of elephant tusks.

He invited me for dinner. I bathed and walked across the lawn. He said, "You can't imagine the game here a few years ago. Wonderful. Incredible." Diana had been to stay with him in his Austrian castle. He said, "Beautiful woman. No. Really. Beautiful."

Colvile, he said, had owned 60,000 acres here on Lake Naivasha, 140,000 at Rumuruti and 30,000 elsewhere. (An estimate near the average: the settlers' view is that Colvile left 200,000 acres when he died.) The Baron said that Colvile owned 29,000 head of cattle ("Incredible. Even by Brazilian standards. No."), and that he had given Diana half the rights to his farms when they married.

ONE DAY towards the end of my stay I came across what looked like a very promising lead. On one of my journeys around the lake I had met by chance the old Somali servant who had worked for Soames, and for several of Erroll's friends. His employer suggested I speak to him, primarily because of his age. When his connection with Soames was revealed, it seemed a stroke of extraordinary luck.

With his employer translating, the Somali spoke, at first, with caution. Translation: "He says that during the brief time he was in Kenya, the servants, in general, liked Broughton. But because he was a newcomer, they couldn't really say."

After a while he simply said, "Yes, I know a lot about Lord Erroll—Bwana Hay—and . . . I would like to tell you about him."

What followed, according to the translation, was a version of the events of January 1941 that was breathtaking in its accuracy. Lapses into hearsay and distortion would have been understandable. But this Somali, forty years later, picked out the prosecution case in great detail, and never put a foot wrong as far as the record is concerned. It was an impressive performance, untainted by the rumour that so often diminished the accuracy of the settlers' accounts.

The affair had been intensely debated between the Somali and his colleagues at the time, he remembered. It was his personal opinion, having discussed the matter with the other servants, that the old man shot Erroll himself. Were any of these other servants still alive? I mentioned

Abdullah bin Ahmed, Broughton's head boy, a witness at the trial. Yes, said the Somali, Abdullah was his closest friend and he lived now in Kilifi. He added that he was convinced that Abdullah knew exactly what had happened, but if I went to find him I was not to say that he had told me this. It was Abdullah who had put out the bonfire on Broughton's instructions, and Abdullah who knew what was burning. Yes, of course the bonfire was discussed between them.

When Broughton left Kenya, he added, Diana had kept Abdullah as a servant, but when she married Colvile, many of the servants, including Abdullah, didn't approve of the marriage. Colvile was like a Masai, he had a Masai driver. Diana was fine. She wasn't rubbish, and she never let common people into her house. But Colvile, this Masai, was mean, and all the servants left. This was only the first time Abdullah left. He was later sacked twice for drunkenness, but he always came back.

Diana got on well with Abdullah despite the drinking. Many years ago, after the incidents that temporarily ended Abdullah's employment, Diana got hold of him, took him back to Kilifi and said, "Work there." He has been on a pension ever since. It is a very long pension. "Diana," said the Somali, "is rather like his mother. She doesn't want Abdullah to get into trouble." He was certain, he repeated, that Abdullah knew who shot Lord Erroll, but it was up to Abdullah to say. He might be scared to talk, but he, the Somali, would give directions where to find him on the coast.

A few days later, in the intense and airless heat that can sometimes descend on that coast, I drove to Kilifi from Mombasa to look for Abdullah, with a journalist friend of mine from Nairobi, Mary Ann Fitzgerald, as interpreter.

At the Kilifi ferry, waiting to cross, we bought guava juice and cashews and looked at the hulks of the old ferry rafts lying seaward on the mud next to the ford. The rare photograph of Diana and Joss together during their brief romance was taken on one of these ferries, which at that time were pulled across the creek on a long chain.

We began enquiring for Abdullah near the market place in Kilifi town, only a few hundred yards away from Diana's coast house, the "Villa Buzzer" (Buzzer being Diana's nickname for Tom). In a general store almost empty of goods except for a large supply of rosewater, and with a huge paraffin fridge as its centrepiece, we heard that Abdullah did live in the vicinity but that he was an old man and very ill. Two small boys guided our car along mud tracks between buildings made of soft coral stone and tin, mangrove poles and mud, each separated from each other by heaps of rubbish. A palm tree growing in the middle of the street blocked our car, and from there we walked, stopping eventually at a narrow wooden door, almost hidden behind a makeshift wall of building blocks.

Abdullah sat on a chair at the end of a dark corridor of bare cream and white walls, dressed only in a *kekoi*, his naked breast and belly bulging in front of him. Wedged in a wooden grille above the door to his room were his only two visible possessions—a toothbrush and a copy of the Qur'an.

The room was rented, and the bed, the sole piece of furniture in the room, was covered in rags. High up on the wall, almost out of sight, were some cheap Indian prints. At first Abdullah's speech came in slow, lazy mouthings, very indistinctly, and he was obviously in some pain. My friend gave a long explanation. Abdullah began to look embarrassed, becoming even more listless. Then he produced one crucial hint to the knowledge he possessed. Broughton, he said, was a good walker, a strong man. But he, Abdullah, was ill, he needed medicine. Would we come tomorrow?

We crossed the creek again and took the day off, lunching at the Ocean sports club and dining at the old settlers' retreat, the Mnarani Club at Kilifi. The next morning, we bought pain killers and fruit, then loaded the two grinning boys into the car. They brought us this time to the market where Abdullah was sitting at the corner of a small clothes stall, wearing a shirt and holding a cane.

Overnight, Abdullah's manner had developed some resolution. I realised that I had taken it almost for granted that he would talk to me after all the trouble I had taken to find him. And I was wrong. It was quite clear, he said, that we wanted to know all about the Erroll murder. "I'm old," he said. "She [Diana] is old too, but she's got money . . . It is a very heavy matter. I don't remember anything. I don't even remember Delves Broughton. I don't remember him any more. It's a long time ago. I've forgotten."

Abdullah thanked us for the medicine, and the fruit we had brought for the children. He said, "Please don't be unhappy that I haven't said anything." He put his wrists together, in the gesture of a prisoner, then made the gesture of knifing. This was the price to pay for speaking. "This is a very heavy matter," he repeated. Abdullah was scared and he was deadly serious. There was no more to be said.

23
LADY
DELAMERE

D I A N A , L A D Y D E L A M E R E , and I first met
face to face in the doorway of her London apartment,
somewhere behind the Ritz Hotel, in late May of 1981.
With a thumping in my heart that I imagined to be audible
in the deadly quiet of the carpeted eighth-floor corridor, I
had rung on her doorbell. I was on the point of turning
back towards the lift, relieved to have any excuse, when
the door was opened by a diminutive maid dressed in
black, striking, it seemed, a crouched and fearful pose. I
later discovered that she was addressed, like Wilks before
her, by her surname, Peterson. I gave my name and Peterson disappeared from the doorway. The heart thumping
had now turned to hammer blows inside the rib cage, and
I began to imagine a bitter poetic justice for my brash
intrusion: I would collapse with a massive thrombosis in
the doorway as she came to greet me, unable even to mouth
the first question. But turning up unheralded had been the
only possible way to approach Diana, and even to arrive
at this unpromising moment had required some planning.

I had discovered by chance, through her network of
English friends, that Diana was coming to England for the
York races in May, and would be staying with a friend in
Yorkshire. At the end of the second day's racing, when
I imagined she would be well installed, I rang her host and

asked to speak to her. I was told, to my consternation, that she was still in Nairobi. My informant had been wrong.

Now I had to explain, albeit in the most general terms, to her somewhat suspicious host—who was also a Kenya landowner—why I wanted to speak to her. He warned me that she would never talk to me about her life in Kenya, and suggested I write her a formal letter of request. For this he gave me her London address—a significant step forward—in the apartment block behind the Ritz Hotel but, as it turned out, provided the wrong flat number. Earlier in the conversation he had also produced, by way of correcting me, the exact date of her arrival. Having now alerted her protective friends, and thus Diana herself, a whole three weeks too soon, my only hope was to wait and chance my luck at her door on the date in question. Letters and telephone calls, once again, would have ended the affair instantly.

The few daily flights from Nairobi arrive in the morning in London, within an hour or two of each other. When the day came, I picked on the flight with the greatest delay, added an hour or two for jet-lag and siestas and decided that 4 p.m. was the right moment to strike. In the meantime I dragged out a Chinese lunch with a friend, and for further moral encouragement rang my publisher, whom I knew had once been a fierce encyclopaedia salesman. He told me that the door would open and the face would say, "What do you want?" He always used to reply, "That's exactly what I've come to talk to you about." He said that this had never failed.

To the porters talking in the hall, more as a password than an enquiry, I said, "Lady Delamere" as I passed. One of them replied, "Eighty-two": I had been on my way to forty-three.

There came to the door, that afternoon, one of the most striking women I have ever seen, wearing an immaculately cut Eton-blue peignoir with blue ribbon bindings along the edges, and with long gold chains strung from her neck. She was younger-looking than I expected, her face longer and leaner than it had been, the ice-blue eyes as penetrating as ever. Any trace of travel fatigue had disappeared under the perfect make-up, though she was not expecting a guest. Dazzled by this apparition, my memory of this first conversation, as I introduced myself, is almost non-existent. I was an author . . . certain characters . . . Kenya . . . grateful for a few minutes' talk. Lady Delamere held the door half-way open. She said she had only just arrived; the flight had been exhausting. Also, she never talked about her private life and didn't think she could be of any help.

I had thought about and speculated on Diana for years: she had become a figure of intense fascination, forever out of reach, who would take her secrets to the grave, leaving a tantalising story untold. If we could ever have talked, even for five minutes, my obsession, at least, would be appeased, and here I was at her door, as if in a recurring nightmare in which I cannot explain myself—the words won't come, she doesn't recognise me and, slowly, the door closes, shutting out the last chink of light. But this was reality and Diana said, "Well, I can't leave you out there in the hall. You'd better come in."

The rented apartment was furnished in a dull imitation of elegance. In the drawing room Diana's daughter, Snoo, was sitting in the armchair. Several photographs of Tom Delamere were already in place in the bookshelves. The contents of Diana's handbag were spread across the carpet. "I'm in a bit of a state," she said. "I've lost my pills." My heart racing, I offered to search for them, imagining all three of us crawling around on the carpet. The pills, as it turned out, were for her heart trouble.

She repeated that she couldn't be of any help to me. She had often been approached to write something—even quite recently by a "charming" London publisher, but had always refused. "I'd rather *die*," she said. Why didn't I write about Tom, a dear, sweet, kind man? Would I like to talk now, to explain what I was after? I said, "Yes," and hastily retracted. The first rule had always been that we should be alone. I took the risk of suggesting an appointment five days later, and Diana agreed.

Already I was struck by her charm and ease of communication, and the instant friendliness. But I was aware that this impression might not last.

When we met the following week, Diana was wearing four strings of pearls, each row separated by diamond buckles on either side of her neck, and impressive diamond earrings. She wore little black shoes with vertical straps, and a black cocktail dress with long sleeves and a long, tight skirt. It made her look slim and tall and showed off her fine figure. Indeed, the disarming perfection of her appearance gave her the imposing look of some great priestess. The exigencies of such *haute couture* were, however, soon apparent: the action of reaching into a low cupboard for a bottle of tonic water forced her into a parody of a curtsey, knees and legs scissoring like a foal struggling to its feet.

As on the first occasion with the handbag, there had been another minor domestic crisis at the moment of my arrival. Peterson, unused to the hand-shower, had severely drenched herself, fighting to bring it under control. Her dress was now drying by the electric fire and Peterson herself was temporarily *hors de service*.

Diana complained of the cold of London in late May. She invariably went out, she said, in a fur coat; the central heating in the block had been switched off on principle at the beginning of May, and she had bought the electric fire which was now drying out Peterson's uniform. This reminded me of Antonia Fraser's observation about Mary Queen of Scots and Diana Delamere sharing the chill of the *femme fatale*. Diana said that most of her day had been taken up with visiting heart specialists. In 1968 she had had a heart attack which had developed into angina. Now the doctor had told her that she couldn't live at the altitude of Soysambu for more than a month at a time, which she found "awful." She had even been told that she shouldn't go marlin fishing. She had told the doctor that it was a terrible winter for fishing anyway.

Her language suggested the 1930s. On the telephone, which rang incessantly, she asked a friend to dinner. "Are you a Wheeler's girl? . . . Do you like fishy?" Discussing the work and effort needed to keep her wardrobe up to standard, she said, "Am I just to let myself *go*?", and later, discussing, also on the telephone, the merits of a fashionable hat maker, she said, "One doesn't want to pay £1,000 for an apple with an arrow through it, *you* know." She was busy with her social life, the race meetings, the charity dinners ("One has to buy something, otherwise it looks *dreadful*"), the weekends and the visits to the doctor. They had told her to take it slowly, not to get upset (a glance in my direction). She would not be going to Ascot. "I can't go to Ascot without Tom," she said to a friend. "I'm going to *dirty* Ascot." (Presumably the Saturday of Royal Ascot week, when, in the absence of Royalty there is no requirement for formal dress.)

Clearly none of the descriptions had done her justice. By the standards of that same world—even of the dense snobbery of the 1930s, when many of the descriptions had originated—she struck me as a woman of considerable style, distinguished and impressive. When I touched on the subject of snobbery and in particular the use of the word "common," her only reply was, "Do people still use that word?" She was neither cold nor hard, although she was very much in control of her surroundings. There was, in addition, something exciting about her—a quickness, a wit and a sense of courage. Certainly she had been a danger to her rivals. "A talent for enjoyment and bringing out enjoyment in others": Connolly had put it precisely.

But she had a reputation as a formidable and fierce opponent if you dared to cross her. It was almost the secret of her survival, and I might have expected at any moment to be shown the door. In particular, everyone who knew her well said the same thing: she had never spoken one word about the events of 1941, even to her close friends, and she never would. It was her unbending rule never to mention it, or to have it mentioned. In that small Kenyan community, if she had let slip the smallest detail, it would have filtered back over the years. It never had.

Our several conversations were conducted in an atmosphere that was charged with wariness and potential conflict. I told her at the first meeting that I wanted to write about Erroll, but only for what the story revealed about Kenyan society at a certain moment, and not for the purpose of ''rehashing a scandal.'' For a writer, I said, it was an irresistible story and always would be, and Broughton in particular was a worthy central character for a novel. This was not a novel, but it might turn into a book of characters as much as anything, and furthermore it would correct some myths, especially about herself. ''I don't care a bit about that,'' she said. ''They've always been murmuring and I don't . . .'' She swept her arm in front of her, leaving the phrase unfinished. ''I didn't do it, if that's what you think,'' she said.

I said that for my generation she was a figure not of scandal but of glamour. She replied that that didn't interest her. I showed her a letter from a friend of hers (typed and with the name removed), praising her and saying how extraordinary it was that such an operatic story with all the stock characters could have happened in real life. Diana said that she too was amazed it had happened. She thought it was ''something that only happened to housemaids.''

She told me immediately that she did not want the past revived. She would oppose me if I wrote about her. She would ''go for me,'' she warned; she would alert her lawyers to watch my publisher. She said that someone I knew well—she gave no name—had advised her, in the intervening five days, to put an injunction on any book, and not to see me, but to refer me to her lawyers. But there was nothing to put an injunction *on*, she said, and she never took such advice without seeing for herself. She always made her own decisions about people.

And yet, as we talked, it was she, apparently, who felt the obligation to put me at ease. She offered me a whisky. "You probably need one." She herself took a Russian vodka with a slice of lemon. Once, in the middle of a sentence which I felt would bring the conversation to breaking point, she stopped me and asked, "Do you like these? One can only eat them if one's not going out," and handed me a tin of garlic nuts. Then, almost as if to explain her reluctance, she said, suddenly, "There are only two men I have ever loved in my life. Tom Delamere and . . ." (she paused for a few moments)—"Joss.

"I always felt that it was because of me that he was killed, although he probably would have been killed anyway. He was that sort of man. I was desperately in love with Joss. It was the first time I had been in love in my life."

She then began to talk hesitantly about the past. I am sure it was the first time for forty years that she had been able to discuss these traumatic events with someone for whom nothing needed to be filled in or explained. She told me that if Tom Delamere had been alive it would not have been possible. They had made a pact never to talk publicly about *anything*. I repeated my fascination with Broughton as a character, and told Diana what I felt he must have been like. "I think Jock probably did do it," she said. "He was slightly mad at the time. I went down to South Africa to get Morris to defend him and he told me that from Jock's reactions he thought he had the first signs of a serious brain disorder. Jock never admitted to me that he had done it, but he never denied it either."

Did she and Joss suspect nothing from Broughton's behaviour before the murder? "I must have been very naïve. I was very young. In retrospect of course it was wrong to take it on face value.'' Joss's attitude, she said, was that Broughton was an old-fashioned gentleman giving his word. He never suspected otherwise. She felt it was awful to treat Broughton like that and she couldn't go through with it, but Joss insisted that the marriage pact should be taken seriously and that it was her life and happiness that mattered.

Diana then repeated the conversation with Gwladys, almost exactly as it appears in the transcript, when Gwladys urged them to go ahead with the romance. Support and approval from the older generation helped Diana make up her mind. Would Erroll have gone through with the marriage? What about the problems of divorce, the rule at the time that three years must elapse before divorce could be granted? She was so madly in love at the time, that it never occurred to her to behave otherwise. There would have been some way round it.

Did she remember anything of the murder night? Did she not hear Broughton coming back in? She couldn't think why she didn't hear it. When something very unpleasant happens, an iron shutter comes down and you can't recall anything, she said. But she did remember that Broughton had given her careful instructions to come in through the french windows, not through the front door, and had given her those keys. Somehow the keys had got muddled up and she couldn't get in that way and went instead to the front door. Broughton had also told her on no account to wake him when she came in. He had taken a sleeping pill and didn't want to be disturbed. He would be very upset if he was woken, and that was understandable, she said.

I said that I thought it odd that soon after the murder she had gone with Broughton on safari. The reason for that, she said, was that she was frightened living in the house at Karen with Broughton. He was having terrible nightmares and would walk around the outside of the house and look at her through the windows. There was something especially frightening about his face looking through the glass, or the open window. She wanted to get out in the open, with some white hunters to protect her. That was why they took J. A. Hunter along.

The trip to India and Ceylon after the acquittal, she said, was "a nightmare. A nightmare. I was so upset and so unhappy that nothing mattered to me, if you know what I mean. I didn't feel anything. I felt I had to set him up on his feet again. I don't know whether he *was* set up." It was the stress of all that, she believes, that had caused her coronary twenty years later.

"He was the most evil man," she said. "He sent me a letter trying to get me to return to England with him. It was appalling. I took it straight to the Attorney-General." I asked whether he had tried to blackmail her. She said, "Yes. But there was no possibility."

She said she knew nothing about Broughton's involvement with the theft of the pearls in Cannes, or that it was one of her own party who had taken them. I told her they had been found in a tree in Doddington Park after the war. "What you say shakes me to the core," she said.

After the blackmail attempt, when Broughton reached England, he sent her a cable which she thought "completely mad." It read, "Enormously admire your guts. Love you and will look after your dogs as if they were my own."

"He was mad," she said, and waved her hand at her head.

She then talked about Colvile with great affection. After the murder he had befriended her, at first, she said, out of pure loyalty to Erroll. The two men had been the closest of friends and one of Joss's first plans for his prospective bride, when everything had been settled with Broughton, was to go to Oserian for the weekend and to introduce her to Colvile. They had planned to travel there the very weekend that Erroll was murdered. Erroll loved Oserian, she said. Even though he couldn't afford to run it, he never wanted to lose it, or even to let it. That was why Diana moved in there immediately with Broughton when they returned from Ceylon and it was also why she persuaded Colvile to buy it as soon as they were married. "If it was anything to do with Joss," she said, "I wanted to do it."

Diana said it was true that Colvile had hardly spoken to a woman before herself. "It was quite amazing when we were together. He was intelligent and nice but very unusual and he could be as hard as nails." He *was* mean, she said, but only with small amounts. That was his French side, inherited from his mother. Colvile lost none of his taciturnity in married life. Once when a friend came to stay and tried to talk to Gilbert, he sat behind his newspaper and wouldn't answer. It was very embarrassing for Diana. The friend eventually said, "I'd better leave. Gilbert obviously doesn't want to talk to me."

She and Colvile would go riding for miles together across his estates. They imported a pack of Atherstone hounds and went hunting lion and buck. They would take pinches of a powerful Masai snuff kept in pouches around their necks. Diana called it "Eau de Boma." "It clears the mind and the head and makes you see the track better," she said. She learned from him how to cull the herds of Boran. He made her sit on the stockade as the Masai drove them in and taught her to look for the cow without milk, a steer that wasn't deep enough in build, a weak calf. In the end she was always harder than he in deciding which ones would have to be slaughtered and Colvile would often reprieve them.

"Gilbert was sad when I left him for Tom," she said. "He always said, 'There's one person who loves and one who is loved.' " She and Tom built him a special suite at Soysambu, so that he could live there whenever he wanted their company. She was the Little White Bear, Tom the Little Brown Bear, and Colvile was Pooh Bear or "Pooey."

Diana then sat beside me on the sofa and showed me

the photographs of Soysambu and her life with Delamere
—her garden, her horses, the sitting rooms. "I had years
of happiness with Tom," she said. "We used to talk to
each other for hours at a time." When I broached the
subject of her celebrated love of jewellery, however, she
became defensive.

"I'm not the one who's mad about jewellery," she
said. "Tom adored it and always used to go into the shop
and ask, 'What's the bargain of the week?' If we saw a
nice piece he would often say, 'Halves, baby?' "

And whoever it was who had described her walking
down to the jetty covered in jewels, was quite wrong. She
never wore jewellery on her fishing boat, she said. Nor
could the Somali have seen her dipping in her pool weighed
down with bright stones. "I never swim in jewellery . . .
I might wear an ordinary little gold ring. I don't wear
jewellery in the daytime . . . I might put on a pair of gold
earrings at lunchtime. I only really wear jewellery at night."

She buried Tom Delamere in the little walled cemetery
she built on Colvile's farm at Ndabibi (the Masai word
for "place of clover"), alongside Colvile and her only
child, who had lived for ten days. She has had fig trees
planted and water piped to the cemetery for the flowers,
and a dog buried at the foot of each grave. She has reserved
her own space between the graves and has written all the
inscriptions: for the child, "So short a life"; for Colvile,
"If you want a memorial, look around you," and for
Delamere, "So great a man."

As I left, she stood up close to me, rolled up one
black sleeve, in imitation of a prize fighter, and said, "It'll
be this." We both laughed and she said, "It hasn't come
to that yet, has it?"

FOUR MONTHS LATER, in September of that
year, soon before her return to Nairobi, we met again.
As usual, I arrived in the middle of a crisis. Diana

had somehow knocked her glass of vodka and tonic and a whole tin of cocktail biscuits off the table—the drink had landed on her pleated dress and the biscuits were strewn about the floor. Peterson came to the rescue, but Diana wanted to change. I said the damage didn't look too bad. "It's me I'm worried about," she said. She reappeared in a dress of blue and white flowers, and now sapphires as well as diamonds. She and Peterson had been discussing the racehorse Shergar, unbeaten until that day.

"It's an odd thing to discuss," said Diana, "but *she's* interested. We don't think Shergar should have been entered for the St. Leger. Don't you agree, Peterson? I hate to see a good horse beaten." Peterson made no sound.

At first I was under suspicion. That week a series on the Erroll murder was running in my old newspaper in Nairobi, written by a visiting American journalist and based, according to the writer himself, largely on our *Sunday Times* article. It contained nothing new, and I convinced Diana that I had nothing to do with it. But it was an unfortunate coincidence. She said the writer was going to get "a very sore ear" when she returned to Nairobi.

In the meantime Diana's memory had been awakened, it seemed, in the process of our meetings, and, although she did not relax her warnings of legal sanctions, we talked on. It was then that I admired her judgment. It was clear to her that the book would be written—that I was committed to it—but instead of accepting the advice of her friends to show me the door, I felt she must have decided that to talk to me could only improve the book from her point of view. There, of course, she was right. When I suggested that, if she were to read a draft, she would object to any mention of the Erroll murder, she replied, "It's not that I mind about. It's the way it's presented."

In that delicate atmosphere there were many questions I left unasked. My persistence in returning to the subject in the four hours we spent together already seemed to me to be straining Diana's hospitality. Yet what she did tell

me was illuminating. First, she made two denials: Broughton and June did not come to the Claremont Road House
later on the murder night, she said, and Broughton's attempted blackmail of her had nothing to do with the jewels,
although she would not say what the subject of the blackmail was.

I asked about her trip to Nyeri, immediately after the
murder. I was surprised, I said, that she had been out of
the house when Broughton arrived from Nairobi. She
couldn't remember why she and June were out, but she
remembered the police arriving the previous night. She
was distraught, and in bed, but she came down to meet
them. "They asked me, 'What do you think happened?'
and I answered automatically, 'He was a very fast driver
and I think he must have crashed and been killed.'

"The last thing I ever said to Joss was, 'Darling,
please drive carefully.' His last words to me were, 'Carefully, darling, but not slowly.' " She believed that
Broughton hid in the bushes at the end of the drive, asked
to talk to Erroll, at some point asked to be dropped off
and then shot him. "He knew the country well. We'd
ridden over it many times," she said.

I said, "I've always been fascinated by . . ."

Diana broke in and said, to my surprise, "Jack Soames.
It was very funny really that I shot better than Jock. He
wasn't a good shot but it's not difficult if you're sitting in
the seat beside someone."

She repeated her regret at not understanding Broughton's mood better: "We were such a foolly crowd not to
know what he was up to." In jail, she said, he was just
the same as ever. The only time he got angry was when
Diana agreed to give back the Erroll pearls to Walter Shapley, the lawyer acting for Erroll's estate. "Joss had given
them to me and told me never to take them off," said
Diana. "Everyone was being horrible about it. They didn't
even belong to the estate, they had been Molly's."

Why, I asked, did June Carberry drive in her dressing

gown to get a jewel box from Erroll's house, as soon as the news of his death came through? Diana said, "It was not a jewel box. Sometimes in life a guardian angel comes to the rescue, and that was one of those extraordinary moments." June, she said, had gone to get a notecase which contained all the love letters that Diana had written to Joss. The irony was that the night before she had asked Joss to burn them. "He said, 'No, darling, I want to keep them.' I thought, 'I'll teach him a lesson,' and I hid the notecase in a box of face tissues." When the police came they took all Erroll's correspondence, she said, but they never found her letters.

She agreed that she and June had joined forces to defend Broughton, but when it was over she hardly saw her again. "I was so surprised. People were perfectly bloody to me after the trial. Many people actively cut me at the time and became friends later. Gwladys never spoke to me again. I couldn't understand why people were so violently against me. Some were genuinely upset that the thing would bring down bad feeling on Kenya in a war. Others were just jealous about anything and anybody. It was much more fashionable to be sorry for Jock. The fact that I pulled myself together and went to the trial every day looking as tidy as I could infuriated some people. I remember the faces . . . I don't want to think about it."

She herself went soon after the murder to Erroll's house to get his two dogs, and a third dog that Fabian Wallis—Erroll's homosexual friend from Happy Valley —had left there before going to Abyssinia. She was very hurt when Wallis sent a message forbidding her to keep the dog and ordering her to deliver it to a friend of his. In the end Fabian Wallis was broke and sad, living in a guest house in Nairobi. His friends organised a subscription to buy him an electric blanket. Diana said, "There'll be no subscription. I'll buy him one."

We turned to Broughton again and I said that if he was guilty, his performance in the witness box was a masterpiece of deception and sang-froid. He was very proud of that performance, she said, and then she told me that the remark to Harragin as he walked out of the courtroom had been simply, "I'm a very good actor." Morris, she said, had thought Broughton guilty.

Towards the end, before he left for England, Broughton became unbalanced, and was tortured with nightmares and various fears. Diana believed that he killed one of Erroll's dachshunds after the trial, out of a jealousy for Erroll which never left him, even after Erroll's death. The final break with Broughton began when Colvile came across an unposted letter that Broughton had written to Vera, saying that he wanted to come back to her, but couldn't remarry her "for tax reasons." Colvile had copied it, mailed the original to Vera, and kept a copy.

The last time she saw Broughton was in a lawyer's office in Nairobi, and it was then that she accused him of murder. "He wanted me to go back to England with him," said Diana. "I didn't want to go but I wanted to say it in front of a lawyer. I told him I didn't want to go back because I believed he had killed Joss. He said nothing. He simply walked out of the room."

For years after Joss's death she felt nothing. "I have always regretted that with Joss it could never have come down to reality. It was so sublime and so perfect, but it couldn't last. I knew that."

The rumour that she and Joss had a row on the night of the murder was far from the truth. It was, she repeated, her eternal regret that she had never fought with Joss in their brief affair. "If you've never had a row, it leaves you much too vulnerable," she said.

Diana and I had now moved into her kitchen. Taking some snacks from the fridge she said, "Peterson said to me today, 'I bought you an egg in May and you haven't eaten it.' In *May*." (It was now mid-September.) It was clear that this was one of Diana's very rare visits to a kitchen. As we sat down to some biscuits and cheese at a small Formica table, she asked me what sort of cutlery we should use. Afterwards she approached the sink and, despite my protests, started to wash up. She poured almost half a cupful of washing-up liquid on to one plate and began dabbing at it with a brush. She said, "I only do it about twice a year. I rather enjoy it. I don't know what everyone's making such a fuss about."

Before I left she told me that she had visited a clairvoyant in the summer near the racecourse at Ascot. "The first thing she said was, 'I'm glad I'm not you.' She said, 'You've had some terrible times in your life but you've always pulled yourself up,' and then she said, 'Your friends take from you, but if you're in danger they wouldn't help you.' I did have a question to ask her: 'Will it happen again?' [referring to the troubles in her life] but after that I didn't want to ask it. The only thing I wanted was a large stiff drink. I just thought I should tell you."

24

THE END
OF
THE TRAIL

ONE OF THE LAST entries in Connolly's note-books is headed ''The End of the Trail.'' These were his notes of an interview in 1971 with Juanita Carberry, June's stepdaughter, who was fifteen years old at the time of the murder. It wasn't quite the end of the trail, as it turned out. But he had come remarkably close to it, and it was only Juanita's reticence that had kept him a few steps away.

In the spring of that year Connolly went to the last day of an exhibition of paintings with the title ''The Death of Lord Erroll'' at the Upper Grosvenor Gallery in London. The paintings were mostly expressionist renderings of the photographs in our magazine layout. The titles, too, were taken from the text: ''One of the better nights''; ''I think wistfully of Madeira now,'' and so on. The artist, Tom Hill, had taken the idea for his series directly from our article, and had sent Connolly an invitation.

On his way out, Connolly glanced at the visitors' book, and noticed Juanita's name, with a forwarding address. When she got a letter from Connolly, Juanita rang him at the *Sunday Times*, and drew a blank: whoever she spoke to had never heard of him. But she persisted and they finally met at the Queen's Elm pub in the Fulham Road, on September 17th, 1971.

Connolly's notes describe the meeting:

JC late. Small, close cropped, medium colouring, nice quiet voice.
Works as a steward on tankers. Knows many languages, fluent
Swahili etc. Lunched at *Le Français*, drinks milk, orders in French.
Impressions: great integrity, sensibility, observation etc.

Juanita had talked first about her family; how June
liked to pass her off as her sister, and to boast that Juanita
could outdrink any man in Kenya—though she only drank
milk—until on the visits to Eden Roc and Cannes, Juanita
began to be attractive to June's boyfriends and the boasting
stopped. She hated Carberry and his cruelty. He had always told her that he was disappointed that she hadn't
been born a male. At Seremai, Carberry had built a "children's wing," remote from the house, whose only occu-
pant was Juanita. "He used to make me race across Mombasa
bay in the tidal wind against a boy who was a strong
swimmer. He took bets on the races, but the father of the
boy was allowed to have a boat alongside—that was his
father's condition. In the South of France he would take
bets on me. If I won I got 100 francs, and if I lost I got
a beating. I became a good speed swimmer." He would
make Juanita, aged thirteen, dive from the highboard. "You
need very strong muscles," said Juanita, "otherwise you
fall backwards. I would go up there and I would start
blubbering because I was terrified, and equally I wanted
to go." Juanita remembered one terrifying day when Carberry ordered her to swim ashore from his yacht which
was moored in Kilindini harbour, a notorious feeding ground
for sharks. She swam once around the boat, then grabbed
the gunwale, pleading to be let back on board. Carberry
stamped on her fingers.

She said that Carberry used to tie tin cans to the horses'
tails, which made them panic and run into trees, and once
she remembers him tying a cat to a drill with centrifugal
weights and spinning it round until its head split open.

Juanita's Grimm's fairy-tale childhood came to an end
when she ran away after the worst of the many beatings
meted out by her father. One day at Nyeri she received a

letter from a girlfriend. June demanded to read it, presuming it to be from a male suitor—and Juanita threw it on to the fire, unopened. She overheard her parents devising her punishment: she was to be beaten with a "kiboko" until she stopped screaming. She said she didn't know how long the beating lasted, because her efforts were concentrated on depriving her father of the pleasure of hearing her cry.

After this Juanita got on her pony and rode to Nyeri police station. "It was a painful ride," she said. "I showed them the weals and asked them to put it in the occurrence book. Then I went to live with my uncle."

Juanita then told Connolly that she didn't want anything she said to be used against Broughton. She had been very fond of him because of their shared love of horses, and his kindness to her in those first few months that he was in Kenya.

She told Connolly that on the morning of the murder she and Miss Rutt were driven to Karen. Broughton took her to the stables to look at the horses and they passed the bonfire, where Juanita saw the pair of gym shoes lying in the embers.

After lunch June, Juanita, Miss Rutt and Diana drove up to Nyeri. Broughton turned up the next afternoon when Juanita was alone in the house. Broughton seemed to think that she knew that he had done the murder. He told her that the police had followed him all the way from Nairobi, and warned her not to be afraid if they came to the house. He was in a very gloomy mood, but she felt later that he was suddenly determined to fight.

Nine years after her conversation with Connolly, Juanita and I were sitting on the second-storey veranda of the Mombasa Club alongside Fort Jesus, high above the palms and the brilliant blue of the Indian Ocean, eating parrot fish and quails. When I first saw Juanita, sitting in a chair waiting for me, I cast her as "tidy-minded" and slightly stern. She began talking about the need for discipline in the world; the problem of too much procreation; Britain going down the drain. But my impression changed as we talked. I could see what it was in her that had attracted Connolly and why she was so popular in her own town. We were frequently interrupted by other lunchers, mostly shipping people and harbour officials. Her face was strong and handsome, her figure athletic. To my surprise and in contrast to her otherwise strictly conservative appearance, I noticed that she wore a fine gold chain around her right ankle. I would have judged her forty, although she was almost fifty-five.

She took me to her house, a modern, airy building, painted white inside and out, with large glass windows looking on the outer entrance of Mombasa harbour. All afternoon tankers and freighters drifted past the point, a few hundred yards beyond the garden. For Juanita, an expert on shipping, the setting is perfect. Much of the year she travels on long voyages with her friend, a ship's captain, and she is at her happiest at sea, she told me, however long the voyage.

Near Juanita's front door, displayed on a pedestal, was a seed-pod the size of a large melon, dark and polished, an exact image of the vulva, as if sculpted from mahogany. So uncanny was this natural similarity that even the pubic hairs were minutely represented on its surface. Against the wall of the veranda, a few steps away, there stood a full-size 'Ylang-'Ylang, the most exotic and sweet-smelling tree on earth—the only true base of the truest scent. Juanita had planted it some years ago and it had grown to its full size. Her bedroom, which I glimpsed for a second, had only the bare minimum of décor: a narrow bed covered with a counterpane of an institutional design—small flowers on bright white. It was made up flawlessly, as if awaiting inspection.

As we talked on the veranda, exchanging the binoculars and looking out to sea, Juanita noticed two over-dressed prostitutes standing on the cliff. "Shall I rush you down there?" she asked.

I asked her what had happened to her after she had

left home. She replied that she never again saw June, whom she felt was indifferent to her, but she bumped into Carberry one day in the Norfolk Hotel, when she was in the army during the war, aged eighteen. "He said, about the beating, 'Do you think I was to blame for that?' I said, 'I've never thought about it.' He said, 'Do you think I was cruel to you as a child?' I said, 'Cruelty is a difficult word to define.' He said, 'I think I was very generous to you since you weren't my child.' Then he told me that he was not my father; that my father was Maxwell Trench [Carberry's partner]. I said, 'I don't give a damn whose child I was. You never acted as a parent towards me.' " Since then Dan Trench and Juanita have embraced each other as brother and sister.

Carberry disinherited her when she went to live with her uncle, Gerald Anderson. So Juanita joined the army when she was seventeen and has supported herself ever since.

"June felt nothing when I left. I felt sorry for her in her loneliness. I hated all that drinking but I felt sorry for her. When she lost her looks, all her friends abandoned her. When I heard she was ill in Johannesburg I wrote and offered to come and see her, but I got no reply." Towards the end, June had spent her days picking up stray dogs in her Rolls-Royce, and she left what remained of her husband's fortune to a dogs' home.

I told Juanita about my involvement with the mystery. I was perplexed, I said, that Connolly had headed his notes of his interview with her, "The End of the Trail." Juanita laughed at that. Then she said quickly, "There is no mystery. He did it. I can tell you that now. He told me himself the following day. He was desperate. They'd been laughing at him. He wanted to unburden himself, poor man. He came up late in the afternoon to Nyeri. Everyone had gone to Nanyuki and I was the only person there. I think that finding nobody there almost broke him.

"We walked down to the stables," said Juanita, "and

I showed him my horse. He told me then that he had shot Erroll. We walked for a bit. We had tennis courts and I remember going down to the courts when he showed me his hand. I wasn't aware until then that he was disabled. He told me not to be frightened when the police came, and he told me about the gun, which he said he had thrown into the Thika falls. He thought the police had followed him and had seen him stop there.''

When Broughton filled in her book of likes and dislikes, she remembers he wrote "loneliness" first, and that his hand shook badly on the "A" of "All animals.''

Diana and June returned, said Juanita, and Diana accused Broughton hysterically and loudly of the murder. She had brought with her Erroll's forage cap and had filled the bedroom with his photographs.

The moment had a great emotional impact on Juanita, and she had asked Broughton no questions. "I felt very protective towards him after that,'' she said. "The key to it was loneliness. He had been provoked to do it. There was nothing premeditated about it. They had gone too far. That last dinner was too much and brought home to him that he had really lost. And the fact is that he was in love with Diana.''

Petal Allen, an exact contemporary of Juanita who had been close to the Carberry family, told me in 1980 that she always remembered one strange thing about the Erroll murder, when she too was fifteen years old. Her friend Juanita suddenly stopped talking, and shut up like a clam. Petal, who knew nothing of my conversation with Juanita, continued, "She was going through the stage of loving her palamino pony more than life itself.'' Could Juanita have known anything? I asked. "Well, she had heard the grown-ups talking,'' Petal said, "and she knew what was going on behind the scenes.''

As the time came for the trial, Broughton left Juanita alone. "I think he knew that he had confided in me and trusted me that I would never let him down,'' she said.

Juanita's evidence would have been enough to convict Broughton, but to the police she assumed naïvety. She said she remembered nothing of the bonfire. (She believes now that Broughton may have removed the gym shoes after she had noticed them.) She believes, too, that Diana knew Broughton had done it, but relented and came round to defend him.

"I can remember having it drilled into me by the grown-ups," said Juanita ("drilling" was the word Wilks, too, had used), "that a man's life hung on it and that every time I spoke to the police I mustn't say anything that might hurt him."

On the day of the murder Juanita had ridden with June and Diana to van Schouten's, the hairdressers in Nairobi. She had noticed that the armstraps were in place inside the car, but it was an old car, she said, and they may have been poorly attached. Juanita thought that Broughton had hidden in the car, shot Erroll from behind, and held on to the straps until the impact of the car with the murram pit wrenched them off.

Juanita's protectiveness towards Broughton had prevented her from telling anyone his secret until this moment, thirty-seven years after his death. She had withheld Broughton's confession from Connolly in 1971 although she had come within a fraction of disclosing it, moving, as it were, from the spirit towards the letter of her secret agreement. How deeply she had buried it in her adolescent psyche—a frightening piece of information entrusted to her by the only adult who had taken her side in the midst of a host of hard-drinking grown-ups, who were constantly pushing her aside and sending her away.

The last I saw of Juanita in Mombasa was in a back street of the town where we had gone, at my request, to find a purveyor of *khat*—the bitter-tasting bark of a young tree shoot widely used on the coast as a stimulant against the enfeebling heat; useful, too, for long hours at the wheel. The sign of the *khat* seller is a small sheaf of shredded banana leaves hung over the door, like a talisman. Having instructed me in the correct chewing method, she presented me with a small bound sheaf of the bark as a parting gift.

The simplicity of her revelation, the certainty of her description, brought on a sudden feeling of exhaustion, as if the obsession had been short-circuited, and the structure of the mystery had collapsed; a kind of post-partum depression before I had even begun to write. I also felt a rush of euphoria at having come as close as I ever thought I would to the end of the trail.

What Juanita had to say was utterly convincing on many levels: so many strands of the story fitted with her short description of the afternoon with Broughton at Nyeri. Nothing is added for embellishment, and no detail is claimed that she can't have heard from Broughton. Her fifteen-year-old impressions of Broughton's state of mind, the loneliness that was about to break him, his horror of being laughed at, the provocations that he had found unbearable, have an added ring of truth—they are separately echoed by others who knew Broughton well at the time, particularly, almost word for word, by the intuitive Paula Long. As Connolly put it:

Such a man can indeed act a part all his life, playing the heavy swell, the grand seigneur, that his money and position have cast him for, yet perpetually rankling from a sense of injury. For a vain man, what insults he had to put up with from the bright young things in this new country. If, indeed, he was besotted with love and jealousy, and treated with arrogant thoughtlessness to boot—"The boy's being terribly difficult." "What are you going to do about it?"; "Try and eat something"—how much could he stand?

"He craved sympathy and affection," said his friend, the Earl of Antrim. Even the hostile Gwladys noticed after Erroll's funeral, "I felt he would do anything not to be left alone"; the letters from Naivasha complained of "terrible loneliness." And there is the melancholy entry in

Juanita's guest-book. He might well have had a phobia about being abandoned. His mother had died when he was two, his father was a distant enemy, his first wife had deserted him. Now his new wife, the young woman with whom he was obsessed, had left him, publicly humiliating him at the same time. Broughton's pride had prevented him from showing how much he cared about losing Diana. He had spent a lifetime hiding his feelings; jealous scenes, fits of rage and absolute demands would have demeaned him and made him look ridiculous. And there was the laughter—while June and Diana lay in bed together, and during the negotiations in the garden when Erroll went inside to fix a cocktail.

Broughton's delicate sense of vanity, as he himself described it, could not stand such treatment. Perhaps his later "confessions" were simply attempts to shore up this wounded vanity, to restore his reputation in the London clubs, where they roared with laughter at his marriage to the blonde which lasted only two months. If so, was he badly disturbed, beginning to imagine the act of murder? Or, if he *had* killed Lord Erroll, were the confessions a way of drawing attention to his fine performance in the witness box, which could only be fully appreciated if the truth were known?

More than anything, it is Broughton's outward show of passivity in the face of such provocation that gives him away. His behaviour, apparently so complaisant, was in truth sadistic. It is as if he imagined that the more accommodating he appeared to be, the more uneasy the lovers might become. By being "so terribly nice about it" he was striking at the heart of their romance, dissipating the excitement of complicity and deceit; by removing all obstacles to their passion he was planting some doubt of its strength in their minds. Attention would be turned away from their drama and towards Broughton's "sweetness." Thus Erroll, used to confronting irate husbands, meekly agreed to bring Diana back home by 3 a.m. on the very night that Broughton had officially handed her over to her lover. This was also meant to humiliate Diana: the couple were now being treated as wayward children.

In the trial Broughton's only explanation for his behaviour was that he was honouring the marriage pact, and it doesn't ring true. He is absurdly literal on the subject:

Q: I am putting it that your wife was your dearest possession and having asked you about such things as land I now ask you here is your dearest possession being taken from under your nose and you take it placidly because you had made a pact?
A: Yes, otherwise there would be no point in the pact.

And here, surely, he is going too far?:

Q: And not even your pride was hurt at the thought of your wife being taken away?
A: She was taken away by a much younger man, a very intelligent man, a very attractive man and a man of very high social position.

Dickinson described Broughton as "jealous and possessive as hell but a bit too damned proud." In view of this, his extreme passivity suggests an anger so fierce that he must at all costs keep it locked up, even to the point where after the murder, and subsequently in jail, and then in court, he proved the exception to Morris's dictum, quoted in his memoirs:

No man who has taken part in an event can lie about it all the time. The conscious mind cannot mount guard over the subconscious indefinitely. The time comes when the conscious mind nods or falls asleep. Then the subconscious asserts itself.

It is no coincidence that Erroll was shot soon after Broughton had made the most extreme gesture of passivity he could muster, at the Muthaiga farewell dinner. Erroll must have had a momentary sense of the danger when he said: "The old boy's being so nice, it smells bad."

Finally, what is the natural reaction of an acquitted murderer or of someone wrongfully arrested? To clear his name by discovering who had done it, by vehemently protesting his innocence, or by exhibiting at least some curiosity about the circumstances of the crime. What action did Broughton take? None. So many of the clues led to Broughton that, had he been innocent, he would surely have shown more curiosity about which of his friends could have organised such an elaborate set-up, which of them might have caused him to be hanged. He never denied his guilt to Diana. He simply told Juanita at a moment of severe emotional stress that it was he who had shot Erroll and that she mustn't be frightened.

The story of Broughton's last days in Africa is indeed a tragic one. Perhaps in the end Africa was to blame. Once Kenya had given Broughton some of his happiest days. In the future it was to provide Diana with her fullest years. She had been accepted. He had paid it one visit too many.

CAST
OF
CHARACTERS

THE CENTRAL CAST

Josslyn Hay, 22nd Earl of Erroll b.1901. Educated Eton. Left prematurely. 1920–2. Brief spell in Foreign Office. Military attaché, High Commission, Berlin.

1924   Went to Kenya with Lady Idina Gordon (q.v.). They married the same year. Founded the "Happy Valley" set.
1928   Became 22nd Earl of Erroll. Divorced.
1930   Married Mary ("Molly") Ramsay-Hill.
1934   Joined British Union of Fascists, for one year only.
1936   Secretary to Production and Settlement Board, Kenya. Member of Legislative Council.
1939   Assistant Military Secretary for Kenya Colony.
1941   January 24. Murdered.

Sir John Henry ("Jock") Delves Broughton (pronounced Brawton) b.1883. Educated Eton. Irish Guards (Captain).

1913   Married Vera Boscawen.
1914   Inherited baronetcy and estates in Cheshire and Staffordshire. Taken off troopship by tender before battalion sailed for France.
1923–7   Various hunting safaris in Kenya. Bought coffee plantations.
1935   Vera left him for Lord Moyne. Met Diana Caldwell (q.v.).
1940   Divorced. Married Diana Caldwell in Durban on their way to Nairobi in November.
1942   December 5. Died.

Diana Caldwell b.1913. Daughter of Seymour Caldwell, the Red House, Hove, Sussex. Married briefly to Vernon Motion.

1940   November 5. Married Broughton in Durban. November 12. Arrived Nairobi.

1943 Married Gilbert Colvile (q.v.). Divorced 1955.
1955 Married Tom, 4th Baron Delamere (q.v.). Lives at Soysambu,
      Elmenteita, Kenya.

Carberry, June née Mosley. b.1912. Third wife of John Carberry (q.v.).
m. 1930. Struck up immediate friendship with Diana on latter's arrival
in Nairobi.

Gwladys, Lady Delamere (pronounced ''Gladys'') née Beckett. b.1898.
m. 1: 1920, Sir Charles Markham; 2: 1928, Hugh, 3rd Baron Delamere
(q.v.). 1938, Mayor of Nairobi. Died 1943.

de Trafford, Alice née Silverthorne. b.1900. American heiress. m.1922,
Comte Frédéric de Janzé (q.v.). Arrived Kenya 1925. Divorced 1927.
Shot and wounded Raymond de Trafford (q.v.) and herself at Gare du
Nord, Paris, 1927. Acquitted of attempted murder. Married de Trafford
1932. Separated after three weeks. Decree nisi, 1937. Died 1941, Gilgil,
Kenya.

Dickinson, Hugh b.1906. Educated Harrow. Posted to Kenya in Royal
Army Signals Corps, 1941. Close friend of Diana. Lives in London.

Poppy, Arthur Head of Nairobi C.I.D. in 1941. Ex-Scotland Yard, sent
to Kenya to organise fingerprint department.

Soames, John Beaucroft (''Jack'') b.1883. Settler farmer at Nanyuki.
Eton contemporary of Broughton.

Wilks, Dorothy South African personal maid hired to look after Diana
at house in Karen. Retired to Durban, South Africa.

OTHER FIGURES IN THE KENYA LANDSCAPE, 1920–41

Bowles, Patricia Alice de Trafford's closest friend. Now living at Kilifi.

Carberry, John b.1892 as John Evans-Freke. Succeeded as Lord Carbery
1898 (family name Carberry). Educated Harrow, Trinity, Cambridge.
Navy, 1914. 1919, became U.S. citizen. 1920, Nairobi, dropped title
and changed name by deed poll to John Evans Carberry. m. 1: 1914,
José Metcalfe, divorced 1919; 2: 1922, Maia Anderson who died 1928,
piloting her plane; 3: 1930, June Weir Mosley of Johannesburg.

Carberry, Juanita b.1926. Daughter of John and Maia Carberry. Lives in Mombasa, Kenya.

Hugh Cholmondeley, 3rd Baron Delamere b.1870. Pioneer leader of the settlers, farmer and politician. 1897, first visit to Kenya. 1903, first settler given right to buy land, at Njoro. m. 1: 1899, Lady Florence Cole; 2: 1928, Gwladys Markham, ex-wife of Sir Charles Markham. Died 1931.

Tom Cholmondeley, 4th Baron Delamere b.1900. Educated Eton (with Erroll). m. 1: 1924, Phyllis Anne, d. of Lord George Scott; 2: 1944, Ruth Mary Clarisse, d. of 1st Baron Mount Temple; 3: Diana Colvile, d. of Seymour Caldwell. Died 1979.

Colvile, Gilbert de Préville b.1888. Educated Eton (with Broughton and Lord Francis Scott). One of the biggest cattle ranchers in the country. m.1943, Diana Broughton.

de Janzé, Comte Frédéric Author of *Vertical Land*. Married Alice Silverthorne in Chicago, 1922. Divorced 1927.

de Trafford, Raymond Playboy. 1924, met Alice de Janzé on her honeymoon in Kenya. 1927, wounded by Alice, Gare du Nord. 1932, married Alice. Separated same year. Decree nisi, 1937. Gaoled three years for manslaughter, 1939.

Drury, Nina née Layman. Formerly married to Jack Soames (q.v.), 1927. Now living in London.

Lady Idina, Countess of Erroll née Sackville b.1893. Daughter of Earl De La Warr. Changed names six times in five marriages to Gordon, Wallace, Hay, Erroll, Haldeman, Soltau. Married Josslyn Hay, later Earl of Erroll, 1924. Divorced 1930. Her house, Clouds, near Gilgil, was the centre of Happy Valley. Died 1955.

Erskine, Sir Derek Managing Director of Erskine and Duncan Ltd, Nairobi. Supporter of Kenyatta pre-independence. Died 1977.

Gregory, Dr. Joseph Irish general practitioner favoured by Nairobi society.

Lezard, Julian ("Lizzie") South African Davis Cup tennis player. Gambler, undischarged bankrupt. Sent to Kenya by his wife and friends, 1939. Posted to Cairo, 1941.

Long, Paula née Gellibrand. Celebrated beauty. Married to "Boy" Long, Elmenteita rancher. Close friend of Alice de Trafford (q.v.). Living in Oxfordshire, England.

Pembroke, Richard ("Dickie") Major, Coldstream Guards. After affair with brother officer's wife, applied for transfer to Kenya, 1940, according to regimental etiquette. Lover of Alice de Trafford, succeeding Lezard (q.v.).

Portman, Hon. Gerald later Lord Portman. At Eton with Erroll and Tom Delamere. On active service in Nairobi in 1940.

Repton, Dushka Russian exile. Formerly married to Guy Repton, settler farmer. Friend of Nina Drury (q.v.). Now living in London.

Lord Francis Scott Younger son of Duke of Buccleuch. b.1879. Eton contemporary of Broughton, Colvile (q.v.). Soldier settler from early 1920s. Became leader of settlers after death of Hugh Delamere, 1931. m. 1915, Lady Eileen, née Elliott, daughter of Earl of Minto.

Eileen, Lady Francis Scott see above.

Wirewater, Nancy pseudonym for Erroll's current mistress in 1940.

INDEX

ABOUT

THE

AUTHOR

James Fox was born in Washington, D.C., in 1945, and was educated at Eton. He has worked on various newspapers in Africa, including *Drum*, and for the *Manchester Evening News*, the *Sunday Times*, and the *Observer* in Britain; he won special commendation in the 1976 British Press Awards for feature reportage. Recently he wrote the script for *The Beryl Markham Story*, which aired on CBS. He lives in London.

27 million Americans can't read a bedtime story to a child.

It's because 27 million adults in this country simply can't read.

Functional illiteracy has reached one out of five Americans. It robs them of even the simplest of human pleasures, like reading a fairy tale to a child.

You can change all this by joining the fight against illiteracy.

Call the Coalition for Literacy at toll-free **1-800-228-8813** and volunteer.

Volunteer Against Illiteracy. The only degree you need is a degree of caring.

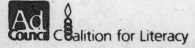

Ad Council Coalition for Literacy

LV-3

THIS AD PRODUCED BY MARTIN LITHOGRAPHERS
A MARTIN COMMUNICATIONS COMPANY